A SINGER IN THE DAWN

REINTERPRETATIONS OF PAUL LAURENCE DUNBAR

Edited by Jay Martin

DODD, MEAD & COMPANY

NEW YORK

ISBN: 0-396-06944-4
Library of Congress Catalog Card Number: 74-104

PRINTED IN THE UNITED STATES OF AMERICA
BY THE CORNWALL PRESS, CORNWALL, N.Y.

A SINGER IN THE DAWN

Also by Jay Martin

CONRAD AIKEN: *A Life of His Art*

HARVESTS OF CHANGE: *American Literature 1865–1914*

THE WASTE LAND: *A Collection of Critical Essays*

NATHANAEL WEST: *The Art of His Life*

ROBERT LOWELL

There came a dark youth singing in the dawn
  Of a new freedom, to a mellow lyre . . .
  Refining, as with a touch of Apollo's fire,
The songs a lowly people sang upon
A toilsome way. . . .

—JAMES D. CORROTHERS,
"Paul Laurence Dunbar"
(1906)

IN MEMORIAM

ARNA BONTEMPS

1902–1973

Contents

FOR PAUL LAURENCE DUNBAR

(Centennial Celebration—Dayton, Ohio—1972)

A man whose life was like a candle's flame:
faint, flickering, and brightened with the poet's light.
He came to earth a butterfly of time
and lifted in his hands the spirit-dust;
gave to the world chameleon his singing heart
and sacrificed upon the altar fame
his glowing candle fire of life and love.
Remembering, we pause to honor him
but knowing well the Ages honor best
his image, frail and pure, while millions here
behold his comet-star and see its flaming trail
burst brilliantly across the burning sky.
We hold aloft his laughter-breaking, black,
and bitter songs, and his immortal name.

Margaret Walker

Jay Martin

FOREWORD: Paul Laurence Dunbar: Biography Through Letters

Toward the conclusion of the Centenary Conference on Paul Laurence Dunbar at which these lectures were first presented, Saunders Redding mused before beginning his speech: "I'm in the unenviable position of following Arna Bontemps, Darwin Turner, Dickson Bruce, Addison Gayle, Kenny Williams. And I'm abashed because they have said, either explicitly or implicitly, and said brilliantly, some of the things I'm going to try to say tonight." Professor Redding's talk, not surprisingly, added one more to the brilliant list he named, as did the presentations of James Emanuel, Gossie Hudson, Myron Simon, and Sarah Webster Fabio. How much more abashed, then, must the editor be who, having heard and read the essays of these critics, must now try to introduce them. My first inclination is to step back at once from such presumption; that inclination, indeed, is so persuasive that I will follow it forthwith. For only Dunbar himself could have anything original to say after so much original thought has been devoted to his life and works.

It is Dunbar himself, then, whom I wish to have speak. And since others have spoken so eloquently of his poetry and fiction, I will confine myself to the less well known,[1] but equally revelatory, personal documents in two collections of his letters in which he portrays his commitment to two sets of standards and values—in one group, to the aesthetic values residing in works of art; and in the other, to the racial values residing in his community. Taken together, these series of letters, show, I think, that Dunbar managed to unite his hopes to be an artist with his desires to represent his people, and to be, in both, equally energetic and aggressive, even while he suffered personally from the way in which both his literary career and also his defenses of his people brought him into contact with the racism so pronounced in American culture in the 1890s and the first decade of this century.

The meeting of Dunbar and James Newton Matthews was accidental, occurring in connection with the gathering of the Western Writers Association in Dayton in 1892, the only year it met in Dayton. Yet their acquaintance on this occasion was to determine Dunbar upon a literary career. Several weeks after the event, Matthews wrote a literary letter about Dunbar to the Indianapolis *Journal* that was reprinted all across the country and read by James Whitcomb Riley, who soon welcomed Dunbar to the company of his followers. In a very direct way, this led to the publication of Dunbar's first book, *Oak and Ivy*; the praise of Matthews and Riley was even used in the advertising and helped to sell the book.

But let Matthews tell the story, as he does in that article:

> A month or two ago, while in Dayton, O., I attended a meeting of the Western authors. About half way down the informal programme the presiding officer announced the reading of a poem by Paul Dunbar. Just the name for a poet, thought I. Great was the surprise of the audience to see stepping lightly down the aisle between the rows of fluttering fans and the assembled beauty and wit of Dayton, a slender Negro lad, as black as the core of Cheops's pyramid. He ascended the rostrum with the coolness and dignity of a cultured entertainer and delivered a poem in a tone "as musical as is Apollo's lute." He was applauded to the echo between the stanzas, and heartily encored at the conclusion. He then disappeared from the hall as suddenly as he had entered it, and many were the whispered conjectures as to the personality of the man, and the originality of his verses, none believing it possible that one of his age and color could produce a thing of such evident merit.
>
> After repeated inquiries I succeeded in locating the rising laureate of the colored race, and called upon him. He was an elevator boy in one of the down-town business blocks. I found him seated in a chair on the lower landing, hastily glancing at the July *Century*, and jotting down notes on a handy pencil tablet. Not having time to converse with me there, he invited me into the elevator, and

> during a few excursions from floor to floor, I gathered from him the following facts: His parents were both slaves, his father having escaped into Canada from the South. His mother is living in Dayton, and he is supporting her and himself on the pitiful sum of $4 per week. He is 19 years of age. In reply to a question, he stated that he had been writing rhymes since he was 13. His favorite authors are Whittier and James Whitcomb Riley. Before leaving I requested him to send me some of his verses in manuscript. Yesterday I received from him a letter enclosing the promised sample of his verse. His spirit seems to be broken. In his letter he says: "My hopes are no brighter than when you saw me. I am getting on no better, and, what would be impossible, no worse. I am nearer discouraged than I have ever been."
>
> Poor Dunbar! He deserves a better fate. Dayton, the terminus of the old underground railway, should be proud of him, and yet, with all his natural brilliancy and capability for better things, he is chained like a galley slave to the ropes of a dingy elevator at starvation wages.

One more sentence remained. "Show me a white boy of 19," Matthews wrote, "who can excell, or even equal, lines like these"; to prove his point, he went on to quote one poem in standard English and one in Western dialect, "A Drowsy Day" and "The Ol' Tunes."

Matthews had portrayed Dunbar's dilemma well and judged his talent wisely. He and Dunbar, after all, had corresponded since the end of July, after the ending of the Western Writers conference, and Dunbar had freely discussed his hopes for his own future in literature and for (as he put it) "the development of a distinctly Western school of poets, such as Riley represents. This may come to pass in that literary millennium, when Chicago becomes a great publishing center, as foreseen by Dr. Ridpath. Until that time the nightingales and thrushes will sing so loud that the modest piping of a homely every day meadow-lark cannot be heard" (July 26, 1892). Both Matthews and Dunbar regarded themselves as Western writers, engaged in writing the great American epic in sections, and certainly this note predominated in Matthews's critique. Dunbar had not yet been forced onto the plantation. Yet, he was already concerned about his future. Privately, after his article appeared, Matthews wrote to encourage Dunbar not to despair. "Dear Friend," Dunbar replied in his elegant script on October 12, 1892,

> For friend you have proven to be; your letter found me still chained to the ropes of my dingy elevator; but it came like a ray of light into the darkness of my discouragement. I want to thank you as much for that kindly, strengthening letter as for your excellent article to the Journal. . . .
>
> They will both do me good. The letter is giving strength to my soul and the article is paving the way for a venture which I am now about to undertake. . . .
>
> I had determined to publish a number of my poems in book form and try to sell them and I would not have wanted a better aid than the write up you gave me.

Dunbar continued by speaking of the two impulses then at war in him, the contrast between his sensibility and the menial, ill-paid work of elevator operator into which he was forced by institutionalized racism. He spoke of the facts that "The Ol' Tunes" had been syndicated by the American Press Association in their "Gems in Verse" column, and he had already attracted fan mail from as far away as Valley Falls, Rhode Island, where a man who had heard of his "sweet gift" asked for a photo and a dozen of his best poems. But, he added, "There have been many things to encourage me but the incongeniality of my work and surroundings cannot but have a depressing effect."

Still, the letters of praise continued to arrive in response to the poems Matthews printed. During the next week he was asked to submit a poem for a book on "bird poetry"—probably "The Sparrow" was written to fulfill this request—he was "receiving many letters from different parts of the country," and when the Fisk Jubilee Singers came to Dayton, Dunbar appeared with them before an audience of over six hundred at the YMCA hall and read his poems, which were received "with an unexpected heartiness." It was a heady time. Even so, his fears over his prospects and his suspicions of a literary career in a white world kept appearing. "With it all," he told Matthews, "I cannot help being overwhelmed by self doubts. I hope there is something worthy in my writings and not merely the novelty of a black face associated with the power to rhyme that has attracted attention." Nonetheless, he clearly was setting out on a literary career and he promised to follow Matthews's advice and to perfect himself as a poet by carefully revising his work, "if I can overcome the utter inability to change a poem that I usually feel." Indeed, he had already based a poem on Matthews's advice, "Keep A-Pluggin' Away," he said.

Clearly, this was a time when Dunbar was being pulled in two ways—toward literature, but also more and more toward entanglement with the politics and prejudices of the white community, where he was likely to suffer. Not even Matthews's article was without ill effects. In a letter begun on November 4, Dunbar wrote, "The republications of your article have greatly inflamed my employer, especially the wage part—he has just had his name in the paper for giving $2000 to charity—he is trying to make me swallow all the insults he can, and will discharge me as soon as he can find another man to work eleven hours a day for $4.00 a week." Matthews wrote back at once with remorse for his remark, but by mid-November "the storm had all blown over," and Dunbar could be ironical about his job. "It's like bad money, I can't lose it."

One more bit of news that Matthews sent also—and very rightly, indeed prophetically—alarmed the poet. A Montreal philanthropist named Ross sent Matthews twenty dollars to buy books for the young poet, with this remark: "I consider that a colored poet of sufficient ability to make a name for himself would do more to enlighten and encourage to ambition the multitude of the colored people in America than almost anything else that could be done for them. They would have someone to look up to—one whose pen would diffuse many wholesome truths to the people of the race, and would imbue others with the desire to emulate his success." True, Matthews had referred to Dunbar's race, but the way in which Dunbar was assigned to be *the* representative poet for black men by the well-intentioned but paternalistic philanthropist must have been alarming. It was the first step in his literary segregation into the role of the white man's concept of the black poet that would torment him for years; for though, as I shall show, he wanted passionately to represent his people, he wished to do so for *their* benefit and not for the mere entertainment or satisfaction of whites. This early the question of dialect verse arose; Matthews, who had printed one of the poems in dialect, opposed Dunbar's dialect work, and Dunbar promised, "I shall write less dialect after this." The attention he had received and the problems it raised could not, however, be so easily solved. He wrote to Matthews, "But indeed this publicity is disturbing me. It upsets me and makes me nervous. I feel like a man walking a slack rope above thousands of spectators, who knows himself an amateur and is every moment expecting to fall." Still, there *was* the matter of the money; and Matthews, who was a practical man, offered Dunbar the twenty dollars outright. But since he was otherwise almost always "compelled to regard my ordinary needs," Dunbar decided to have the luxury of the books—Crabb's book of *Synonyms* and Harper's *Cyclopedia of Poetry* among them.

Clearly, the currents of Dunbar's future were already beginning to swirl and foam and eddy around him, and he was beginning to move with them. His economic circumstances were intolerable and unstable. How could he foresee a future tied to the ropes of his dingy elevator? He knew that writers like Riley were well supported by sales and readings, yet he had not yet been able to sell a single poem. Even though his verses were more and more widely reprinted by newspapers, he was not protected by adequate copyright laws. At this time he often saw his only prospects as arising from professional preparation, and he thought of preparing for the law. "I have always had the desire to go to college," he told Matthews pragmatically, "but must confess to having little faith in the 'on flow'ry beds of ease' method. It would do me good to be able to fight my own way through a good school; but if it be denied me, why all I can do is to resign myself." As Saunders Redding suggests in his essay in this book, Dunbar, like his black contemporaries, was not allowed to choose his own career, his life's work; it was being chosen for him. More and more it seemed that the elevator cage would open only through a literary career, in the directions that Matthews and many others after him would point for Dunbar. He could not choose *whether* to follow the directions of others—only *which* circumstances designed by others to choose. Always conscious of the circumstances of his destiny, Dunbar would complain to Matthews that he could get no employment, since people had come to think of him as a writer, and he added, strikingly and decisively: "It is not I but those people who have made up my mind for me, that I must 'adopt literature as a profession.' "

In this state of powerlessness, it took only the slightest push to move Dunbar in a given direction, and Matthews had provided that thrust. Later, Dunbar himself clearly saw the intimate connections that I have been tracing between his literary career and his association with Matthews. In a letter of December 12, 1893, he described his literary fortune of the year and concluded, "I am beginning to feel timidly hopeful and at each step I take ahead, I thank and bless you for it, for you were the Moses that led out my enslaved powers." By planning *Oak and Ivy*, Dunbar was moved in the direction of Matthews's praise. But by deciding to make a career of poetry, he was also moving in the direction of his own considerable literary talent. In late November 1892, when he received his "first money for a poem, two dollars for a little piece to a child's publication in New York," he could write "I am beginning to hope" (November 29, 1892). He started a flurry of activity, as he told Matthews:

> I got together some of my best work, so I thought, and sent it off as follows: Sonnet–N.Y. Independent–A Poem–N.Y. Sun, Poem, Ladies Home Journal–Story to Washington Post, rejected, then to Chicago Post, rejected, then to Chicago News rejected, then A.K. Kellogg Newspaper Co. rejected.–Sketch to the Cincinnati Commercial Gazette. Now all of these were returned except the one I mentioned, to the L.H.J. (February 7, 1893).

And of course, *Oak and Ivy* appeared just before year's end. Then, Dunbar's literary genius was wound in the coil of events that Matthews had initiated. He spoke to Matthews about a prose sketch he was preparing for *Youth's Companion*, and continued–as we almost hear another cage open and then close with a click–"I have acted upon your advice and am trying to work into stories the old tales of the South that I have been hearing since early childhood. Whether they will get into the papers or not I cannot foretell, for it is so hard to get a hearing for a new voice in the literary world." From thinking of himself as a Western writer, Dunbar was moving toward the Plantation Tradition; and, for good or ill, *Folks from Dixie* and "Chrismus on the Plantation" were in his future.

Dunbar wrote several other letters in 1893 to Matthews as his literary career blossomed—letters that described financially successful readings in Detroit and Toledo, his articles on the 1893 World's Fair in Chicago, his attendance at the summer meeting of the Western Association of Writers, his hopes for favorable reviews of *Oak and Ivy* from the Chicago *News Record* and the *Interocean* as well as the suggestion that Matthews review it, and progress reports on sales, all summarized in Dunbar's concluding remark in a letter of May 2, 1893: "I would that I could make my living with my pen."[2] It is appropriate to go no further in his letters to Matthews, for here he reaches the conclusion that he had been making for all this time. During the next decade he would make a living as a professional writer. And he would produce the sketches and novels that the critics in this volume discuss so illuminatingly. However one judges his work—and I judge much of it to be highly successful, especially through the brilliant dramatic sense that informs it—undeniably, in becoming a writer he was thrust toward genteel society and the pressures to satisfy its various demands. And he was, the letters to Matthews show, so moved almost imperceptibly, until it would seem that he could not move back.

But he did move back, and in the letters to which I now turn, he showed both a confidently positive identification with his community, his peoplehood, and also a very aggressive capacity to defend it against attacks of dominant society. In turn, we must see in these letters evidence of the support that his sense of community gave him, providing the power that lay in back of what James Emanuel calls the "racial fire," and, less explicitly, the imaginative energy of much of his poetry and fiction. While he was being drawn as a writer into a society that would often treat him with indignity, precisely because he was a black man he also had available to him the strengths of his black community. I do not think that the importance of this influence upon Dunbar has been fully recognized, even though in an earlier essay titled "Paul Laurence Dunbar: The Rejected Symbol" Darwin T. Turner pointed out the importance of his articles of protest, and in this volume, Kenny Jackson Williams shows the importance of the anonymous black community of Dorbury, in *The Fanatics*. Even before these, too,

W. S. Scarborough, the president of Wilberforce, remarked that the work of Dunbar was "pre-eminently racial. . . . He felt for his race, and . . . he sang with the heart and tongue of the people." My own comments derive largely from theirs, but I will also look closely at Dunbar's letters and articles.

During Dunbar's youth, five thousand blacks lived in Dayton, constituting nearly ten percent of the population. For several reasons they comprised a rather special community. As the Northern outpost for the underground railroad, and as a center for abolitionist activity, Dayton had long been a center for free Negroes. For some of the same reasons, the black community in it was fairly self-sufficient economically. Black churches were extremely active in Dayton and nearby Springfield, and provided centers for intellectual and social life. Churches also provided a rich source in the 1890s for racial-awareness movements, where the proposals of Douglass, Alexander Crummell, and others were avidly discussed. Finally, as racist attacks on blacks increased after Reconstruction ended, the community tended to draw close together to form a cohesive, interactive unit. These were all potential sources of self-esteem for Dunbar and formed his sense of a worthy self in relation to others.[3] That he recognized this and drew upon these sources is evidenced in his first literary work—his editorship of the *Tattler*, a newspaper established specifically to represent the black population of Ohio. In his "Salutatory"—his first editorial—Dunbar very clearly described the needs of his community, proposing to satisfy these needs through his paper:

> Dayton with her sixty thousand inhabitants, among which are numbered five thousand colored people, has for a long time demanded a paper, representative of the energy and enterprise of our citizens. It is this long felt want which the Tattler now aspires to fill. Her mission shall be to encourage and assist the enterprises of the city, to give our young people a field in which to exercise their literary talents, to champion the cause of right; and to espouse the principles of honest republicanism. The desire which is the guiding star of our existence is that some word may be dropped in our columns, which shall reach the hearts of our colored voters and snatch them from the brink of that yawning chasm—paid democracy.
>
> There are materials to make a successful newspaper in this city, if they can only be combined and utilized. And we must ask the co-

operation of a generous public in our attempt to do this. Every one can give us some aid: first by subscribing to the paper: for local pride if nothing else should prompt you to do this; next by advertising; and thirdly by contributing. You should subscribe, first because knowing as you do that a city having so many colored inhabitants as Dayton should support a newspaper, you would feel it your duty; then because it will benefit you by keeping you posted on all current matters. The literaries shall be represented and all the lodges shall find their notices readily published by us, and we shall have items of interest from many other cities. Why you should advertise with us can be told in few words, because it is money in your pockets.

Grocers, blacksmiths, restauranteurs, all should advertise, and boarding house keepers should not forget that the paper will go out of town and their "ads" will be noticed in other cities so that when people come from those towns here, they will know where to stop. So advertise and advertise soon.

Lastly, contribute because there is no better way for ambitious young men and young ladies to bring themselves before the public than by writing for a live newspaper.

With these few introductory words, the Dayton Tattler makes its initial bow to the public, demanding the recognition which is its right.

In the same issue of the *Tattler* Dunbar aggressively took up the question of race, addressing his fellow black editors and the black populace. He begins deceptively, by declaring, "A great mistake . . . made by editors of the race is that they discuss only one question, the race problem." But, he says, "A quarter of a century of discussion . . . has worn it thread bare, . . . no new idea has been presented upon this subject for the last ten years." Then, just as he seems about to dismiss the race problem, quite conventionally, as constituting an irrelevant issue, he turns surprisingly back: "We do not counsel you, debaters, writers, and fellow editors, to throw away your opinions on this all important question; on the contrary we deem it one worthy of constant thought. But the time has come when you should act your opinions out, rather than write them. Your cry is, 'we must agitate, we must agitate.' So you must but bear in mind that the agitation of deeds is tenfold more effectual than the agitation of words. For your own sake, for the sake of Heaven and the race, stop saying, and go to doing."

In the second number of the *Tattler* (December 20, 1890), Dunbar continued his attack upon white institutions as well as his defense of the black community; his paper, he said, was "for the colored people of Ohio." He spoke of black political power, concluding, "The colored voters in the last election were very much like cats. When they were tramped upon, they turned around and scratched." In another Dunbar article, under the head of "Negro Superstitions," he clearly was taking black behavior as his norm and attacking white misstatements. Controverting an article that had appeared in the *Herald,* he argued, "This idea about the Negro race being more superstitious than any other is erroneous, any way. Many of the most absurd superstitions of the time can be traced to the old Puritan founders of the country."

Though Dunbar was but eighteen when these issues of the *Tattler* appeared, he showed that he had fully absorbed a black point of view. The development of black enterprise, the molding of an ethnic political opinion, the creation of a distinctive black cultural and artistic mode, the need for vehicles of communication in the community, the development of black pride, the involvement of all black institutions in one organ, the creation of black consciousness and the development of self-esteem in individuals, a call for social agitation, and attacks upon white denigrations of the black community—these themes are all rapidly but unmistakably adumbrated in the observations with which Dunbar began his paper. In his first issue he had urged his readers, "We should have by the second week, two hundred subscriptions from young men alone. Young men save a dollar and a half from pleasure and help support a colored journal." But those dollars, doubtless, were devoted to Christmas gifts; for after five or six issues the paper folded. Yet, those issues show in very bold terms the clarity and conviction of Dunbar's commitment to the black community.

It seems clear that Dunbar was consciously attempting to reach his brothers, by prose or verse. Prose journalism seemed to be the more likely route, and in 1894, on his way to a second editorship, in an article for the Chicago *Record* Dunbar paused to consider the history and progress "Of Negro Journals" as evinced in "the tone of its press." He begins by declaring that "even a cursory glance over the past history of his journalistic achievements will show that the Negro's newspaper . . . has not merely kept pace with his evolutions, but rather led the way. It was the voice of an oppressed people." Then he goes on, strikingly, to show an intimate acquaintance with the history of black newspapers. "Freedom's Journal, the Ram's Horn and the North Star," he says, "awakened public opinion and paved . . . the way to emancipation" as "the first shoots of an intellectual growth in a people who were popularly supposed to be incapable of any such development." With emancipation achieved, he continues, this "separate and distinct press" would seem to have had no further call for existence. But, "as soon as the head of slavery was cut off the Negro found that the monster was like Hydra, and that there were a dozen more very aggressive heads newly arisen that needed destroying." Under such circumstances of multiplied oppression, he concludes sardonically, "five papers arose for every head. Subsequently, this proposition has been maintained, which accounts for the 250 papers published by colored people in the United States today." Even more self-consciously than in his editorials for the *Tattler* Dunbar was attempting to protect, and perhaps advance, the interests of the black community through journalism. It is not surprising to find him, as early as 1893, in correspondence with other black writers—Joseph Seaman Cotter, J. Edwin Campbell, and William Edgar Easton—who were all attempting to create a distinctive black literature. Nor was it surprising that in May of 1895 he assumed the managing editorship of the Indianapolis *World*, another black paper.

That editorship was only a temporary job. But Dunbar was more and more committed to the literary life. In pursuing that career, he would move away from the black community of Dayton, to such literary centers as Washington and New York. But his own positive view of the black community was not diminished; if anything it increased. Again we can find the evidence for this in the dispatches he continued to send to the newspapers. These speak for themselves—particularly one of mid-December 1898, published in the Chicago *Record* under the title "Recession Never":

It would seem that the man who sits at his desk in the North and writes about the troubles in the South is very apt to be like a doctor who prescribes for a case he has no chance to diagnose. It would be true in this instance, also, if it were not that what has happened in Georgia has happened in Ohio and Illinois. The race riots in North Carolina were of a piece with the same proceedings in the state of Lincoln. The men who shoot the Negro in Hogansville are blood brothers to those who hang him in Urbana, and the deed is neither better nor worse because it happens in one section of the country or other. The race spirit in the United States is not local but general.

To the outsider, unacquainted with the vagaries of our national prejudice, the recent and sudden change of attitude of the American toward the Negro would appear inconsistent, to say the least. We are presented with the spectacle of a people gushing, through glowing headlines, over the bravery of its black heroes. In an incredibly short space of time—almost too brief, it would seem for the mental transition of the individual, much less the nation—we find the mouthpieces of this same people chronicling the armed resistance of the community to the Negroes in the exercise of those powers and privileges which are the glory of the country for which the colored men fought. The drama of this sudden change of heart is incongruous to the point of ghastly humor.

The new attitude may be interpreted as saying: "Negroes, you may fight for us, but you may not vote for us. You may prove a strong bulwark when the bullets are flying, but you must stand from the line when the ballots are in the air. You may be heroes in war, but you must be cravens in peace.

It is true, as has been insistently urged, that it would be expedient for the Negro to forego his suffrage and climb to worth and to the world's respect by other means. By other means: That is the cry of the miners when they ask him out of the mines. It is the word of the whole commercial world when they ask him out of everything—the American shibboleth. Relinquish! Relinquish! And from the dust of the very lowest places, the places that grind men's souls and kill ambition, the Negroes seek to climb to places of worth and respect.

In order to cool the passions and allay the prejudices of the superior race the entire self-effacement of the Negro would be expedient—as expedient as it would be cowardly; and, say what you will of the American people, their respect is not to be won by cowardice. Let those suffering people relinquish one single right that has been given them and the rapacity of the other race, encouraged by yielding, will ravage from them every privilege that they possess. Passion and prejudice are not sated by concession, but grow by what they feed on.

The Vaudois, hiding like wild beasts in their mountain fastnesses, shot like goats upon their own hills, purpling with their blood the streams of their own valleys, France could hate, but dared not despise. The Indian himself, ground to dust under the heel of civilization, driven to death by the greed of a stronger people, will not be remembered with a sneer. But for the Negro honor is dangerous; only cowardice is safe.

The African is told that he is not yet ready to participate in government, because he has not yet learned to govern himself, and the race which preaches this proves its own right to political domination by the rioting, the rapine and the slaughter, with which for weeks past the civilized world has been scandalized. Since when was ever a psychological [thesis] published with [and defended by] a musket?

After all, the question is not one of the Negro's fitness to rule or to vote, but of the right of the whites to murder him for the sake of instruction. Not a groan that the Romans wrung from the hearts of the conquered Britons, but echoed and re-echoed in the sound of her own fall. Every drop of blood that France drew from her own suffering Huguenots on St. Bartholomew's day but called its brother to the hungry sod on that awful 14th day of July. Rome sated her thirst for blood and called it civilization. France indulged her barbaric fancy and named it religion. America strides through the ashes of burning homes, over the bodies of murdered men, women and children holding aloft the banner of progress.

Progress! Necessity! Expedience!

But why is it necessary to excuse these acts of sophistry? Is not murder murder? Is not rapine rapine? Is not outrage outrage?

The whites are stronger than the blacks. Why not then say to them openly: "We don't like you; we do not want you in certain places. Therefore when we please we will kill you. We are strong people; you are weak. What we choose to do we will do; right or no right. There is no one to wage with us a holy war in the cause of humanity."

Even the church has attempted to explain and palliate and we are told from the pulpit that the Negroes have been taught a salutary lesson: that the whites must prevail. The murderers of Wilmington are congratulated upon the effort they have made toward civilization and purer government. And some of this within a stone's throw of the nation's capitol. When the reckoning shall come, what shall such ministers say? They have not stoned martyrs but they have burned their shoulders with the coats of those who did; and every such is an accomplice dyed with the same blood of the men who stood redhanded over the murdered blacks. And yet, what else could we expect from the pulpit, when we remember that less than forty years ago with the same smug complacency, it was finding excuses for slavery and in tracing out the divine intention?

The passions of the people often need a spiritual backing, and shame to say, we have a clergy always ready and willing to furnish it, whether it be when man restrains his fellow men from the exercise of his national rights or murders him for pursuing his political dues. It is a disgrace to the honor of their calling, a reflection upon the intelligences of their heroes, and an insult to the God they profess to serve.

The text for better and for different sermons might be found for those divines in Paul's first epistle to the Corinthians. It is as apt to-day as it was then, and it applies to the American people with no less strength than it did to the older race. "Take heed," said the apostle, "lest by any means this liberty of yours become a stumbling block to them that are weak."

We are comforted with the statement that the sudden enfranchisement of the Negro was a mistake. Perhaps it was, but the whites made it. The mistakes of life are not corrected in that way. Their effects are eternal. You cannot turn back the years and put ten millions of people into the condition that four millions were in thirty years ago. You cannot ignore the effects that have ensued, the changes that have followed, and make the problem of to-day the problem of 1865. It is a different one. The whole aspect of the case has changed. The Negro has changed. Public opinion has shifted. Try as you will, though it has grown away, you cannot put the plant back into the seed. Of course you can root it up entirely; but beware of its juices.

Thirty years ago the American people told the Negro that he was a man with a man's full powers. They deemed it that important that they did what they have done few times in the history of the country—they wrote it down in their constitution. And now they come with the shot gun in the south and sophistry in the north to prove to him that it was all wrong.

For so long a time has the black man believed that he is an American citizen that he will not be easily convinced to the contrary. It will take more than the hangings, the burnings and the lynchings, both north and south, to prove it to his satisfaction. He is not so credulous as he was. He is a different man. The American people cannot turn back the tide of years and make him what he was. And so it was an entirely new people with whom they have to deal. It is an entirely new problem which is presented to them for solution. Why then should it not be met with calmness, justice, breadth and manliness which should characterize a great nation?

If the problem is as much the Negro's as the white man's—and I do not say that it is not—he is doing his best to settle it. He is acquiring property. Yes he even builds churches to the religion whose servants preach his damnation. He is going forward. Such catastrophes as the southern riots, terrible though they be, are but incidents in his growth, which is inevitable. The principle of manhood is springing to life within him. Every year men are being educated to live for it. Every year to some—to many, it seems—God gives the better grace to die for it.

Commentary on this essay would be superfluous, since in every particular it clearly emerges from the same unified consciousness of blackness—filled out with public self-confidence—that we saw operating eight years earlier in his *Tattler* commentaries. Originally written for *McClure's*, the magazine in which the muckraking movement began, and which included Ida Tarbell, Lincoln Steffens, and Ray Stannard Baker on its staff, this article proved too strong for *McClure's* to print. The rake, as that magazine then conceived it, was not designed to throw up racial muck.

Only a few days later, Dunbar took up the same pen of fire once again to discuss the problems of "The Negroes of the Tenderloin" in a letter to the New York *Sun*. Perhaps the first article that called attention to the racial problems of the northern cities, in this piece Dunbar feelingly described the "crowds of idle, shiftless Negroes that throng" the East Side. Then, his soul went out to his people:

I look on at it all, and, though I feel fear for our civilization, I must confess that the strongest emotion in my heart is pity for the

> poor people themselves and for their children. They are my brothers, and what touches them touches me. I can look on at the vice and degradation of Whitechapel and the Seven Dials with less emotion than I can upon the misdeeds of the Tenderloin. For the former I sorrow in the name of humanity; for the latter I grieve on account of my race, which already has so much to overcome. Do you say that this is too narrow a view, too selfish? If it is so, it is because I have been forced into it. As a race, we are thrown back upon ourselves, isolated from other Americans, and so brought into a more intimate communion one with the other. Fifth Avenue cannot feel for Cherry Hill as the better class of Negroes must feel for their degraded brethren, because the former are not so closely identified with each other. The sight of a dweller in Fifth Avenue does not suggest a denizen of Cherry Hill; but the sight of one Negro suggests a race.

His is a vision of horror, of human degradation, of a lost humanity and shattered community. His people, Dunbar says, "have given up the fields for the gutters. They have bartered the sweet-smelling earth of their freshly turned furrows for the stenches of a metropolitan alley, . . . they do not walk like clodhoppers, but they creep like vermin." Dunbar's cry of pain echoes through his letter—it is the black man he calls to, the "simple, common folk" for whom he said he designed his songs, the lowly black community of his earliest life. Eugene Debs, somewhat later, identified himself with the working class in words that are famous. But who knows Dunbar's defense of his people, his sense that the black struggle is classless? "So if the better class Negro would come to his own he must lift not only himself, but the lower men, whose blood brother he is. He cannot afford to look down upon the denizens of the Tenderloin or to withdraw himself from them; for the fate of the blacks there degraded, ignorantly vicious as they may be, is his fate."

Dunbar, it is clear, was not writing these articles from the point of view of the dominant society—he preserved a very clear sense both of the injustice done to his people and also of the inner integrity that the black community retained in spite of all outside pressures. We can fairly say, I think, that in the nineteenth century Dunbar recognized the need for self-esteem and for what Jarrett has called "black arrogance" or an aggressive attitude toward his world. In this Dunbar was following in the tradition of such black leaders as Douglass, for whom he worked in 1893, and Alexander Crummell, with whom he lived in London in 1897. Certainly he and Du Bois were the two most powerful spokesmen around the turn of the century against the problems of the color line. Two themes run through all of Dunbar's newspaper dispatches: an assertion of the worthiness of black life and an exposure of the pathology of the white denial of that worth.

One more letter by Dunbar, written to *The New York Times* as a sardonic commentary on the ironies of Independence Day in America, appeared on July 10, 1903, and is an astonishing example of the clarity and dignity of Dunbar's perceptions of the tragic course of race problems in America.

> Belleville, Wilmington, Evansville, the Fourth of July, and Kishineff, a curious combination and yet one replete with a ghastly humor. Sitting with closed lips over our own bloody deeds, we accomplish the fine irony of a protest to Russia. Contemplating with placid eyes the destruction of all the Declaration of Independence and the Constitution stood for, we celebrate the thing which our own action proclaims we do not believe in.
>
> But it is over and done. The Fourth is come and gone. The din has ceased and the smoke has cleared away. Nothing remains but the litter of all and a few reflections. The skyrocket has ascended, the firecrackers have burst, the roman candles have sputtered, the "nigger chasers"—a pertinent American name—have run their courses, and we have celebrated the Nation's birthday. Yes, and we black folks have celebrated.
>
> Dearborn Street and Armour Avenue have been all life and light. Not even the Jews and the Chinamen have been able to outdo us in the display of loyalty. And we have done it all because we have not stopped to think just how little it means to us.
>
> The papers are full of the reports of peonage in Alabama. A new and more dastardly slavery there has arisen to replace the old. For the sake of re-enslaving the Negro, the Constitution has been trampled under feet, the rights of man have been laughed out of court, and the justice of God has been made a jest, and we celebrate.
>
> Every wire, no longer in the South alone, brings us news of a new hanging or a new burning, some recent outrage against a helpless people, some fresh degradation of an already degraded race. One man sins and a whole nation suffers, and we celebrate.

Like a dark cloud, pregnant with terror and destruction, disenfranchisement has spread its wings over our brethren of the South. Like the same dark cloud, industrial prejudice glooms above us in the North. We may not work save when the new-come foreigner refuses to, and then they, high prized above our sacrificial lives, may shoot us down with impunity. And yet we celebrate.

With citizenship discredited and scorned, with violated homes and long unheeded prayers, with bleeding hands uplifted, still sore and smarting from long beating at the door of opportunity, we raise our voices and sing, "My Country, 'Tis of Thee"; we shout and sing while from the four points of the compass comes our brothers' unavailing cry, and so we celebrate.

With a preacher, one who a few centuries ago would have sold indulgences to the murderers on St. Bartholomew's Day, with such a preacher in a Chicago pulpit, jingling his thirty pieces of silver, distorting the number and nature of our crimes, excusing anarchy, apologizing for murder, and tearing to tatters the teachings of Jesus Christ while he cries, "Release unto us Barabbas," we celebrate.

But there are some who sit silent within their closed rooms and hear as from afar the din of joy come muffled to their ears as on some later day their children and their children's sons shall hear a nation's cry for succor in her need. "Aye, there be some who on this festal day kneel in their private closets and with hands upraised and bleeding hearts cry out to God, if there still lives a God, 'How long, O God, How long.' "

This was the last of the articles Dunbar was to write, but as powerfully as any he wrote in more than a decade, it asserts and defends the nobility of his people. So it well serves as his last such pronouncement. In 1903, too, his literary career was also ending; his production thereafter came virtually to a halt as future collections of his work were gleaned from earlier writings. It was coincidental, but not inappropriate, therefore, that less than three weeks after this last article appeared, and after a long silence, Dunbar should have received a letter from James Newton Matthews. On August 1, 1903, he hastened to reply—in the last letter he wrote to Matthews before his friend died. The excitement of youth is there again, I feel, in the letter—but it is deeply mixed with the sadness of the end of Dunbar's life:

Are the skies going to fall?

My dear old friend, I have never been more surprised in my life than I was this morning. I have been writing to you oft and on until about three years ago and could never get a response, and here all of a sudden you come to life. I am so glad that I cannot wait until I am well enough to write you by hand but send you this little, old handshake on a machine. It is very, very good to hear from you again, though I am sorry to know that your eyes are not good. Let me hope that they will soon be better.

* * *

With very, very grateful remembrances of all your kindness to me, I am

Sincerely your friend,
Paul Laurence Dunbar.

In these pages I have only tried to present Dunbar as revealed in his relevant letters and articles as he saw himself from the perspectives of two areas of his experience which were crucial to him—his role as a writer and his relation to his people. These are often identical and always close to his more explicit concerns. In the pages that follow, Dunbar is discussed with great insight and force from a variety of perspectives. I will not attempt to speak for the authors of these essays or make any effort to summarize or compare the positions they take, since the contributors to this volume speak so well for themselves.

Even though I am fully possessed by the desire to hurry the reader along to those essays, I wish to make one further observation, the effect of which is intended to bring Dunbar's life and work into a very direct relation to the present. After all, most of the contributors to this volume were first brought together in person, at the University of California, Irvine, to honor Paul Laurence Dunbar and, by their lectures and their presence, to celebrate the occasion of the hundredth anniversary of Dunbar's birth. There were several things that were extraordinary about this conference, and it is only to speak of these that I would detain the reader still further.

The first extraordinary thing about it was its very existence. By this I do not simply mean that the money was made available to fund it—though to gather these funds took four months of my almost daily effort, and the gathering of scholars that took place between November 2 and 5, 1972, was only, finally, made possible by the collaboration of the Program in Comparative Culture, the Committee on Student Affairs and Lectures, the School of Humanities, the Extension Division, the Graduate Council, and Daniel G. Aldrich, Jr., Chancellor of the University of California, Irvine. Certainly, I wish to acknowledge the material importance of their aid.

But what I really mean to refer to is the *existential* nature of the conference. This occasion was, I make bold to say, a historic one in which black and white scholars gathered together to honor the achievement of an eminent poet, the first time that a black poet has been so honored by a major university in the United States. While by the nature of their distinction and dignity, Arna Bontemps and Saunders Redding naturally took precedence of a sort—and were honored jointly by belated birthday cards in a tender ceremony—still, a genuine sense prevailed that here scholarly men and women had assembled to do honor, with their best talents, to a fellow human, a poet, and a man of great distinction. Long before the conference began, I described the program to a colleague in the English Department, for during that time I was always speaking of *the* conference that I was so busy at planning. He is of a rational, analytical bent, and after I finished he said, "That's the second time you've pointed out that both black and white critics are collaborating on this celebration. It must be important to you." It was. James Emanuel has observed about the writing of American literary history, "American literature might never record, with regard to black literature, any thoughtful consensus among its stellar critics, for they have generally failed to give that literature the respect of serious examination," and he has condemned the "silent white giants of the academy for their unforgivable long neglect." I myself find no reference to Dunbar in such presumably "standard" "objective" works of scholarship dealing with Dunbar's period as Warner Berthoff's *The Ferment of Realism,* Larzer Ziff's *The American 1890's,* Grant C. Knight's *The Critical Period in American Literature,* and Fred Lewis Pattee's *A History of American Literature Since 1870.* Certainly it was important that in this centenary conference black and white critics should have joined together not only to deepen our mutual sense of black writing, but also to expand our conceptions of American literature.

It remains important to me, then, and to all of us, that for perhaps the first time in the history of criticism in America black and white scholars have joined together in close personal association to study and honor a literary figure—and thus to honor each other and the occasion itself.

All during the planning for this gathering I had in mind two statements. The first is by Ralph Waldo Emerson:

> The world is young: the former great men call to us affectionately. We too must write Bibles, to unite again the heavens and the earthly world. The secret of genius is to suffer no fiction to exist for us; to realize all that we know; in the high refinement of modern life, in arts, in sciences, in books, in men, to exact good faith, reality and a purpose; and first, last, midst and without end, to honor every truth by use.

The other is Marcus Garvey's:

> If we are to have world peace, it will only come when a greater inter-racial conference is called. When Jew will meet Gentile; when Anglo-Saxon will meet Teuton; when the great Caucasian family will meet the Mongolian, and when all will meet the Negro, and then and there straighten out the differences that have kept us apart for hundreds of years, and will continue to keep us apart until Doom's Day, if something is not done to create better racial understanding.

These have been hard times for visionaries, for Emerson, for Dunbar, for Garvey, and for all of us who would seek to allow no fictions to exist and to honor our truths, and ourselves, with good faith and honest purpose. New bibles and new worlds are not easily born.

But this is really what the centenary conference on Paul Laurence Dunbar was about. And as it unfolded the observation of another visionary came to me as having expressed what we were learning to begin to do, together. Thirty-five years ago Richard Wright spoke of the need for writers, "white writers and Negro writers alike," to end "mistrust and isolation." "Writers faced with such tasks," he said, "can have no possible time for malice or jealousy. The conditions for the growth of each writer depend too much upon the good work of other writers. Every first rate novel, poem, or play lifts the level of consciousness higher."

And so does such a criticism as we have here. The conference is over, as the life of Dunbar is. But the spirit of humanity that is unmistakably infused in both that poet's life and the papers written about him remains to sustain what Garvey called the "common fraternity of progress and achievement, that will wipe away the odour of prejudice, and elevate the human race to the height of real Godly love and peace." If that spirit was capable once of moving men's hearts, it can be again, for the readers of this book.

NOTES

1. Dunbar's letters to Matthews have never before been published. The texts of Dunbar's letters on racial problems have never been reprinted since they appeared in newspapers between 1890 and 1903.
2. He was succeeding so well and so rapidly that by December 23, 1893, he told Matthews, "I have at present no regular employment but am trying to live by my pen."
3. There has been extensive research by black psychologists on the growth of self-esteem and its relation to the community. In particular I have in mind Edward J. Barnes, "The Black Community as a Source of Positive Self-concept," in *Black Psychology*, ed. Reginald L. Jones (New York: Harper & Row, 1972); V. Jarrett, "Black Arrogance: A Key to Survival," Chicago *Tribune*, October 25, 1970; Barbara A. Sizemore, "Separatism: A Reality Approach to Inclusion?" in *Racial Crisis in American Education*, ed. Robert L. Green (Chicago: Follett, 1969); Andrew Billingsley, *Black Families in White America* (Englewood Cliffs, N.J.: Prentice-Hall, 1968); and James Comer, "Self-Esteem and the Black American Future," *Renaissance 2: A Journal of Afro-American Studies* 1 (1971), 3–5.

I

REMINISCENCE

Saunders Redding

Portrait Against Background

I refuse to call this a lecture. Certainly in the formal academic sense it is not, nor was it my intention for it to be. I shall not lay out a series of assumptions and critical postulates or explore literary theories and scholarly resolutions to the various problems a close examination of Dunbar's work discovers—problems that are both narrowly aesthetic and broadly cultural, sociological and historical, psychological and metaphysical. One does sometimes get tired of both the means and the ends of academic scholarship and one gets tired of manipulating scholarly apparatus. I am chucking all that now. What I have to say in the next few minutes is in the nature of a memoir, the recapturing of a memory, a reminiscence, if you will. It is highly subjective, as of course all literary studies eventually boil down to being. If I say flatly I like Dunbar and his work, or most of it at any rate, I am making a subjective judgment which I straightaway qualify. I did not say, remember, that I have nothing but admiration for the poet and the writer. There are certainly components in his character and items in his canon that are admirable, but there are also things from which one turns with feelings of embarrassment. But let me get on with my reminiscence.

When I was a child a signed photograph of Dunbar hung over the mantel in what was called "the back parlor." This room was separated by an arched and curtained doorway from the front parlor, which was reserved for the entertainment of rather special company, like a visiting clergyman or other dignitary, and on one occasion, Charles Gilpin. He had come to Wilmington, Delaware, to play the title role in *The Emperor Jones* in the segregated and only legitimate theatre in the town. The hotels, too, were for whites only, and for three nights and two days Gilpin was a welcomed guest in our family's home.

I mention him particularly because after he had gone I learned in a dinner table conversation between my parents that Mr. Gilpin had known Paul Dunbar many years before, in the first half of the first decade of this century. He had known him in New York, where black artists, writers, singers, entertainers and figures in the sports world used to gather in Marshall's Hotel in the San Juan Hill section of what is now mid-Manhattan between Fifty-first and Fifty-seventh Streets west of Fifth Avenue. I estimate now that the time of Gilpin's acquaintance with Dunbar was about nineteenth hundred and two, or three, and Dunbar was no longer at the zenith of his fame. The poet's best work in both poetry and fiction was behind him and he was only three or four years from the close of his life.

And it was quite a life. In the operation of the vaunted American system of values, his choices were severely limited, as indeed they were for all of his black contemporaries. He could not really choose a career or a profession. Indeed, he had yearned to be a lawyer. Nor could he either accept or reject the hazards and the rewards of the career he was persuaded to follow. And this matter went even deeper. His search for identity was never completely successful because society never acknowledged him as the person he thought he was. He could not choose to be wholly himself. He had to make his life conform to one or another stereotype and to live up to the white man's models.

This was not easy for him. It is difficult for any man to achieve a definition of self in American society. You must find a slot to fill and a category that represents what you feel to be the essence of yourself that you can take to heart and be a part of. If no category is available, you have to make one. To accomplish this on a personal level is difficult enough, but to correlate the view that others have of you with your image of yourself is far more difficult. Coming to early manhood in a time when Booker T. Washington's accommodationist philosophy seemed to give validity not only to the prevailing paternalistic concept of race relations, but also to the dominant stereotypes of the black man that supported the concept, the difficulty was compounded for Dunbar. Chief among the stereotypes he had to contend with or reconcile himself to was that of the Negro as an irresponsible child, completely dependent upon the largess, the good will, and the loving kindness of white people, and eternally happy with this state of affairs and in this situation.

Paul Dunbar knew that this was not the way things really were. He sensed something sinister beneath the prevailing attitude and he saw behind the interchangeable mask of degradation, self-abasement, and clownishness his people wore another people altogether. This generated in him a certain ambivalence, a kind of double consciousness he found it difficult to deal with:

We wear the mask that grins and lies,
It hides our cheeks and shades our eyes—
This debt we pay to human guile;
With torn and bleeding hearts we smile,
And mouth with myriad subtleties.

Why should the world be over-wise,
In counting all our tears and sighs?
Nay, let them only see us, while
    We wear the mask.

We smile, but, O great Christ, our cries
To thee from tortured souls arise.
We sing, but oh the clay is vile
Beneath our feet, and long the mile;
But let the world dream otherwise,
    We wear the mask!

Forgive him if he gave some substance to that false dream in at least a hundred poems and a score of stories. The easiest way for the black man to survive in white society is to go with the flow. This passive attitude cannot be simultaneously held with an individual concept of existence based on individual pride and goals. A black man could not follow the dictates of white society and remain at peace with himself. A new, different, and personally established identity had to be created. Forgive him if in the days when he read his poetry to select audiences he made the dream seem real with mimetic performances and by dancing to the rhythm of his dialect jingles.

After one such literary concert in Newport, Rhode Island, a staid and imperiously aristocratic white lady rose while the all white audience was still applauding, waited for silence and said, "Paul"—she had never seen him before much less met him—"Paul," she said, in a most complimentary and gratified tone, "I shall never again wax impatient and cross at the childish antics of my servants, members of your race. Tonight, you have made me understand and love them." Following this remark, the applause was resumed more enthusiastically than before, and Paul Dunbar fled through a side door to an anteroom where his wife waited. There he dropped to his knees before her, buried his head in her lap, and wept convulsively.

Though there are many apocryphal Dunbar anecdotes, I can assure you this one is not apocryphal. I heard it from Paul Dunbar's widow, who besides being my high school English teacher, was also a family friend. She lived just around the corner and was occasionally in our home. She was Mrs. Alice Dunbar-Nelson then, having married sometime before a widower with two children who were my friends. "There was much bitterness in Paul which he had to suppress," Mrs. Nelson said more than once. If you play the game to survive, will the knowledge of your spiritual position keep you from being dominated? Hardly. Read *The Uncalled*, which, his widow said, was Dunbar's spiritual autobiography, in which, for the sake of credibility, he represents himself as a white youth. And in both *Along This Way* and *Black Manhattan* James Weldon Johnson suggests the same sense of suppressed bitterness and frustration.

But one does not have to go to these sources. Dunbar himself was very explicit. From London he wrote to a friend in 1897, "I see now very clearly that Mr. Howells has done me irrevocable harm in the dictum he laid down regarding my dialect verse." William Dean Howells was then the most outstanding and the most highly respected American literary critic. And what was the dictum he laid down? Here is what he wrote in the Introduction to Dunbar's first regularly published volume of poems, *Lyrics of Lowly Life*. He wrote,

> Yet it appeared to me then, and it appears to me now, that there is a precious difference of temperament between the races which it

> would be a great pity ever to lose, and this is best preserved and most charmingly *suggested* by Mr. Dunbar in those pieces of his where he studies the moods and traits of his race in its own accent of our English. We call such pieces dialect pieces for want of some closer phrase, but they are really not dialect so much as delightful personal attempts and failures for the written and spoken language. In nothing is his essentially refined and delicate art so well shown as in these pieces, which, as I ventured to say, *describe the range between appetite and emotion,* with certain lifts far beyond and above it, *which is the range of the race. He reveals in these a finely ironical perception of the Negro's limitations,* with a tenderness for them which I think so very rare as to be almost quite new. I should say, perhaps, that it was this humorous quality which Mr. Dunbar had added to our literature, and it would be this which would most distinguish him, now and hereafter. (Italics mine)

Years later, Dunbar's bitterness found explicit expression in "The Poet":

> He sang of love when earth was young,
> And love itself was in his lays.
> But ah, the world, it turned to praise
> A jingle in a broken tongue.

Do not think that the poet was repudiating all of his poetry in a "broken tongue." His righteous complaint was that his poems in standard English were slighted or completely ignored by an audience that seemed to think it ludicrous for a black poet to express in pure English the nice sentiments, the laudable attitudes, and the higher passions the blacks were assumed not to think, feel, and experience. But if we accept the testimony of his widow and the evidence of the poems themselves, Dunbar labored harder on and put more of himself into his standard English poems than those in dialect. In such pieces as "Black Samson of Brandywine" and "The Conquerors" he tried to establish his people's rightful claim to their humanity and their share in the American heritage. In other works in standard English, and especially in his lyrics—for his was essentially a lyric gift—he proclaimed his own share in the Western heritage of ideas and ideals, of wonder and glory, of moral victory, and the ever-present hazard of moral defeat.

So, what is Paul Dunbar's place? For certainly he has a place in the corpus of American literature. But as I did not do some years back, I would now demur at trying to establish that place on objective grounds. Subjectively, he inspired in me a sense of wonder for the richness and complexity of the real, though unseen world of the heart and mind, and he inspired in me an overwhelming sorrow for the fragility of the human spirit yearning toward the ideal. And that, I submit, is enough. And that, I hold, is sufficient reason for the honor this celebration bestows upon him.

Arna Bontemps

The Relevance of Paul Laurence Dunbar

The name of Paul Laurence Dunbar was in every sense a household word in the black communities around Los Angeles when I was growing up here. It was not, however, a bookish word. It was a spoken word. And in those days it was associated with recitations which never failed to delight when we heard or said them at parties or on programs for the entertainment of the church-folk and their guests. I was still in grade school when I first heard a program chairman asking a prospective participant if he knew a "Dunbar piece" he could recite. A knowledge of Dunbar's poetry and the pleasure it gave when spoken with a note of mimicry and a touch of pathos was all it took to melt our hearts and make us one.

A time came when "The Party," "When Malindy Sings," "In the Morning," and "When de Co'n Pone's Hot" was dear to my childish contemporaries as country music is to Nashville folk today in Tennessee. Soon we were familiar enough with the basic repertoire to call for favorites by which certain speakers were known or remembered. The Dunbar poem had become a recognized hallmark.

I never attempted to say a Dunbar piece myself in those days. I had no confidence in my ability to cope with the dialect or the impersonations, but I yielded to none in my rapture when others performed them. Performed was indeed the word for this kind of entertainment. You didn't *say* a Dunbar poem—you *performed* it. And this may have been one of the elements that distinguished it from much of the other poetry one heard or read in school in those days.

In such a turned-on environment it was inevitable that I would occasionally hear remarks or asides that shed flashes of light on the personality of the individual behind the poetry. And the first inference I drew was that the name Dunbar belonged to the generation of my parents. So it came as no surprise later on when I learned that Dunbar had been born in Ohio the same year that my own father had been born in Louisiana.

This led me to ask further questions. Neither of my parents had ever met Dunbar, but both seemed to know that the poet was no longer living, that he had been dead a long time in fact. This knowledge saddened me. It meant that we were talking about a very young individual whose life had been brief, and this prompted someone who was standing nearby to suggest that poor Paul had drunk himself to death. It was a horrid thought and it promptly put an end to conversation.

In the days and years that followed I decided to reject that image of the poet and to erase it from my mind. But in doing so, however, I nearly erased Dunbar himself from my thoughts through the final high school year and the first year of college. I remember distinctly that it was at the beginning of my second year at college in northern California that I was one of those students attending a social evening at which new members of the college faculty and their families were introduced. The entertainment provided for the evening consisted of musical numbers and suitable recitations accompanied by modest explanations or introductions. Most of what the others offered us on this lackluster occasion has not remained with me. But my ears perked up and I became attentive when suddenly I began to hear a voice speaking in a drawl and dialect that I know well. It turned out that she was the wife of the new head of the music department of the college and I for one didn't have to be told that she was from the deep, deep South. What surprised me was a statement in her introductory remarks in which she mentioned that her number would be a selection from the beloved American poet Paul Laurence Dunbar. I suppose I was a little sensitive about the prospect of hearing a white faculty wife imposing the dialect of the white Southern region, which I myself did not use at the college, but understood very well and rather liked, in a college community that I feared might not hesitate to pin on me an image of the Plantation Style of speech and behavior. Behind that in my subconscious there may have lurked also that embarrassing and only half-remembered statement about "poor Paul" drinking himself to death. In any case I braced myself while she performed—very effectively as I recall—Dunbar's unforgettable "The Party."

For the next couple of years I studied music with this lady's husband and noticed that he was familiar with at least three of Dunbar's lyrics that were widely known and "beloved," to use her word, in their musical settings. "An angel robed in spotless white,/ Bent down and kissed the sleeping night" was one. "Thou art the soul of a summer's day,/Thou art the breath of a rose" is another. And "Lay me down beneaf de willers in de grass." None of these gentle indicators was sufficient to arouse in a casual English major, like myself, a curiosity in the main body of Dunbar's writing or, in professors of English of that era, a reasonable concern for the black experience in the United States as reflected in the life and times and writings of the young man who epitomized all three and had died so painfully, so tragically, so prematurely during my own infancy and within the adult lives of my teachers.

Three years later I was in New York and caught up in the afflatus of the Harlem Renaissance. And here again Dunbar's shade reappeared abruptly. In quick succession I met three men who had been Dunbar's personal acquaintances and friendly associates. All of their names are known to you now. But in 1924, Richard B. Harrison was little known beyond Chautauqua and Lyceum circuits. He had accepted a post in a black college in North Carolina and remained there for seven years. But recently he had achieved a contract with a concert bureau and was making extremely modest appearances in churches and at small social gatherings arranged by the churches themselves. Harrison's name was completely unknown to me when a hostess at one of these gatherings announced the program she was about to present to her guests. An elderly gentleman with long white hair—as I think back I am reminded of others I have known recently, but long white hair was rare then—dressed in dark preacher-style clothes came on and began performing with great ease and command and with a mellow organlike voice everybody's favorite Dunbar numbers. He spoke, in between, of his personal association with Dunbar and told how his own slave father had made his way to Canada over the underground railroad, the same route that Dunbar's parents had taken to Dayton. Young Richard B. left home as a boy and came to Detroit, where he caught the eye of the drama editor of the Detroit *Free Press*, began to appear professionally as a reader, and to dream of performing classics in real theater —a dream that was not fully realized, incidentally, until forty years later, when a casting agent offered him the leading role in *The Green Pastures.*

It thus became my privilege to hear Harrison's Dunbar program at a small church party in Brooklyn in 1924, and seven years later, to occupy a seat in the gallery on the opening night in 1930 when *The Green Pastures* made stage history. And Richard B. Harrison, who was neither born nor raised in the South, by way of his association with Dunbar's projections of the folk from whom both of them had sprung, became the agent for a new awakening of the plantation tradition in American literature and drama. I did not see Harrison again to speak to him after the acclaim of *The Green Pastures* made him a celebrity, nor did I question him further at the Saturday night church party in Brooklyn about his personal memories of the poet he had known in lowlier days.

But between the two occasions, and with comparable surprise, I became acquainted with a second of Dunbar's one-time friends and associates. James Weldon Johnson's friendship with Paul Laurence Dunbar had been especially significant. They were near the same age, just a year apart. Each was aware of the other's talents. Each recognized the sparks of ambition that the other made no attempt to hide. Moreover, I am sure it was more than obvious to each that a certain possibility of friendly competition existed between them. If there was in the United States in the 1890s another lyrical black talent that might have awakened envy in one so prodigiously sufficient as young Dunbar, James Weldon Johnson represented it. While Johnson's poetry as such had lit no fires at the time their acquaintance began, Dunbar was being widely hailed. Yet it is easy to see, even at this distance, aspects of the personality of the college-bred Jim Johnson—his good looks, his suave sophistication, his command of languages, and his ability to turn his hand from one artistic and scholarly challenge to another—qualities that might have been admired, if not indeed envied, by a sensitive youth, even one so endowed as Dunbar, given all the circumstances. Obviously, nothing of this kind came between them. Friendship seems to have been born instantly and to have continued for the rest of their lives.

My own introduction to James Weldon Johnson occurred just a few months after the meeting with Richard B. Harrison. By then I had celebrated my twenty-second birthday and had started sending specimens of my own writing to editors and publishers. When one of these writings won a prize in a contest, I learned that on the panel by which it had been judged there had been several names that I recognized. One was Robert Frost. Another was William Rose Benét. Still another had been James Weldon Johnson, the only black on the panel. This was all intensely interesting to a young wanderer from such an outlying province as southern California and I began to fill my lungs with the heavy air of New York's awakening Harlem.

Stimulated, yes. But I was lifted into orbit soon afterwards when I received a letter from someone in Long Island who said he was planning a literary afternoon in a church out there at which James Weldon Johnson was to be featured as a representative of the older generation of black writers in our country and had asked him to suggest one of the newest ones to appear with him. I assumed my name had come to his mind because of his presence on the panel of judges. But I suspect now he may have recommended others more eligible who had not happened to be available.

In any case, I went, read some poems, and accepted Johnson's invitation to ride back to Harlem with him in his chauffeur-driven automobile. As we were about to leave, a very pretty young woman ran to the car to thank him for his remarks that afternoon as well as all the happiness his writing had given her over the years. He seemed enormously pleased and invited her to sit between us in the back seat and ride back with us to Harlem. I won't go into the conversation between the three of us on that Sunday afternoon drive, with first the old lion, and then the embarrassed young one, trying to top the other's compliments to our vivacious fellow traveler. Of course, I was out of my depth and should have kept my mouth closed, but they were both considerate and tried to spare me embarrassment at being so outclassed.

After we dropped Johnson's pretty admirer at her doorstep, I asked him about Dunbar. What did he know about that poet? This appeared to strike a spark. In the two decades since the other's death, Johnson's admiration had continued and, if anything, increased. He described Dunbar's medium height and slenderness and I got the impression that Dunbar's friends never considered him robust. His manners and his manner of speaking, however, had impressed Johnson as impeccable. No trace of the plantation speech rendered so lovingly in Dunbar's poetry could be heard in Dunbar's own talk. His voice, Johnson told me, was a perfect musical instrument and he knew how to use it with extreme effect. Johnson did not tell me exactly how or when he first met young Dunbar, but I gathered it had been several years before publication of *Lyrics of Lowly Life*. For Paul had been quite unknown when their paths first crossed. Their friendship was confirmed and cemented at the height of Dunbar's fame when Johnson, still living in Florida, arranged for Paul to come to Jacksonville for a public reading. The occasion was highly successful, with a large mixed audience thrilled not only by the modest dignity of the new celebrity, but also by the young man's uncommon ability as a reader. Jim Johnson had then gone a step further and arranged for Paul to give another reading of his poetry in the parlors of the St. James Hotel in that city, and invited him thereafter to remain and visit with himself and his brother Rosamond and their family as long as he would like.

Paul had remained about six weeks, during which time Jim had registered a number of impressions that had remained indelible in his memory. "As courtly as Paul's manners were, as polished as was his speech, as modest as his behavior, there remained under his polite tongue a sac of bitter sarcasm that he could spit out in self-defense as needed or use on people he did not like." A young man who happened to be living in the Johnson home at that time seemed to become the object of Paul's strong disfavor during this visit and Paul did not hesitate to express disapproval of traits this young man exemplified—roughness, a cocksure manner, and what Paul had called a vulgar streak, were all quietly and effectively denounced in the polished phrases of the slender and modest celebrity. Paul Dunbar and Jim Johnson had exchanged opinions on subjects that we will be discussing here in the centenary of the young man's life and work. The question of dialect, the impact of the formless forms of Walt Whitman on poetry, as well as the poet's odd dietary whim. Every night Dunbar demanded, and Jim Johnson scrupulously provided, as a bedtime snack, a raw onion with salt and a bottle of beer. I have told this to students who shook their heads at the thought of raw onion and salt as libation but broke into smiles at the mention of the chaser. While Paul remained in the Johnson home in Jacksonville, Jim's brother Rosamond set two of Paul's poems to music, and one of them, "Li'l Gal," became a standard art song in the decades following Paul's death. It was still going strong at the time and Jim Johnson recalled the circumstances under which the poem became the song, and the song the favorite of so many concert singers, including Paul Robeson, who kept it in his program, along with such other memorable favorites as "Water Boy."

At the time which I am recalling James Weldon Johnson was employed by the NAACP where he, shall we say, was creating the role in which Roy Wilkins is now appearing. He was not, in my opinion, the leading figure in the operation, as is Wilkins today. That burden, it seemed to me, was carried by the editor of *The Crisis* (the official organ of the Association), W. E. B. Du Bois, and who, I learned a year or two later, had also been associated with Dunbar. But Du Bois was not the hail-fellow-well-met that Jim Johnson was, though both wore a courtly dignity quite suited to the mauve decade in which Dunbar's star reached ascendancy. What I learned from Du Bois about Dunbar during rehearsals of his daughter's marriage, which he was directing, incidentally, and in which my role was that of an usher in 1928, was that just thirty years prior to the happy occasion in Harlem for which we were preparing, he and Paul Dunbar, both shining in the limelight in their different ways, had appeared in joint public lectures. Du Bois had been warmly drawn to Dunbar, as had Johnson. And the same can be said of Frederick Douglass and Booker T. Washington before them. None of these mighty men, so far as I can gather, complained about Dunbar's writing of dialect poems and stories, though opinions by others on the subject have often been divided. Though a great controversy over the relative merits of Booker T. Washington's and Du Bois's programs for the advancement of the black infancy of freedom in the United States had shaken and almost shattered the unity of their adherents, Dunbar was loved and admired by both.

Then as now, in his life and in his writing, Dunbar projected an image in which laughter and suffering were somehow balanced:

> I know why the caged bird sings, ah me,
> When his wing is bruised and his bosom sore—
> When he beats his bars and he would be free;
> It is not a carol of joy or glee,
> But a prayer that he sends from his deep heart's core,
> But a plea, that upward to Heaven he flings—
> I know why the caged bird sings!

In the era in which he wrote his poetry black and unknown creators of blues songs began using, to express the same sentiment, "laughing to keep from crying." And in the Harlem of the strolling twenties, when Richard B. Harrison, James Weldon Johnson, and W. E. B. Du Bois were recalling the friend of their own youth from whose brave heart, whose pride, and whose sadness they continued to draw courage, a beautiful new generation appeared and reached out as if to touch hands with the poet to whom they somehow felt indebted.

While still a student at Central High School in Cleveland, Ohio, the young Langston Hughes tried to write for his school paper what he thought of as a Dunbar-style poem. More than ten years later, he included it in his collection *The Dream Keeper*:

> I had my clothes cleaned just like new,
> I put 'em on, but I still feels blue.
> I bought me a new hat, sure is fine,
> But I wish I had back that ole gal o' mine.
> I got new shoes, they don't hurt my feet,
> But I ain't got nobody for to call me sweet.

At about the same time his twin star in the shower of stars that fell on Harlem in that decade, Countee Cullen, set down in his very first book this epitaph for Paul Laurence Dunbar:

Born of the sorrowful of heart,
  Mirth was a crown upon his head;
Pride kept his twisted lips apart
  In jest, to hide a heart that bled.

Later, many years later, observing discontents on campuses where I worked or lectured, I became curious to know how the poet who had meant so much to so many during his life and since his death had fared in the esteem of the newest generation whose unction had produced, as I thought, more inspired action than inspired lyricism. It did not surprise me that their first quick reaction was to brand his laughter, his tenderness, and his dialect as handkerchiefed, perhaps Tom-ism. But it didn't take them long to discover that militance had been in his heart, in his head all the time, and that he had not hesitated to speak his mind in troubled times. In the end it seemed to me that they were cross with Dunbar about just one thing, and in this I was inclined to agree with them. He owed no one an apology for writing what he called "a jingle in a broken tongue." Even though his dialect was Plantation Speech, I heard them insist, it was honest and it was the best of Plantation Speech. Moreover, it transcended the Plantation Tradition from which it appeared to spring. While some of the joy may have been lost in the difficult reading of phonetic dialect, the ear seldom complained. And in his poems intended mainly, no doubt, to be read aloud, Dunbar is picked up by a tradition older than the plantation—the oral tradition—and becomes as relevant as Robert Burns, say, or today's stereo vogue.

PAUL LAURENCE DUNBAR VIEWS THE SWORD OF TOUSSAINT L'OUVERTURE, CHICAGO EXPOSITION 1893

for Etheridge Knight

Four hundred years of exploitation
Edged the blade

And black Toussaint exposed
The rent in white imperial veils
As the tropic sky burst with
Dark thunder and the lightning

Of the saints. Orisha from Guinee.

Ogoun unchained
The blade before his eyes
Cut down and cleared

Perfumed materialism of Versailles
And flicked the latch for Legba

Where spirits wandered on the razor edge
A king's highway

Open the jails! Undo the chains!

Spirits loosed in the world and slaves
Set free. And young Paul's tongue
A floating in his mouth struck blind

The hatred with our common speech,
Yes it will come St. Paul will come will come
To us as once to you so young and gaping

Before the opening of a better world.

Lorenzo Thomas

II

THE POETRY OF PAUL LAURENCE DUNBAR

Darwin T. Turner

Paul Laurence Dunbar: The Poet and the Myths

At a time when Afro-Americans are redefining and reevaluating their culture, it is important to reassess the images and merits of blacks who earlier gained recognition for their contributions to that culture. Paul Laurence Dunbar is one who deserves such a reexamination. As I have suggested in an earlier essay, emphasis upon him as a symbol has tended to obscure the actual image of the man and his work.[1]

Even in poetry, the art form on which he wished his reputation to be based, Dunbar's achievement is obscured by myths resulting from a tendency to repeat tales about him rather than examine his work critically.[2] The result, I think it is fair to say, is that Dunbar's literary reputation has declined with succeeding generations. Dunbar's contemporaries enthusiastically accepted him and occasionally excessively praised his work. Countee Cullen and the Renaissance writers respected his name but lamented his need to prostitute his talent to the demands of publishers. Readers today seem to ignore him except to chastize him as inferior to James Whitcomb Riley or as a writer who betrayed his people by caricaturing them. Neither current judgment seems to present a complete or even accurate appraisal of Dunbar's work.

I wish to suggest the need for a careful reevaluation of Dunbar's poetry by examining six popular myths about his versification, his tone, his subjects, his diction, his attitudes toward his black characters, and his competence or talent. Unless these myths can be corrected, the actual strengths and weaknesses of Dunbar will rarely be recognized.

Versification

In her biography, *Paul Laurence Dunbar and His Song* (New York: Dodd, Mead & Company, 1947), Virginia Cunningham imagines Dunbar indolently observing a little child. Dunbar smiles, a thunderbolt of inspiration strikes, and "Little Brown Baby" springs from his mind, as maturely perfect as Athene from the head of Zeus. Although this fancy of Virginia Cunningham's may be minimized as merely a manifestation of the layman's romantic concept of poetic inspiration, the fact remains that her sketch conforms to a popular image of Dunbar as a natural—i.e., instinctive or unconscious—versifier.

If Coleridge had not informed posterity that "Kubla Khan" originated in a dream, few readers would have suspected that the poem did not result from careful construction. No one imagines that T. S. Eliot looked at a middle-aged man and, in poetic frenzy, scribbled "The Love Song of J. Alfred Prufrock." "Rendezvous with America," a relatively simple piece in comparison with Melvin Tolson's later work, immediately impresses readers with the skill and judgments responsible for its creation. Emphasis upon Countee Cullen's stylistic similarities to earlier poets, praise of Langston Hughes's use of the rhythms of black music, attention to Claude McKay's use of the sonnet form for social protest—all suggest critical awareness that these poets were consciously striving for particular artistic forms and effects.

It is easier, however, to think of Dunbar as a natural versifier, an unlettered bard—in the dialect poems at least. The homely thought and imagery, the smooth meter, the conversational tone, the simple diction, and the apparent speed with which he could produce literature—six volumes of original poetry, in addition to four novels, four collections of fiction, and numerous miscellaneous pieces within a twelve-year writing span—all these characteristics suggest that easy, spontaneous writing which is all that might be expected from a young black elevator operator whose formal education ended with graduation from high school.

The myth obscures the fact that Dunbar, seeking distinction as a poet, consciously and extensively experimented with meter and rhyme throughout his career.

Even in his first major volume, *Lyrics of Lowly Life* (1896), Dunbar experimented with forms, metrical patterns, and rhyme schemes. In "Ode to Ethiopia," for example, he used *rime couée,* a somewhat complicated structure of a six-line stanza composed in iambic feet. The first, second, fourth, and fifth lines have four feet; the third and sixth have three. The first and second lines and the fourth and fifth lines are rhymed couplets. The third and sixth lines rhyme. The first stanza of the ode illustrates the pattern:

O Mother Race! to thee I bring
This pledge of faith unwavering,
  This tribute to thy glory.
I know the pangs which thou didst feel
When Slavery crushed thee with its heel,
  With thy dear blood all gory.[3]

In "Beyond the Years," he modified the pattern by writing a seven-line stanza with a different rhyme scheme. The first, second, fourth, and sixth lines contain four iambic feet; the others, two. The first two lines rhyme. Alternating rhymes are used in the other five. The first stanza is,

Beyond the years the answer lies,
Beyond where brood the grieving skies
  And Night drops tears.
Where Faith rod-chastened smiles to rise
  And doff its fears,
And carping Sorrow pines and dies—
  Beyond the years.

He used the formal Alexandrine line both in the serious "Longing" and in the sentimentally humorous "The Spellin'-Bee," written in "white" dialect.

Dunbar also imitated the more popular patterns, iambic pentameter and tetrameter. One of his most praised early poems, "Ere Sleep Comes Down to Soothe the Weary Eyes," is written in iambic pentameter and a difficult-to-sustain rhyme scheme. The rhyme scheme is a, b, a, b, a, c, a, c, a. The ninth line repeats the first. The first stanza of the poem is the following:

Ere sleep comes down to soothe the weary eyes,
  Which all the day with ceaseless care have sought

The magic gold which from the seeker flies;
  Ere dreams put on the gown and cap of thought,
And make the waking world a world of lies—
  Of lies most palpable, uncouth, forlorn,
That say life's full of aches and tears and sighs—
  Oh, how with more than dreams the soul is torn,
Ere sleep comes down to soothe the weary eyes.

"Mystery" is in blank verse; "The Path" is a sonnet; and in "Nature and Art," two sonnets relate the fable of the wedding of Queen Nature to Art. As one might expect because of his dependence on English traditions in poetry, Dunbar relied on iambic pentameter for his most serious ideas. "Frederick Douglass" and "Columbian Ode" are examples.

Dunbar often wrote iambic tetrameter, a rhythm which he considered suitable for serious poems, such as "Whittier" and "The Master Player"; for didacticism, as "Not They Who Soar"; for self-revelation, as "The Poet and His Song" or "The Dilettante"; for descriptions of nature, as "Sunset" or "Spring Song"; for love poems; and for serious or comic narratives, such as "Ione" or "The Rivals." Sometimes Dunbar varied the stanza lengths and rhyme schemes. In thirteen poems of iambic tetrameter in *Lyrics of Lowly Life*, for example, he used thirteen different rhyme schemes.

Although Dunbar experimented with dactylic feet in "Ode for Memorial Day," with anapestic in "To Louise," and with trochaic in "Song of Summer," "Alice," and "A Negro Love Song," he later favored patterns of skillfully combined anapests and iambs. Thus freed from some of the rigidity of iambic tetrameter and pentameter, he could develop more easily the phrasing essential to his poetry, which he conceived of as an art form to be presented orally. "The Lesson," "The Cornstalk Fiddle," "The Lover and the Moon," "The Rising of the Storm," and "Conscience and Remorse" exemplify Dunbar's skill in writing this combined meter. The first stanza of "The Lesson" is an illustration:

My cót wăs dówn by̆ ă cýprĕss gróve
  Ănd Ĭ sát by̆ my̆ wíndŏw thĕ whóle níght lóng,
Ănd héard wĕll úp frŏm thĕ déep dárk wóod
  Ă mócking-bírd's pássiŏnate sóng.

The most obvious examples of combined anapests and iambs, however, are seen in his early dialect verse. Often, the lines are in trimeter: the first line consists of an anapest, an iamb, and an iamb with a feminine ending; the second line consists of an anapest followed by two iambs. This pattern characterizes "The Seedling," "An Ante-Bellum Sermon," "A Banjo Song," "The Lawyers' Ways," "Deacon Jones' Grievance," "After a Visit," and "The Ol' Tunes." Variations are seen in "The Apple Tree" and "Keep A' Pluggin' Away." Sometimes Dunbar diversified the pattern by substituting a strong stress for a first syllable of the anapestic foot. The first stanza of "An Ante-Bellum Sermon," for example, is the following:

We is gáthahed hýeah, my bróthahs,
In dis hówlin' wíldanesś,
Fu' to spéak some wórds of cómfo't
To each óthah iń distréss.
An' we chóoses fú' ouah súbjic',
Dís—we'll 'spláin it bý an' bý;
"An' de Láwd said, 'Móses, Móses,'
An' de mán said, 'Hýeah am Í.' "

Since Dunbar is best known for his poetry in dialect, the rhythm of this poetry is the one with which he is identified. Most commonly, in his dialect poetry, the feminine ending for the first line and the anapestic beginning of the second force a pause which compels the reading of the poem in trimeter. The occasional stress at the beginning of a line and the stress closing the alternate line emphasize the very strong, sprightly rhythm to a degree which, I believe, makes the form ineffective for sustained melody. Ideal for humor and not-too-serious sentiment, the form is difficult for poems of serious emotion or thought.

In books written after *Lowly Life*, Dunbar improved his rhythmic skill by freeing himself from inversions and by using sprung rhythm consciously for comic effect. He developed the pattern for his dialect poetry even further. While retaining his basic pattern, he more often used a fifteen-syllable line with a stressed or unstressed syllable beginning the line of iambic feet. The eighth syllable is often a feminine ending, forcing a pause and so closely relating to the seventh that a skipping half-step breaks the line. Of course, variations occur. Sometimes the first syllable is stressed, or the ninth is not stressed. Sometimes, an amphibrach is sounded, or a caesura follows the ninth syllable. Characteristically, however, the rhythm is a catchy one, beginning with a strong beat, broken in the middle of the line by a quick step, and ending with a strong beat. The pattern can be illustrated by the first lines of "Angelina":

> When de fiddle gits to singin' out a ol' Vaghinny reel,
> An' you 'mence to feel a ticklin' in yo' toe an' in yo' heel;
> Ef you t'ink you got 'uligion an' you wants to keep it, too,
> You jes' bettah tek a hint an' git yo'self clean out o' view.

While perfecting a pattern for dialect poems, Dunbar continued his experiments in his standard English verse. Perhaps his most interesting later experiments in standard English poetry are attempts to imitate musical rhythms. In "The Valse," for instance, he duplicated the waltz rhythm with reasonable success.

Dunbar's lines do not always scan for the eye and for the metronomic finger; but, more often than not, when the poems are read aloud, an unsuspected, necessary pause or the necessary prolongation of a sound teaches a reader that Dunbar mastered rhythm far beyond the bookish imitations by earlier American poets. More than most English and American poets of his time, he depended upon quantitative meter and perfected a rhythmical phrasing. If he had not clung so deliberately to rhyme—both end and internal rhyme—he might have received more attention as an early American experimenter with rhythms depending on oral phrasing rather than upon traditional patterns of English metrics.

Tone

A second myth about Dunbar concerns the tone of his writing. Recalling the gaiety of such poems as "When Malindy Sings," "The Party," and "When de Co'n Pone's Hot," or the sentimentality of "When the Old Man Smokes" or "Chrismus on the Plantation," many readers picture Dunbar as a poet of light and gentle emotions. His pleasures are judged to be simple—fishing, eating, sleeping, whistling; his emotions are assumed to be light, except when an occasional memory of the past calls forth a tear. The picture, in fact, approximates the stereotype of the antebellum slave as portrayed by Joel Chandler Harris and Thomas Nelson Page. Truly, the youthful serenity of *Lyrics of Lowly Life*, the collection which includes the best of his early poetry, is reflected in the dominance of images of trees, flowers, sunshine, and blue skies. Also abundant, however, are images of dreams, wealth, tears, armor, and warfare. Each of these latter images appears in more than fifteen percent of the poems. These, perhaps, merely reflect the characteristic thoughts of youth. But the appearance of images of wealth in twenty percent of the poems indicates clearly that Dunbar's dreams frequently centered on the money he needed to support himself. The most surprising images are those of blood and chains, which appear in more than ten percent of the poems. These scarcely are what one would expect from a gay child of nature.

Dunbar's second major collection, *Lyrics of the Hearthside*, was published in 1899 after three emotionally exciting years during which he had won recognition abroad as well as in America. Although his tour in England during the spring and summer of 1897 had failed financially, it had added to his literary reputation in America. After returning to the United States, he completed his collaboration with Will Cook for the musical *Clorindy* and began work at the Library of Congress as a clerk. In 1898, he married Alice Moore, a talented poet, and, encouraged by his wife, decided to earn his living as a writer. In 1899, however, his success was interrupted by severe illness—first, pneumonia; then, tuberculosis—which necessitated a summer in the Catskills and a fall trip to Colorado.

The emotional turbulences of this period reflect themselves in the images in *Lyrics of the Hearthside*. Although some biographers assume that the idea of death obsessed him only after 1902, images of death rise sharply in *Hearthside*, appearing in twenty percent of the poems. In contrast, images of nature, wealth, and daydreams diminish sharply. Although nature images continue to be important, they now constitute only one-fourth rather than three-fourths of the images. Strangely, the only images to increase in percentage, other than those of death and love, are images of animals.

Dunbar's third major book of poems appeared in 1903. The years since his publication of *Hearthside* had been marked with sorrow. In 1902 he and his wife had separated, for reasons not explained to the general public. After apparently regaining his health as a result of a trip to Colorado in 1899, Dunbar was weakening rapidly. He was depressed also by the conviction that he had failed as a writer. Although he had published four collections of poetry, two collections of stories, and four novels by 1902, he confided to James Weldon Johnson his belief that he had not improved. *Lyrics of Love and Laughter*, however, like *In Old Plantation Days*, the short-story collection published in the same year, seems an almost deliberate rejection of unpleasantness. Since Dunbar conventionally used birds such as the lark, nightingale, robin, and jay as symbols of escape and of happiness,[4] it is not surprising that images of birds increase. They appear in almost forty percent of the poems. Images of wealth and daydreams virtually disappear, and images of death subside to the level of *Lowly Life*.

The final two years of Dunbar's life were marked by illness and loneliness. His acceptance of the inevitable is reflected in the changes in images in *Lyrics of Sunshine and Shadow*. The increase in images of children (twenty-five percent of the poems) and images of mothers (fifteen percent) suggests that Dunbar may have wished to regress to a past when he had been protected by his mother. Other images of animals, armor, and wealth return to levels corresponding to those of *Lowly Life*. The bird images decline, while images of death rise to the level of *Hearthside*.

Subject

Corresponding to the myth which pictures Dunbar as a poet of gaiety is one that presents him as a pastoral poet concentrating on rural blacks and nature as subjects. Again an examination of his poems refutes the myth.

The subjects of *Lyrics of Lowly Life* are those to be expected from a sentimental young poet. In one-third of the poems he expressed his philosophy of life, described love, and worshipped nature. Less frequently, he eulogized individuals and institutions and satirized human behavior. He wrote narratives about and satirical portraits of whites as well as blacks, and he also wrote consciously didactic moralizings.

In *Lyrics of the Hearthside*, either because editors demanded more Negro portraiture or because he realized his talent for characterization, Dunbar created more speakers. He wrote about love three times as often, as would be expected of a man living through a period of courtship and marriage. Sobering from youthful immaturities, he less often offered philosophical or moral advice. Although he wrote more poems affirming faith, inspiration, and the hope of life after death, for the first time he developed theses of doubt and skepticism. His own illness seemed to change his attitude about death. In *Lowly Life*, he had written elegies and dirges for other people. Now he contemplated the inevitability of death for all men, himself included.

In *Lyrics of Love and Laughter*, his book of escape, he described moods of indolence more frequently. He continued to praise the joys of love, but he became preoccupied with love lost because of betrayals. He explored new subjects: dancing and music, conscience and guilt, and children. The variety of subjects and themes emphasizes the contrast between the happy mask Dunbar wished to present and the bitter, despairing self that he could not completely conceal.

In *Lyrics of Sunshine and Shadow*, his characteristic tone is sorrow rather than sunshine. He seldom wrote on the subject of death, but he seldom wrote optimistically. In one-third of the love poems, he lamented lost love. His thought was clouded by doubt which he tried to evade by conceiving utopias or by dreaming of childhood.

Of further irony in the myth about Dunbar's subjects is the fact that, although Dunbar undoubtedly appreciated nature, he could not, as his wife, Alice Dunbar-Nelson, once explained, give original expression to his feelings.[5] His outdoor scenes, even those peopled by blacks, are painted canvases. Dunbar's best poetry lives inside the house, drowsing beside a popping fire, burrowing beneath the bed covers to shut out the morning summons, mentally tasting and devouring the food still cooking on the stove.

A reason for Dunbar's weakness in expressing nature is that he derived his awareness of it from English pastoral poetry rather than from observation. In *Lyrics of Lowly Life*, for example, although he referred to trees and flowers in more than seventy-five percent of the poems, he did not create pictures. He wrote almost abstractly of scenes in which flowers grow, trees blossom, birds sing, and the sun shines. He gave no color, no shape to these abstract forms. When he was the most specific, he merely named traditional plants of poetry—the rose, the poplar tree, and the lily—or traditional birds—the lark and the nightingale.

Although he was no more sensuous in his descriptions of nature in the dialect poems, there he at least abandoned his books as sources of his images. Even in the dialect poems, however, Dunbar did not describe the nature he saw in southern Ohio or Washington, D. C.

Diction

A fourth myth relates to Dunbar's diction. A surprising number of individuals who can identify Dunbar as a poet seem unaware that he wrote the majority of his poems in the most elegant nineteenth-century English which he could manage. Even fewer readers seem to recognize that Dunbar wrote not one but two distinctive varieties of dialect poetry. Well known, of course, is his use of a "Negro" dialect; less frequently perceived is his creation of a "white" dialect suggesting the speech of residents of Kentucky, Ohio, and Indiana.

Failure to note Dunbar's careful distinction, which William Dean Howells praised, can result in amusing misinterpretations of Dunbar's poetry. For example, "Deacon Jones' Grievance" is sometimes read and discussed as a black churchman's protest against the new singing style in churches. Actually, Dunbar is reported to have written the poem in memory of the complaints of a German music master, and Dunbar's effort to separate the poem from the context of Afro-American life is evidenced by the fact that he very clearly used his "white" dialect for the speaker.

Differences between the two dialects are readily apparent to the perceptive reader even though some sounds—such as *ef* and *ez*—occur in both dialects, and certain final consonant sounds—*d*, *f*, and *g*, particularly—are omitted in both. In the "Negro" dialect, more sounds are omitted or substituted than in the non-Negro. For instance, in the "Negro," *d* is substituted for initial *t* or *th*, *e* for long *a* (*mek* for *make*), short *a* for short *o* (*drap* for *drop*), *f* for final *th* (*beneaf* for *beneath*), short *a* for long *i* (*lak* for *like*), *ah* for *er*, *ar*, or *ir* when it is the final sound (*ah* for *air*, *hyeah* for *hear*), *er* for *ow* with the sound of long *o* (*swaller* for *swallow*), etc. Dunbar commonly elided medial *r* except when it introduces a syllable (*co'n* but *farin'*). He also elided unpronounced medial vowels.

Although Dunbar defended apparent inconsistencies by arguing that he was imitating diverse Negro dialects, the inconsistencies sometimes obtrude in the dialect of a single speaker. For instance, in "The Deserted Plantation," he substituted *pa'lor* for *parlor*, but *er* and *ner* for *or* and *nor*; he wrote *there* as *da*, but its rhyme partner, *air*, as *ah*. Occasionally also he forgot to make all necessary changes in spelling. For instance, *racah* is not the *raissah* (or *racer*) which Dunbar wanted.

Well-known poems in which Dunbar used "Negro" dialect are "When Malindy Sings," "When de Co'n Pone's Hot," "Noddin' by de Fire," "The Party," and "In the Morning."

In contrast, Dunbar identified the "white" dialect by different substituted sounds—short *u* for medial short *i* (*fust* for *first*), short *i* for medial long *o* (*riz* for *rose*), or *er* for long *o* (*swaller*, as in the Negro dialect, but also *persess*), short *i* for medial short *u* or *e* (*sich* or *git*), *o* for medial long *u* followed by *r* (*shore* for *sure*), short *e* for medial short *u* (*jest*), and short *u* for medial short *o* followed by *r* (*fur* instead of *for*). Much more frequently than when writing Negro dialect, Dunbar used eye dialect; for example, *wuz* and *ust*.

Poems in which Dunbar uses "white" dialect are "An Easy-Goin' Feller," "When a Feller's Itchin' to Be Spanked," "Possum Trot," and "The Rivals."

A few lines will illustrate the distinctions between the two dialects. A passage from "The Spellin'-Bee" imitates the dialect of white Americans of the Midwest:

That spellin'-bee had be'n the talk o' many a precious moment,
The youngsters all was wild to see jes' what the precious show meant,
An' we whose years was in their teens was little less desirous

O' gittin' to the meetin' so's our sweethearts could admire us.
So on we went so anxious fur to satisfy our mission
That father had to box our ears, to smother our ambition.

A second passage, from "Temptation," is in the dialect Dunbar wrote for Negro speakers:

> I done got 'uligion, honey, an' I's happy ez a king;
> Evahthing I see erbout me's jes' lak sunshine in de spring;
> An' it seems lak I do' want to do anothah blessid thing
> But jes' run an' tell de neighbours, an' to shout an' pray an' sing.

Attitudes Toward Black Characters

One of the major controversies about Dunbar centers on his characterization of blacks. William Dean Howells introduced Dunbar to the American public as a poet whose major contribution to American literature would be a sympathetic interpretation of his people. But blacks themselves have disagreed about the authenticity of Dunbar's interpretation. Some obviously enjoy the characterizations in "The Party" and "How Lucy Backslid." Others, however, argue that Dunbar did not know Southern blacks and was contemptuous of them. These readers insist that Dunbar merely perpetuated the stereotypes of blacks as shiftless, lazy, easily satisfied people concerned with nothing except eating, sleeping, and making love. It cannot be denied that in "The Deserted Plantation" and "Chrismus on the Plantation" Dunbar does picture slaves who are nostalgic for the days before the war and love the former master so much that they continue to work for him without financial compensation. It is doubtful, however, that Dunbar would have considered these derogatory images. To the contrary, as I have suggested in "Paul Laurence Dunbar: The Rejected Symbol," he probably would have judged these to be evidences of a virtue which should be brought to the attention of white readers in the hope of persuading them to stop abusing a people who had served them faithfully.

If these pictures of the loyal freedman are eliminated from discussion, a major reason for the allegation that Dunbar perpetuated demeaning stereotypes may result from the failure to perceive the parallels that Dunbar drew between the character and habits of blacks and those of whites. That is, because readers fail to distinguish "Negro" dialect from "white" dialect; they assume that all characters in the dialect poems are intended to represent black people. Consequently, they do not perceive that Dunbar ascribed to his white characters certain traits or habits which are considered part of the traditional derogatory stereotypes of blacks.

For example, "The Rivals" pictures a fickle white girl who leaves a dance with Hiram Turner while two white youths are brawling for the privilege of escorting her. "The Cornstalk Fiddle," not in dialect, pictures a white youth who enjoys dancing as much as do the black admirers of "Angelina." The white who is confused by the debate between lawyers at the courthouse in "The Lawyers' Ways" is identical in perception (or lack of it) with the black narrator who is confused by the "Speakin' at de Cou't House." Black "Scamp" 's love for his mother is identical with that of the unnamed white narrator of "Appreciation." Both boys enjoy the tenderness and affection of mothers who feed, care for, and comfort them. What's the difference that the black boy gets bread and molasses while the white gets bread and jam? Certainly, no black narrator is more amusing than white Deacon Jones, who tried to join the "weak-voiced" soloist because all the other singers left him "a singin' there alone!" One suspects that black Malindy in "When Malindy Sings" might have caused the white narrator of "The Ol' Tunes" to stop complaining about solos. The white coquette in "The Wooing" is no more virtuous and no less easily attained than the black one in "A Coquette Conquered." No black lover is more sentimentally ridiculous than the garrulous young white in "A Confidence" or the white kiss-stealer in "Breaking the Charm." The young black lover in "Dely" seems more sincere than either when he describes his love for Dely, whose special charm is that she is not a mulatto but "brown ez brown kin be." No black character is more nostalgic than the white narrator of "Possum Trot," and no black gossip is more hypocritical than the Irish narrator of "Circumstances Alter Cases."

Other examples could be introduced to suggest that Dunbar, assuming similarity of character between blacks and whites, was as ready to satirize one group as the other. Yet, perhaps because they fail to recognize the white characters in the dialect poems, many readers assume that he satirized only black characters and idealized his whites.

Dunbar's Talent

A final myth is that William Dean Howells prevented recognition of Dunbar's literary excellence by his emphasis upon Dunbar's value as an interpreter of black people. Dunbar himself is partly responsible for this myth. Wanting to be remembered as a writer of standard English verses, he blamed Howells because editors preferred the dialect pieces.[6] Actually, however, Howells evaluated Dunbar's talents perceptively. Dunbar's standard-English verse is talented but not exceptional. His unique contribution to American literature is his dialect poetry.

Benjamin Brawley insisted, but with insufficient explanation, that Dunbar's standard-English poetry fails Matthew Arnold's touchstone test. It lacks memorable lines or passages which are distinguished by trenchant thought and illuminating imagery. The thought too often is drowned in the sentimentalism characteristic of much of American poetry during the nineteenth century. The imagery, if particularized at all, is a copy-book imitation of sights and sounds familiar to the English lyricists who were his models, but foreign to the Ohio-born Dunbar.

Nevertheless, Dunbar possessed many poetic talents. He was rhythmically adroit. He characterized skillfully. He created suspense and humor. He might have utilized these talents effectively in comic or dramatic narratives and dialogues written either in dialect or in standard English. But when he wrote in dialect, he felt less constrained. Having few models he sought familiar images. No nightingales perch in trees above rills and streams; instead, whippoorwills whistle from the brush beyond the creek. Furthermore, his sentimentality seems less offensive to cynical readers of the twentieth century when it is partially damned by dialect. Enlivened and enriched by sprightly rhythm, amusing themes, homely images, and credible characters, the dialect poems offer compensations for the lack of powerful emotion or imagery or thought.

I must reemphasize that this appraisal does not imply that

Dunbar could not write competent standard English poems. Quite to the contrary, as Howells observed, Dunbar wrote very well, even in his earliest published work. But Dunbar effectively appraised the strengths and limitations of most of his standard English poems when he described them as "graceful little verses." Within twenty-five years after Dunbar's first major collection, the poetry of America was the intellect-torturing verse of T. S. Eliot and the mind-dazzling imagery of the Imagists. Dunbar's "graceful little verses" were shattered and swept under a rug before World War I. His laughing, weeping people of dialect danced and gossiped and flirted their insouciant ways into World War II.

Conclusion

Perhaps after the myths about Dunbar are corrected, Dunbar the poet will be seen more clearly. He was an artist for the folk—not just for black people, but for all common people who live close to nature, who enjoy music (especially singing), who love and laugh among friends, and who pursue the simple pleasures of hunting, fishing, eating, telling stories to children, and napping by a fire. Although such people are identified with the pastoral tradition, Dunbar wrote about them most effectively when he placed them in their homes; for he knew and loved the hearthside scene far better than the outdoors. And he wrote most freely when he used dialect. Then he described the coquettes, young lovers, and the sleepy boys he knew rather than the Phyllises of English poetry. In the simplicity of dialect he restricted himself to homely appraisals of life and rarely attempted explicit sermons about living.

One fact, however, must be underscored: Dunbar was an artist for the folk but not a folk artist. He was not a rural bard singing unconsciously; he was an educated, conscious creator of rhythmic songs, of likable people, and desirable retreats from a materialistic, urbanized age.

NOTES

1. Darwin T. Turner, "Paul Laurence Dunbar: The Rejected Symbol," *The Journal of Negro History* 52 (January 1967), 1–13.

2. During a three-day period, speakers at this conference will present more critical commentary on his literary skills than has been published in the past thirty years. To my knowledge, there has been no significant study of Dunbar as a poet since Victor Lawson's *Dunbar Critically Examined* (Washington, D.C.: Associated Publishers, 1941).
3. This and all subsequent quotations of Dunbar's poetry are taken from *The Complete Poems of Paul Laurence Dunbar* (New York: Dodd, Mead and Company, 1913), and reprinted by permission of the publisher.
4. He also used the owl as a symbol of sorrow.
5. Alice Dunbar-Nelson, "The Poet and His Song," *A.M.E. Church Review* 31 (October 1914), 6. In Schomburg Collection.
6. Lida Keck Wiggins, *The Life and Works of Paul Laurence Dunbar* (Naperville, Ill.: J. L. Nichols & Company, 1907), p. 107.

James A. Emanuel

Racial Fire in the Poetry of Paul Laurence Dunbar

The reputation of Paul Laurence Dunbar, America's first professional black poet, changes gradually but surely, in accordance with massive alterations in the fortunes and prospects of his race. As a literary phenomenon, this fact is just, especially regarding writers who, like Dunbar, choose to serve as interpreters of their people. Their once-authentic works, if they become dated, at least remain historically useful; and their gleams of prophecy, if brightened by the course of events, are adduced as evidence of particular genius and integrity. On the other hand, their excellences of style and substance that transcend the commanding interests of their day endure to nourish that unity of spirit that keeps mankind alive to art.

Black literary criticism, prefigured as a racially oriented tradition by Benjamin Brawley before the 1920s, has continually assessed Dunbar as a poet. In the 1920s, James Weldon Johnson recognized Dunbar's primacy as the first black American poet to combine sustained technical mastery with an objective but sympathetic penetration of racial experience. In the 1930s, Sterling Brown minimized his poems about slavery and dispraised his failure to reveal explicit hardships in his poems about black folk life; but in the latter poems Brown admired the pastoral details so engaging to the poet himself, as well as the humor, rhythm, and humanizing affection for black peasants. In the 1940s, J. Saunders Redding stated Dunbar's profound significance in the first decades of this century: that his poems "proved that even with the arbitrary limitations imposed upon them by historical convention, Negro writers could rise to heights of artistic expression." [1]

In the 1950s, a comment just as general, but psychologically more speculative about Dunbar's racial drive, came from Richard Wright, who saw Dunbar as a poet who tragically failed to resolve a "fatal conflict" in himself. Wright concluded,

> He tells us but little of what he really felt, but we know that he tried to turn his eyes as much as possible from that vision of horror that had claimed the exclusive attention of so many Negro writers, tried to communicate with his country as a man. Perhaps no other Negro writer ever demanded more of himself than Dunbar did, and that he achieved so much, that he did manage to wring a little unity out of the blatant contradiction that was his life, is truly remarkable.[2]

And near the end of the 1960s, Darwin T. Turner concluded that black readers today have demanded too much of Dunbar, that they have overlooked the crucial fact that he was "a talented, creative, high school graduate whose views reflect the limited knowledge of many historians, economists, and social philosophers of his day." [3]

Racial fire in their authors is deeply prized by most black readers of the 1970s. If unsupported by traditional virtues, its perishability as art is deemed of little consequence. Black people are crying up a literature of psychological need, not a literature of aesthetic power. Its truth is to be acted out as freedom. Its beauty is to be felt as justice. In the face of these new but predictable imperatives, the critic who looks back to Dunbar must secure for him a fair hearing. He must determine, at the minimum, by examining the 417 works in Dunbar's *Complete Poems* (1913), how often and how intensely the poet exhibited that racial fire so important today. The observations in this paper, based upon such an examination, suggest Dunbar's continuing value according to this one criterion.

Judging a man and judging his literary expression are two different enterprises. Even as men do not always speak of those matters most vital to them, authors do not invariably write at length or at all about what touches them most deeply. One might, without being the least charitable, assume that all black men feel racial fire. In the May 1972 number of *Black World*, Preston Wilcox's review of Robert Beck's *The Naked Soul of Iceberg Slim* contains an all-too-rare comment on black men: "How many can allow their dads to become Uncle Toms and still love them, knowing that every Black man has stood up to white people at least once?"

Dunbar, too, stood up to whites in his own way. For example, reading his poetry at the West End Club in Toledo, Ohio, at the age of twenty, just after a Dr. Chapman had spoken unfavorably of black people, Dunbar retaliated with his only weapon, his fervid reading of his "Ode to Ethiopia." Benjamin Brawley records that the young poet, while reading, seemed to have "taken upon himself the defense of all his people from the slurs and slanders to which they were daily subjected." [4] Darwin T. Turner, in his essay "Paul Laurence Dunbar: The Rejected Symbol," gives some details of the poet's newspaper articles between 1898 and 1903 in which he strongly protested specific racist brutalities and injustices.

The vicious murders of black people during the elections of 1898 in Wilmington, North Carolina, which roused condemnation by Dunbar in the Chicago *Record*, and which were graphically depicted by Charles W. Chesnutt in his novel *The Marrow of Tradition* (1901), occurred in a year in which there were 101 lynchings. At the height of Dunbar's national popularity, white publishers were printing books and magazines filled with venomous propaganda debasing black people, among them Thomas Dixon's notoriously racist novel, *The Leopard's Spots* (1902), which presented the black man as "a possible beast to be feared and guarded." Dunbar's combination of dark countenance and artistic talent gave the lie to bigoted claims that white ancestry alone accounted for any competence that a black man might have. His talent, however, could not save him from discrimination in employment after graduation from high school, nor brighten his hopes during the following hard years that led to his contemplation of suicide in November 1894. In 1898, his fame as a poet could not protect him from the insulting assumptions of the Albany, New York, hotel manager who thought him crazy and sought to have him arrested for claiming reserved accommodations prior to his public reading.

In short, Dunbar resented, sometimes actively, the racist enormities in the daily national environment; and he felt the irritations and stings of prejudice in his personal life. But his historical perception of racism was limited, for he knew little of Africa and could scarcely have known much about the vast American experiences of his race that are slowly penetrating our curriculums today. He inherited little conscious bitterness from his parents: as slaves, his father had been semiskilled and perhaps literate and his mother had been a house servant in a Kentucky home which Brawley describes as "one of culture" (p. 12). Further, Dunbar was aided in his climb to fame by a succession of white friends, among them Dr. James Newton Matthews, whose public praise attracted the attention of James Whitcomb Riley; William Lawrence Blacher, who financially guaranteed the poet's first volume, *Oak and Ivy* (1893); the attorney Charles Thatcher, who offered to pay for Dunbar's college career and who sent money to keep the Dunbar home in Dayton, Ohio, from being lost; and Dr. H. A. Tobey, who secured readings for the poet and helped defray the costs of his second volume, *Majors and Minors* (1895).

Dunbar's racial attitude, conditioned by his knowledge and personal experience, was also affected by his temperament, which Sterling Brown has described as kindhearted and forgiving,[5] and which Benjamin Brawley has called "gentle, with a keen sense of the comedy of life" (p. 73). To the amalgam of man and poet belong, too, the elements of commercialism and poetic aim. Regarding the former, it is only the rare professional who can or will ignore the public taste that controls his livelihood. Dunbar's repeated complaint to James Weldon Johnson that he was constrained to write dialect poetry in order to maintain his audience indicates his dilemma.

Dunbar's poetic purpose, on the other hand, seems to reflect the ambiguity of his racial views. His forthright letter of July 13, 1895, to Dr. Tobey records his ambition "to be able to interpret my own people . . . and to prove to the many that after all we are more human than African" (Brawley, p. 37). But the opening lines of his well-known "The Poet" say, "He sang of life, serenely sweet, / With, now and then, a deeper note"—an imbalance and disproportion that could not interpret the lives of black people, unless those occasional deeper notes were thematic in poems ethnically profound in ways open only to genius inspired by knowledgeable love of race. Dunbar, answering a reporter's question at the Waldorf-Astoria on February 12, 1899, said that black poets "must write like the white men. I do not mean imitate them; but our life is now the same" (Brawley, p. 77). The poet's idealism, illusion, and personal thrust of spirit are evidenced in these three excerpts. To try to prove to any man that black people are "human" is a tragic waste of energy, and to believe that black men lead lives that are the same as those of their American countrymen is to impose wishful logic upon an irrecoverably irrational system; but Dunbar's humane idealism relieves him of blame for these misconceptions. He obviously believed in the sweet and serene possibilities of life and love, so much so that deeper notes were almost intrusive in his poetry. But a poet's intrusive themes, those that force themselves with little or no initial welcome onto his page, speak for him as a man. It is this kind of theme, in the main, nerved by Dunbar's racial fire, that is the subject of the following remarks.

In the *Complete Poems*, there are at least ten works that, in referring to oppressive conditions endured by black people during and after slavery, do not usually emphasize resentment on the part of the protagonist or the poet. In the early poem "A Banjo Song," the music of that instrument is "de greates' joy an' solace / Dat a weary slave kin know." The tight little black world, restricted to evening and to a single family and its cabin, is very slowly released from its "keer an' trouble" in this poem that does not quite manage to sound gay. Dunbar shifts to Reconstruction times or later in "The Old Cabin," in which the protagonist remembers when slavery "helt me / In my mis'ry—ha'd an' fas'." Whippings and the block and the lash are referred to, but the old man forgets them in the joy that accompanies his recollection of tumbling children and laughing, dancing friends around his former cabin door. The slavemaster figures in this poem, however, for his gorgeous mansion and hunting dogs pleasantly merge with the ex-slave's other memories.

The instruments of oppression are mentioned in two other poems, one romantic and one didactic. In "Parted," the slave protagonist is being sold down the river, a fate that "ain't so bad's hit seem," he has been told. Much worse is being parted from his sweetheart, whom he calls "my lady," and for whom he says "I'll stan' de ship, I'll stan' de chain, / But I'll come back, my darlin' Jane." In "Joggin' Erlong," Dunbar opens with a cliché connecting the darkest hour and the dawn, then gives his reader, in what becomes the refrain, sound advice on how to survive life's manifold troubles: "des' keep on a-joggin' wid a little bit o' song." The second of the three stanzas begins with a different mixture: the doubtful and the true. Employing his single reference to slavery, the poet says:

> De whup-lash sting a good deal mo'
> De back hit's knowed befo',
> An' de burden's allus heavies'
> Whaih hits weight has made a so';

then he continues, with a significantly ambiguous modification of his allusion to black people, by picturing a weary traveler who is whipped by tribulation. If the traveler, whipped " 'Twell he ain't got stren'th to stan'," is the identical sojourner that suffers in black folk songs, the poet has deepened his racial meaning. Concerning Dunbar's assertion about repeated lashings, one might consider Frederick Douglass's autobiographical comment, in Chapter 6 of his *Life and Times*: "He was whipped oftener who was whipped easiest." But it is uncertain whether the poet refers to unhealed scars or to the unaggressive psychology of what Douglass refuted as "the doctrine that submisison to violence is the best cure for violence."

Today, when women in general, in the public sense, and black women in particular, within the fraternity of black poets, are subjects of increasingly clear-sighted reflection, it is gratifying to note that Dunbar contributed his insight. In his undistinguished occasional poem "On the Dedication of Dorothy Hall" (at Tuskegee Institute), the fourth stanza merits attention:

> The women of a race should be its pride;
> We glory in the strength our mothers had,
> We glory that this strength was not denied
> To labor bravely, nobly, and be glad.

The poem closes with a commendation of "the striving women of a struggling race." The stanza is lackluster in comparison with those in Langston Hughes's "The Negro Mother," Sonia Sanchez's "blk / wooooomen / chant," and Mari Evans's "I Am a Black Woman." But its unsentimentality indicates that Dunbar was thinking of the grim facts of black women's special trials, not platitudes about motherhood.

Lynching, the obvious physical extreme of oppression, is the source and subject of one of the ten poems under discussion. "The Haunted Oak," written and published in 1900, could have been based on one of the 105 lynchings that occurred that year, but it was inspired in Washington, D.C., by a story that Dunbar heard an old black man relate concerning his nephew in Alabama who had been hanged on an oak tree by a mob of whites after having been falsely accused of "a grave crime" (Brawley, 88). According to the story, shortly afterwards the leaves on the limb used for the lynching yellowed and fell off; and, unlike the rest of the normal tree, the offending bough shriveled and died. Townspeople began to call the tree "the haunted oak." Dunbar, using the ballad form to enhance the superstition, personifies the tree and makes it the most sensitive and remorseful participant in the crime.

Perhaps the narrative style and the limitation of feeling and thought to that tolerable in the personification prohibit strong individual expression on the author's part. On the other hand, it is relatively easy to miss the sharpness of the satire in the following crucial stanza describing the nightriders:

> Oh, the judge, he wore a mask of black,
> And the doctor one of white,
> And the minister, with his oldest son,
> Was curiously bedight.

Within the racial context, what more economical, low-tension attack could have been launched against the lie of white justice, the lie of white solicitude for the sick, and the lie of white godliness?

Satire and despair, both derived from racism, inform most of the other four poems that reflect oppression of black people. Although the sonnet "Harriet Beecher Stowe" speaks of "wrongs and cruelties" redressed by "the sword of justice," another sonnet, "Robert Gould Shaw," refers to the Civil War as hopeless and closes with these cynical lines addressed to the martyred regimental commander: "thou and those who with thee died for right / Have died, the Present teaches, but in vain!" "Speakin' at de Cou't House" finds the black protagonist amidst whites listening to political campaigners. He derides the actions of the audience and relates as follows the concluding words of the present speaker, whom music has ushered forward as a "conkerin' hero":

> An' he said de colah question,
> Hit was ovah, solved, an' done,
> Dat de dahky was his brothah,
> Evah blessed mothah's son.

The black observer is momentarily affected by the happy response of the crowd until he hears an onlooker warn that next week's speaker, named Jones, will take a contrary stance. The point of Dunbar's satire is that the liberal white politician-as-hero offers nothing but temporizing hypocrisy, and that such undependable aspirants to daily power, numerically meaningless among representative politicians like Jones, provide little hope for black citizens.

Unremitting despair, not really cancelled in its final lines by the image of dawn in a better afterworld, pervades the last poem in this group, "When All Is Done." Its third stanza, which follows, carries the full weight of its racial emphasis:

> For I have suffered loss and grievous pain,
> The hurts of hatred and the world's disdain,
> And wounds so deep that love, well-tried and pure,
> Had not the pow'r to ease them or to cure.

The words "hatred and the world's disdain," because they apply with tragic singularity to the poet's race, although not to him personally, show Dunbar's individuality flowing into the mass identity of his people. Wounds that true love cannot ease are, unarguably, the deepest ravages of the human spirit.

Sometimes, when using slavery as his temporal setting, Dunbar is more explicit in expressing the attitudes of his characters toward their environment. Two poems, which have not endeared the author to many black readers in the 1970s, represent this category: "The Deserted Plantation" and "Chrismus on the Plantation." In the former, an old ex-slave laments the departure of his companions in bondage and thinks of himself as "a lover till de las' " in remaining behind. He says,

> So I'll stay an' watch de deah ole place an' tend it
> Ez I used to in de happy days gone by.
> 'Twell de othah Mastah thinks it's time to end it,
> An' calls me to my qua'ters in de sky.

Readers today would deem this man still a slave and would consider his misplaced love a pathetic example of the perversion of feelings inherent in the slave system.

"Chrismus on the Plantation," equally stereotyped in the attitude of the ex-slaves, has their spokesman, "ol' Ben," thus address their poor old master, who is urging them to leave because he can no longer afford his recent innovation of paying them for their labor:

> ". . . you wants us
> to fu'git dat you's been kin',
> An' ez soon ez you is he'pless, we's
> to leave you hyeah behin'.
> Well, ef dat's de way dis freedom
> ac's on people, white er black,
> You kin jes' tell Mistah Lincum
> fu' to tek his freedom back."

Mockery of this frequently quoted decision—like the decision in "The News," the preceding work in the *Complete Poems*—should not obscure the fact that Dunbar is praising in these black people specific virtues like compassion, courage, endurance, and group solidarity. Some of their conjectural relatives and friends who escaped slavery by means of the Underground Railroad shared the same virtues, but had an additional combination of pride and daring that governed their visions. Dunbar, as Sterling Brown has observed, was "definitely a poet of the happy hearthside and pastoral contentment" (p. 34); and perhaps his attachment to what might be called fireside virtues made him minimize the societal blindness with which they can coexist.

Five other poems by Dunbar, not outdated, reveal a sublimated racial fire. All praise black soldiers fighting for their own and the nation's freedom. The poet's memory of his father, who died when Dunbar was twelve, might well have figured in the inspiration of these works. Joshua Dunbar had fled slavery in Kentucky and used the Underground Railroad to escape to Canada. A few years later he returned to enlist in the Fifty-fifth Massachusetts Infantry, the second regiment of black soldiers recruited in the North. The poem "Black Samson of Brandywine" exemplifies what authors in the 1970s will increasingly do. Developing material found in a book describing "a giant Negro armed with a scythe" during the Battle of the Brandywine in the Revolutionary War, Dunbar pictures his hero's destructive powers, then adds,

If he was only a chattel,
  Honor the ransom may pay
Of the royal, the loyal black giant
  Who fought for his country that day.

Noble and bright is the story,
  Worthy the touch of the lyre,
Sculptor or poet should find it
  Full of the stuff to inspire.

The other four poems are about black soldiers in the Civil War, in all of which the heroes evidence the historical truth of black men's enthusiasm and bravery in fighting for their freedom —without equal pay, or with none, before 1864. (It might be noted in passing that historian Lerone Bennett, Jr., in his *Before the Mayflower* [1962], counts 449 Civil War battle actions in which black troops "struck man-sized blows for their own freedom" [p. 175].) "Whistling Sam," a favorite with audiences in Dunbar's time, and one of the two poems about black soldiers that are written in dialect, uses musical notations to exemplify the tunes Sam whistled to cheer his fighting comrades. The other dialect poem, "When Dey 'Listed Colored Soldiers," is narrated by the recruit Elias's sweetheart, who learns black pride as well as the tragedy of war through his service and death.

The remaining two Civil War poems reflect more of black history and do so more vigorously. Dunbar's optimistic purpose in praising the might of black soldiers is revealed in "The Unsung Heroes" when he writes that poets should glorify them "Till the pride of face and the hate of race grow obsolete and cold." In deference to the hopes of Dunbar, and to long-neglected facts, the most thoughtful or moving lines in these poems deserve quotation. In "The Unsung Heroes," after attributing the war to "the slaver's cruel greed," Dunbar mentions some of the main places where black soldiers distinguished themselves:

> Ah, Wagner saw their glory, and
> Pillow knew their blood,
> That poured on a nation's altar,
> a sacrificial flood.
> Port Hudson heard their war-cry
> that smote its smoke-filled air,
> And the old free fires of their savage sires
> again were kindled there.

The final Civil War poem to be mentioned, "The Colored Soldiers," is slightly more informative about these battles; but the following details might help illuminate the references. During the attack on Fort Wagner in South Carolina, Colonel Robert Gould Shaw, the commanding officer of the Fifty-fourth Massachusetts Infantry, and a black standardbearer died side by side. Another black sergeant, William H. Carney, who picked up the fallen man's flag and led the next attack, was awarded the Congressional Medal of Honor. In the same summer of 1863, against the almost impregnable Port Hudson on the Lower Mississippi, black troops from Louisiana made six successive attacks, trying to aid General Grant in his campaign against Vicksburg. Benjamin Quarles, in *The Negro in the Making of America* (1969, revised edition), quotes *The New York Times* of June 13, 1863, as declaring that "No body of troops—Western, Eastern or rebel—have fought better in the war" (p. 120).

A condensed account of the third battle can be quoted from Peter M. Bergman's *The Chronological History of the Negro in America* (1969):

> The worst example of Confederate slaying of Negro troops was at Fort Pillow, Tenn., on April 12 [1864]. A Confederate cavalry force under Maj. Gen. Nathan B. Forrest captured the Fort garrisoned by Negro soldiers. Wholesale slaughter followed, and every

> sort of atrocity took place. Approximately 300 soldiers, many of them wounded, plus women and children, were killed (p. 239).

Lerone Bennett, Jr., after elaborating with gruesome details, adds,

> At Memphis, a few days after the Fort Pillow Massacre, Negro soldiers dropped to their knees and swore remembrance. After April 12, 1864, Negro soldiers entered battle with the cry, "Remember Fort Pillow" (p. 176).

In writing "The Colored Soldiers," Dunbar must have had the above mentioned or similar facts at his disposal: from memories of talk by his father (who spoke particularly about Fort Wagner, according to Brawley [p. 14]), from conversations with older people, and possibly from George Washington Williams's *A History of the Negro Troops in the War of the Rebellion* (1888). At any rate, in his strongest war poem he devotes the second and third of eleven stanzas to criticism of Uncle Sam for scorning black would-be recruits until military reverses forced a change of policy. After commending the eager fearlessness of the new enlisted men, he sets forth the essence of his praise of black soldiers and his condemnation of Confederates as follows:

> From the blazing breach of Wagner
> To the plains of Olustee,
> They were foremost in the fight
> Of the battles of the free.
>
> And at Pillow! God have mercy
> On the deeds committed there,
> And the souls of those poor victims
> Sent to Thee without a prayer.

The eighth stanza argues thus for equal citizenship:

> They were comrades then and brothers,
> Are they more or less to-day?
> They were good to stop a bullet
> And to front the fearful fray.
> They were citizens and soldiers,
> When rebellion raised its head;
> And the traits that made them worthy—
> Ah! those virtues are not dead.

An almost indefinable mixture of caution, humor, and something close to cynicism in Dunbar links "The Colored Soldiers" and the next category of three poems: a group in which the flame of black resistance is concealed. One cannot be certain, in examining the already quoted lines about Fort Pillow, why Dunbar asks for mercy on the *souls* of the black victims, but requests mercy on the *deeds* of the Confederate killers. Mercy is bestowed upon humans, not upon things and actions. The poet seems either cautious about damning the whites directly, or subtly unwilling to invoke mercy for them. The same mixture of qualities marks the protagonist, not the poet, in "An Ante-bellum Sermon," a preacher who cautiously protects himself from white oppression while humorously revealing his cynical estimate of black solidarity. Comparing the Lord's freeing of the Hebrews through Moses to the future deliverance of slaves, he says,

> Fu' de Lawd of hosts is mighty
>   When he girds his ahmor on.
> But fu' feah some one mistakes me,
>   I will pause right hyeah to say,
> Dat I'm still a-preachin' ancient,
>   I ain't talkin' 'bout to-day.

Addressing his slave listeners more directly, he continues:

> An' de love he showed to Isrul
>   Wasn't all on Isrul spent;
> Now don't run an' tell yo' mastahs
>   Dat I's preachin' discontent.

After this prudent interruption—in which the poet refers obliquely to the harsh Black Codes that included punishment for instigators of discontent among slaves—the preacher adds these remarks typical of the rest of the poem:

> So you see de Lawd's intention,
>   Evah sence de worl' began,
> Was dat His almighty freedom
>   Should belong to evah man,
> But I think it would be bettah,
>   Ef I'd pause agin to say,

Dat I'm talkin' 'bout ouah freedom
 In a Bibleistic way.

The humor in "An Ante-bellum Sermon," which accommodates the preacher's aggressive spirit to his belief that white supremacy is unbreakable by ordinary humans, contrasts with the grimness of the other two poems about concealed racial fire: "Vagrants" and "We Wear the Mask." The spiritual anguish in the protagonist of "Vagrants" is shown in this middle portion of the three-stanza poem:

We do not love, we are not friends,
 My soul and I.
 He lives a lie;
Untruth lines every way he wends.
 A scoffer he
 Who jeers at me:
And so, my comrade and my brother,
We wander on and hate each other.

Whatever scant validity exists in the self-hate theory imposed upon black people by psychologists is pinpointed in these lines about a split psyche that needs only an infusion of today's Black Consciousness.

The mask theme that controls "Vagrants" is best expressed by Dunbar in the poem that most often moves readers of the 1970s to credit him with racial fire: "We Wear the Mask." Significantly an early poem, it is spoken *by* black people and *for* black people. Too well known to demand full quotation here, it nevertheless has features that should be mentioned. In the opening lines, for example—"We wear the mask that grins and lies, / It hides our cheeks and shades our eyes"—Dunbar is careful to show that the *mask* is grinning, not the black man. Although the poet's use of the word "lies" is probably simple, it might not be. If the mask is lying to the wearer, the anguish of the black man shown in "Vagrants" is brought into play. If the mask is lying to white people, the psychology later explored by Ralph Ellison's Dr. Bledsoe and the grandfather and the black physician in *Invisible Man* enters the poem. The hiding of cheeks and eyes is the concealment of those features that reveal tears and that give quality to smiles. To be blinded to these parts of a person's countenance is to be blinded to his special humanity—which Langston Hughes considered artfully in writing his well-known poem "Minstrel Man." Skipping to the end of the stanza, where Dunbar says that black people "mouth with myriad subtleties," one notes the precise usage of the verb "mouth," which intensifies the mask theme by suggesting pretense, affectation, grimacing, and distortion of one's genuine features. In attributing to these actions "myriad subtleties," Dunbar indirectly commends the imaginative creativity that black people have been forced either to waste or to narrow because of the vagaries of white racism.

The wealth of implication in only three lines of this poem indicates what a thorough examination of it ought to yield. It must suffice here to make two more observations. By indicating in the second stanza that the world would be "overwise" in sympathetically enumerating the miseries of black people, Dunbar recognizes that individuals risk their psychological equilibrium in immersing themselves too long or too deeply in the catastrophes of others. In short, they know too much for their own good. And when that unwanted knowledge brings guilt, real or assumed, for the almost irremediable ills of victimized millions, the wisdom of sympathetic involvement diminishes. Although Dunbar questions the prudence of such commitment, he sees the trap that white bigots have set for themselves: they continue dreaming. Let them dream, concludes the poet, knowing that dreamers have only two destinies: they either die in their sleep or they wake up. And when these wake up, they will face what William Blake and Edgar Allan Poe foresaw in mystical terms as the destruction of the mind.

Dunbar's racial fire generally glows best when he is not advancing directly upon what his war poems call "the foe." His language can flare when he supports the aggressiveness of black civilian and military warriors. At least four poems show his strong racial feeling through such means. In "Frederick Douglass," the poet sinews his lines with the power of the freedom fighter who

> . . . sent his arrows to the very den
> Where grim Oppression held his bloody place
> And gloated o'er the mis'ries of a race.

And he was no soft-tongued apologist;
He spoke straightforward, fearlessly uncowed;

* * *

To sin and crime he gave their proper hue,
And hurled at evil what was evil's due.

Dunbar, no doubt feeling the toughness of his language, says:

He dared the lightning in the lightning's track,
And answered thunder with his thunder back.

The image of a warrior in his armor links the poem on Douglass (who "died in action with his armor on!") to the poem "The Warrior's Prayer." The protagonist of the latter, after refusing to ask the Lord to do battle on his behalf, prays as follows:

Still let mine eyes look ever on the foe,
Still let mine armor case me strong and bright;
And grant me, as I deal each righteous blow,
Strength for the fight!

Another poem, entitled "Right's Security" and first printed, like the piece on Douglass, about a year after that black hero's death, holds up the image of embattled minorities in its final stanza:

Right arms and armors, too, that man
Who will not compromise with wrong;
Though single, he must front the throng,
And wage the battle hard and long.
Minorities, since time began,
Have shown the better side of man;
And often in the lists of Time
One man has made a cause sublime!

The fourth poem that supports black aggressiveness, entitled "Philosophy," might not seem to do so at all. In dialect, it counsels ripping off the mask, the false grin that, Dunbar specifies, denies the misery, hunger, and circle of predicaments that leave the black man "mad ez sin." The importance of wearing or not wearing what the poet calls "a sickly so't o' grin" is easily recalled by a few historical and contemporary references—the historical ones certainly known to Dunbar. Frederick Douglass, in his work already cited, discusses the "very common and very indefinite . . . crime" of a wrong facial expression. The Black Codes, tightened after the rebellions led by Denmark Vesey and Nat Turner, made such a facial offense punishable by flogging, branding with a hot iron, or mutilation. In the summer of 1925 in Jackson, Mississippi, Richard Wright was fired from his job as porter in a clothing store for not grinning enough. Near the end of the 1960s, there appeared essays by black writers, Nathan Hare among them, asserting their right to be angry about racist deprivations. And in the same period, drawings and photos of black men made it clear that the national press considered their frowns revolutionary. Therefore, it is no small matter for Dunbar to suggest, even in satirical dialect, that black people should not "giggle w'en dey's nuffin' in de pot."

In the final poem to be considered, "To the South on Its New Slavery," twenty stanzas long, Dunbar speaks directly to the "foe." The poet begins by expressing pride in his blackness ("the long kiss of the loving tropic sun") and continues on to offer cogent arguments, striking what he calls "deeper chords, the notes of wrong," to attack the systems of peonage and convict leasing so abusive of black people. He asserts that his race has earned the respect of the South by caring for its best children and by saving its plantations during the Civil War through labor and loyalty certain to prolong slavery. But "Mother South" emerges guilty only of a slackening in her former upright posture; and during that interim after which she will again take her "dusky children to [her] saving breast," she can regain her glory by negating the "rumors" of her hatred for these black people who have loved her. It is the nation, not just the South, that slumbers and "takes its dangerous ease." Dunbar, then, speaking directly to the powerful South, could not, like Douglass, dare the lightning in the lightning's track.

These twenty-five poems contain substantially whatever racial fire Dunbar could express in verse. Certain conclusions can be drawn about each of the categories into which these poems have been grouped for discussion. In the ten poems that contain rather objective references to historical oppressions, Dunbar typically emphasizes folk music and dancing, romantic love, or dogged perseverance as the means by which black people have survived in spiritual health. His style and thought are rather pedestrian in his single commentary on the role of black women; but his satire is subtly bitter in his treatment of lynching, and humorously realistic in his appraisal of politics. Blunt pessimism tones one poem in this group; unrelieved despair marks another (and it might be added that, among all of Dunbar's poems that use his personal voice, well over thirty are markedly sad). In his two poems depicting slaves sentimentally attached to their kind masters after the Emancipation Proclamation, the author does not violate human nature, but he irritates militant readers of today.

In those five poems in which Dunbar sublimates his racial aggressiveness through praising black heroes in the Revolutionary and Civil wars, he makes it clear that the soldiers knew they were fighting for their race as well as for their country. In two of those poems, the author memorializes heroism and tragedy that every black person ought to know today. In the three poems expressive of concealed racial militance, Dunbar bolsters the still faltering image of the black preacher, concisely dramatizes the restlessness of spirit necessitated by racism, and in "We Wear the Mask" skillfully condenses the implications and the fate of American prejudice. In five other poems, one finds positive support of black resistance. Here Dunbar's language is forthright and vigorous in praise of Frederick Douglass (who had given him a job at the age of twenty) and in admiration of fighters for civil liberties; but humorous dialect softens his hard philosophizing in another instance. An additional poem in this category, although it adduces large historical truth to support the author's pleading for his race, remains essentially a plea—addressed to the South that has responded to love with hatred.

Dunbar, as a sensitive black man who felt no inherent inferiority to other people, had to feel racial fire in resistance to prejudice. The fact that this fire glows in only one poem out of every twenty that he wrote is not dispraise of him as a man or as a poet (nor does the number or proportion of the poems have anything to do with their quality). Most of these poems are average representatives of his competence, but several evince unusual power of thought or expression. Although Dunbar knew that many white people would buy his poems, in "The Lesson" he recalled his purpose: "I sang a lay for a brother's ear / In a strain to soothe his bleeding heart." The lines indicate his sentimentality, which is now construed as weakness. But at least Dunbar knew who his brothers were. And he knew they needed to be reminded that, in and out of slavery, their kind had clung to survival and to humanity through folk art, folk fun, and love.

NOTES

1. "American Negro Literature," in *Black Expression*, ed. Addison Gayle, Jr. (New York: Weybright & Talley, 1969), p. 231.
2. "The Literature of the Negro in the United States," from Richard Wright's *White Man, Listen!* (1957), as found in *ibid.*, p. 209.
3. "Paul Laurence Dunbar: The Rejected Symbol," *The Journal of Negro History* 52 (January 1967), 13.
4. Benjamin Brawley, *Paul Laurence Dunbar: Poet of His People* (Chapel Hill: Univ. of North Carolina Press, 1936), p. 50.
5. *Negro Poetry and Drama* (Washington, D.C.: Associates in Negro Folk Education, 1937), p. 36.

Dickson D. Bruce, Jr.

On Dunbar's "Jingles in a Broken Tongue": Dunbar's Dialect Poetry and the Afro-American Folk Tradition

A major problem confronting readers of Paul Laurence Dunbar's dialect poetry is the question of to what extent the poet can be considered an interpreter of the people whose speech those verses purported to capture. In part, the problem grows out of what we know about Dunbar's own view of his work. His feelings about the dialect poetry were fairly ambiguous. He wanted to make his mark in the literary world as a poet, plain and simple,[1] and he felt, probably rightly, that his identity as a dialect poet, coming as a result of William Dean Howells's famous review, had done him "irrevocable harm." [2] As Dunbar told James Weldon Johnson, it was not that he wanted to write dialect poetry, but that, "I've got to write dialect poetry, it's the only way I can get them to listen to me." [3] That Dunbar wrote in dialect to please a white audience and gain a hearing for his more serious efforts has led many readers to place that work within the minstrel tradition and to give Dunbar a place alongside the worst proponents of plantation stereotyping.

Yet, there is also evidence to suggest that Dunbar did not reject his efforts in dialect out of hand. The same Dunbar who confessed to James Weldon Johnson that he only wrote the verse to gain a hearing also had to admit that he "could write it as well, if not better than anybody else I knew of." [4] If he used his readings in dialect to get an audience for what he considered his more literary endeavors, he also seems to have performed those readings with great zest.[5] Dunbar's own attitudes towards his dialect verse were no more one-sided than critical opinion has been. He certainly did not consider it to be his best work, nor does it seem to have been the poetry on which he concentrated his efforts. Nevertheless, he did consider himself to have been a good practitioner of his art—he was thoroughly embarrassed when a performance of his work came off like a minstrel show [6]—and he felt himself capable of putting into poetry the life and language of his people.

It was the latter view which predominated among the critics of his own time. Moreover, it is important to note that those who appreciated Dunbar's dialect writing were not just white critics steeped in the plantation tradition, for the dialect verse also ranked high in the estimation of writers for black magazines and books which were published in Dunbar's time. Far from feeling that the dialect verse held black Americans up for ridicule, these critics saw it as Dunbar's forte, capturing accurately the way of life of the rural black Southerner in the generation which had gained freedom from slavery.

John Livingston Wright, in an early study of Dunbar, James D. Corrothers, and Daniel Webster Davis printed in *The Colored American Magazine*, felt rather strongly that the dialect verse was Dunbar's best work, and remarked on the poet's "fineness of feeling, that delicacy and daintiness of touch that characterized his work, that subtle and accurate perception and spiritual philosophizing." [7] In quoting examples in order to acquaint readers of *The Colored American Magazine* with Dunbar's writing, Wright chose two poems in literary English—"With the Lark" and "Life"—and four pieces of dialect writing, including "A Plea," "Time to Tinker Roun'," "Accountability," and "Foolin' Wid de Seasons."

A more pointed appraisal of Dunbar's poetry appeared in *The Voice of the Negro*, shortly after Dunbar's death. Edited in Atlanta by J. Max Barber, *The Voice of the Negro* was the major forum for black intellectuals who were openly critical of the accommodationist policies of Booker T. Washington.[8] The sentiments its contributors expressed were not likely to be in accord with anyone who held black people up for ridicule and mockery. Thus, it is important that the magazine's posthumous tribute to Dunbar, written by George Davis Jenifer, pointed out that

> Little of his work in the vernacular tongue rises above the mediocrity of every-day magazine verse—much of it is not as clever. It were an injustice to his people, therefore, and to his own memory—for he was ever modest of spirit—to rate him higher than he ever really attained as a writer of pure English verse.[9]

Perhaps, Jenifer felt, if Dunbar had lived longer, he might have attained the status of a great American poet, in literary English. Dunbar's strength, however, was that,

> Finding significance in the passions of simple black folk, he has lovingly set forth with picturesque truthfulness the sensuous joys, the broad humor, and the simple pathos of their lives. Moreover, he has preserved to our literature a life and patois that are doomed to pass with the diffusion of greater light among the colored people of the South.[10]

Jenifer's comments seem unusually patronizing for having appeared in a journal like *The Voice of the Negro*, but they were merely an extension of what the editors themselves had written a little earlier in their obituary of the poet. Calling him "the greatest poet that the Negro race has yet produced," they wrote, "he gave us a vivid interpretation of an era in the history of this country that is swiftly vanishing in the past, Dunbar's pictures of dusky maids in gay calico dresses and showy feathers are natural and easy." [11] Speaking further of his accomplishments, the editors noted that, "As a lyrical interpreter of the appetites and spiritual strivings of the older generation of Negroes, Dunbar excelled all others, and it may be said of most of his writings that they showed an artistic feeling and genuine poetic ability." [12]

Even Mary Church Terrell, President of the National Association of Colored Women, and an independent woman who took strong stands on behalf of black Americans,[13] acknowledged the value of Dunbar's dialect verse. Although, as a friend of the poet, she recognized and empathized with his own misgivings about the verse—and her tribute to him focused on his efforts in "the classic style of English composition"—she also wrote that "he had mastered more fully than most writers of Negro verse the real genius of the race whose characteristics his verses portrayed." [14] And in fact, after Mrs. Terrell had joked with him about using his illness as an excuse to receive sympathy from beautiful girls, Dunbar wrote the following little dialect verse for her:

> Look hyeah, Molly
> Ain't it jolly
> Jes' a loafin' 'roun'?
> Tell the Jedge
> Not to hedge
> For I am still in town.[15]

Edward H. Lawson, writing in *Alexander's Magazine* shortly after Dunbar's death, went his fellow critics one better when, commenting on Howells' review, he pointed out that

> It is practically impossible for a cultured and aristocratic white breast to thrill one-half so joyously at the representative dialect and cultured poetry of Paul Dunbar, as the breast of him or her who has been, beneath an ebony skin, in every situation that this poet of the lowly life describes.[16]

Lawson went on to praise Dunbar for having preserved "southern Negro speech" in his "immortal lyrics." The editor of *Alexander's* fully agreed with what Lawson had written, and in the obituary of Dunbar declared that

> Dunbar did much to dignify the race problem by portraying in a vivid manner the quaint customs, the weird folk-lore, and the aspirations of the ex-slave class in the southern sections of our country.[17]

It would be possible to quote other critics, but the point which emerges from a reading of the criticism of Dunbar's dialect poetry which appeared in turn-of-the-century black-American writing is the unanimity of critical opinion. The harshness with which more recent critics have viewed Dunbar's dialect poetry does not seem to have been present in the criticism appearing during his lifetime, nor were there any apologies for the dialect verse. Dunbar's critics could have chosen to condemn his dialect writing by silence if they did not choose to attack the man directly, but, in fact, all went to great pains to proclaim not only its depth and breadth, but also the accuracy with which the poet had portrayed at least some part of black-American life. They further agreed with the poet himself that no one around was any better.

Yet, they also agreed in assigning Dunbar's portrayals to a particular time and place. Not one of the critics seems to have felt that the life Dunbar's poetry described was the life of turn-of-the-century black America. Instead, they felt the poet's writings related to an older time and another place; particularly, they felt that the life Dunbar had captured was that of the rural Southerner, born in slavery. While they viewed Dunbar's interpretations as entirely accurate, then, they also felt that the poems were interpretations of a way of life that no longer fit black America, and, indeed, of a way of life that would soon disappear.

Dunbar seems to have agreed. He told an interviewer, "I believe I know my own people thoroughly. I know them in all classes, the high and the low." [18] He had imbibed as a child in Dayton, he believed, the way of life of those who had once been slaves. His father and mother had both been held in bondage, though his father had escaped it before the Civil War, and Dunbar could remember listening to his parents and their friends talk about the old life in the South. He even went so far as to say that, even though he lived in Dayton, his real environment was not Northern, but Southern.[19]

Dunbar maintained his associations with ex-slaves even as his career grew. During his drinking sprees, he'd "sit for hours listening to 'roustabouts' and absorbing odd expressions which he would later convert into poems." [20] When he lived in Washington, he would often invite old antebellum friends in for beer so that they might tell him "before the war" stories, and these, too, he would convert into verse.[21] Even though he himself did not speak dialect, and even though he had not lived in the South for any length of time, Dunbar was not out of contact with the people about whom he wrote, for he was exposed to their reminiscences and their ways of looking at things throughout his life.

Nor was Dunbar the kind of man who would have held black Americans up for ridicule. Although he only rarely spoke out on racial matters in what was, perhaps, the most trying period in contemporary black-American history, he showed himself to be vitally concerned with events in the country that affected black Americans. There is a tone of protest in some of his poetry and prose, and he is known to have spoken out against both the growing racism in American society during the period and the accommodationist response of such a man as Booker T. Washington.[22] Moreover, he felt he had enough influence within the black community that when rioting broke out in New York City in August 1900, the poet visited homes in the riot-torn areas in an attempt to restore peace.[23] Neither money nor the hope of a wider audience would likely have been enough to have persuaded Dunbar to make a mockery of his people, and, indeed, he resented very deeply any attempts to identify his dialect writing with the minstrel tradition.[24]

Neither Dunbar nor his black critics believed that the dialect poems made black people look ridiculous; for both the poet and those who evaluated his work felt that his picture of at least antebellum Southern life was an accurate portrayal of the thoughts and feelings of those who had lived during the period. That it should have been accurate was due to the fact that Dunbar was familiar with both the people and their traditions, having known both since childhood. It is not surprising, then, that the poetry which he came to write does in fact show a strong dependence upon both the folk traditions and the historical perspective which those who had endured slavery carried with them.

One of Dunbar's more popular dialect poems was "An Ante-Bellum Sermon."[25] It was quoted with approval by those who wrote in black publications, and it caught much of the flavor of Afro-American folk tradition. The poem, which is supposed to be a sermon by an antebellum slave preacher, is a thinly disguised articulation of the slaves' hope for freedom, expressed in the story of Moses and the pharaoh. As such, the poem captured several of the major themes not only in the religion of the slaves, but in their view of the world.

The focus of the poem, and what gave it its punch, was the slaves' need to keep anything other than the religion imposed upon them by the plantation owners under wraps. What slave religion seems to have been, and what the masters thought it to be, were two very different things. The slaves were supposed to receive their religious instruction from sanctioned preachers, white or black, who preached only one acceptable message: "Servants, obey your masters." Freedom, these preachers said, was to be found in heaven, and awaited only those who had been good and obedient while here on earth.

There is plenty to suggest that for most black Southerners of that time, such a religion was no religion at all. According to one ex-slave who was interviewed in the 1930s, the mistress had built a church on the plantation and had hired an acceptable black preacher. "She had him preach how we was to obey our master and missy if we want to go to heaven, but when she wasn't there, he come out with straight preachin' from the Bible." [26] In the days immediately following the Civil War, as the white South attempted to reconsolidate its power and the Ku Klux Klan was ravaging the country, one man remembered that black people used to gather for church meetings in the arbors out in the woods: "De preachers would exhort us dat us was de chillen o' Israel in de wilderness an' de Lord done sent us to take dis land o' milk and honey." [27]

These reminiscences were not unusual, nor did their message of freedom and citizenship fall on deaf ears. The slaves often went off, away from the surveillance of the plantation owner and his assistants, to hold prayer meetings on the sly. There, they would gather to sing old hymns and to pray for a freedom they were sure would come to them in this life. Such private prayer meetings seem to have been fairly common among the slaves and their subject was almost always the freedom from bondage which they thought the Lord would give them.

Religious language, further, has always been one way in which black Americans, particularly under slavery, could make their true feelings known. One need not posit a secret code behind the spirituals, for example, to see how the singing of those religious songs expressed strivings which were not entirely religious. W. F. Allen, Lucy McKim Garrison, and C. P. Ware recorded a spiritual during the Civil War, which, though very old and quite widespread, actually led to the jailing of some of its singers. In one verse the singers proclaimed,

We'll soon be free
We'll soon be free
We'll soon be free
De Lord will call us home

while in another they sang,

We'll fight for liberty
We'll fight for liberty
We'll fight for liberty
When de Lord will call us home.[28]

Although, to be sure, the religious implications of the song were important, the secular thrust of the words was not lost on either the slaves or their white auditors.

In a trickster-type folktale from Virginia, a slave was also said to put religious language to a more profane purpose. John was the plantation chicken-raiser, trusted by the master, and was known to expropriate a chicken for his own use, every now and again. Once, however, the master caught him:

> Nex' day Mahster call him: "John, what did you steal my chicken fo'?"—"Mahster, let me tell you dishyere one t'ing. I done saw in de Bible dat de man had to reab whey he labor. Mahster, I done labor raisin' dose chickens." [29]

Dunbar himself, in fact, showed the strength of religious language in a Fourth of July oration in which he made use of the words of the spiritual tradition. In a blistering attack on white America, the poet proclaimed,

> With citizenship discredited and scored, with violated homes and long unheeded prayers, with bleeding hands uplifted, still sore and smarting from long beating at the door of opportunity, we raise our voices and sing, "My Country, 'Tis of Thee"; we shout and sing while from the four points of the compass comes our brothers' unavailing cry, and so we celebrate. . . .
>
> But there are some who sit silent within their closed rooms and hear as from afar the din of joy come muffled to their ears as on some later day their children and their children's sons shall hear a nation cry for succor in her need. "Aye, there be some who on this festal day shall kneel in their private closets and with hands upraised and bleeding hearts cry out to God, if there still lives a God, 'How long, O God, How long.' " [30]

But, in "An Ante-Bellum Sermon," Dunbar caught more than just the superficial aspects of the religious language of the slaves, for, in this and other religious poems, he also showed himself to be aware of the beliefs that lay behind the language. The plantation owners tried to set their slaves' eyes squarely on the hope of a world to come, but, as one preacher put it, they "knew there was something better" [31] to be hoped for than a life in the hereafter. They reflected such knowledge in their private prayers for freedom, in their spiritual songs, and in their own accounts of what religion had done for them. Dunbar recognized the foundation of the slaves' hope in most of his religious poems, and among these is the dialect masterpiece, "An Ante-Bellum Sermon."

Benjamin Mays has referred to the traditional conception of God among black Americans as "compensatory," in that belief in God usually rests on a kind of "shallow pragmatism" based upon what God can do for the individual.[32] Mays's description may be couched in overly critical terms, but he has defined the core of the religion developed by American slaves. As Dunbar also understood, the God of those who were held in bondage was *not* an otherworldly God whom one would meet only in heaven. Rather, He was a God who was close to people, giving them strength to make it through this life. As one convert described his experience to an interviewer, "When I had finished [shouting] I had a deep feeling of satisfaction and no longer dreaded the whipping I knew I would get [for having gone off to pray]." [33] Another man, having been sold off to "the meanest man . . . ever God created," remembered that, "I lived through it all, praying to God every day for deliverance, and it came" when slavery was abolished.[34] The strength which the Lord gave may have been "compensatory," as in the case of the man who no longer dreaded a whipping, or it may have been related to the hope for freedom, as in the case of the individual who prayed for deliverance, but the hope of the believer was for something better while here on earth and not for the sanctioned hope of heaven as put forth by the master and those who represented him.

This was clearly intended by Dunbar's preacher. The poet set the "Bibleistic freedom" which his preacher was definitely *not* talking about in sharp contrast to the freedom which would lead to the recognition of black people as citizens. In one of his literary poems, Dunbar made the same point:

Take up your arms, come out with
  me,
Let heav'n alone; humanity
Needs more and Heaven less from
  thee.
With pity for mankind look
  'round;
Help them to rise—and Heaven
  is found.[35]

The religion Dunbar expressed in this poem, as in "An Ante-Bellum Sermon," was particularly concerned with life in this world, not in a world not yet known. Dunbar was concerned with sustaining and improving man's lot while in this life, and he recognized that far-off hopes could do little for a people in captivity. But even when the poet was not concerned with change and improvement, the this-worldly character of religious belief dominated his writing on the subject, as in "A Plantation Melody":

O brothah, w'en de tempes' beat,
An' w'en yo' weary head an' feet
  Can't fin' no place to res',
Jes' 'membah dat de Mastah's nigh,
An' putty soon you'll hyeah de cry,
  "Lay low in de wildaness." [36]

Dunbar articulated what seems to have been the essence of the religious beliefs of black Americans who experienced slavery. Told to be obedient and to hope for rewards in heaven, they recognized the plantation owners' religious instruction as a sham, and looked, instead, to a God who would carry them through their trials and, perhaps, lead them to freedom. Taught to pray for heaven, they prayed for freedom. Taught to sing of the God they'd meet above, they lifted their voices to proclaim,

We have a just God to plead-a our cause,
  To plead-a our cause, to plead-a our cause,
We have a just God to plead-a our cause,
  We are the people of God.[37]

The God of black Americans living during slavery was, however, more than a good friend upon Whom one could count for strength and support. Their God was a Being Who permeated the life of the world; He did not merely assist those who called on Him; rather, He was responsible for everything that occurred. Speaking directly of Dunbar's poetry, Benjamin Mays has pointed out that one implication of such a belief about God is the feeling on the part of the believer that "whatever happens, it happens at the will of a potent God; that it is useless to grieve and worry about abuses and maladjustment; that God's will moves on and it is irrevocable."[38] Mays may have described the implication in terms that are a bit too fatalistic, but he has also identified a basic underpinning of the religion of American slaves.

The deterministic cosmology described by Mays shows up very clearly in Dunbar's version of "An Ante-Bellum Sermon." The slaves saw that God's will was moving irrevocably towards their freedom and their vindication, and they prayed to the Lord to send a Moses who would deliver them out of bondage. Just as Dunbar's preacher talked about the hope of freedom, based on Bible precedent, when he said,

> But when Moses wif his powah
> Comes an' sets us chillun free,
> We will praise de gracious Mastah
> Dat has gin us liberty . . .

the slaves might have sung,

> Come along Moses, don't get lost,
> don't get lost, don't get lost,
> Come along Moses, don't get lost,
> We are the people of God,

a song which, though very old, became quite popular in the South during the Civil War.[39] A woman who had been in slavery, commenting on the economic ruin of the postwar South, expressed the same view of the world:

> I owned a nice home in Warren, Arkansas. I sold it to come up here. De folks down dere said dey would sure miss seeing me walking around down dere with my white apron on, but I believed in immigration like de Bible said. So I just immigrated from de South up here to de North. God said de plantations would grow up and de hoot owls would have 'em and dey is doin' it. Growin'

> up into wilderness. *God planned dem slave prayers to free us* like he did de Israelites, and dey did.[40]

The credit, in Dunbar's poem as for the singers and the woman, went to God and, more specifically, God's plan for the world. God had even planned that the slaves would pray for their own freedom. Dunbar's preacher expressed the same idea in the poem:

> So you see de Lawd's intention,
> Evah sence de worl' began,
> Was dat His almighty freedom
> Should belong to evah man. . . .

There was implicit in Dunbar's poem, as in the discourse and singing of those who had lived through slavery, a view of the world in which God was responsible for every event. Mays describes the view as a kind of fatalism in which anything that happens is to be accepted, and Dunbar, in other poems, also articulated that view. In the poem, "Faith," for example, he wrote,

> Dey ain't no use in mopin' 'round
> an' lookin' mad an' glum
> Erbout de wintah season, fu' hit's
> des plumb boun' to come;
>
> An' ef it comes to runnin' t'ings
> I's willin' to retiah,
> De Lawd'll min' de wintah an'
> my mammy'll min' de fiah.[41]

This poem echoed the sentiments of the better-known "Foolin' Wid de Seasons" in its acceptance of life as it comes and in the belief that all things have a place in a Divine plan.

Yet, there is little in "An Ante-Bellum Sermon" to suggest a fatalistic approach to the world. The idea of God's plan was central, but it was not used to rationalize existing conditions. Just as the woman saw in God's plan a reason to have left the South and a vindication of her people in the grown-over plantations, so Dunbar's preacher saw in the Divine plan a hope for a "mighty reck-'nin' day" when his people would gain citizenship and freedom. The cosmology underlying slave religion, which Dunbar articulated in his "Sermon," acknowledged the existence of some kind of plan in which everything had its place, but the belief in such a plan was hardly fatalistic in the sense that the individual would accept everything that came and neither grieve nor worry.

The notion of a Divine intention at work in the world came through in Afro-American tradition in religious discourse, particularly on the subject of freedom, and it lies at the base of Dunbar's poetic sermon. Because of this, the poem did a good deal more than simply express a traditional motif—the relationship of the Exodus story to the situation of black people in American slavery—in verse form. Instead, the poet went much deeper, since he had clearly understood the philosophical basis of that relationship, and made a poem in which he accurately conveyed what the Israelites' history had to do with people living in a different land at a different time.

The degree to which Dunbar had successfully assimilated that cosmology is shown not only in the "Sermon," which draws on a specific folk motif, but also in a poem dealing with more mundane matters, "Accountability." [42] The poem is an elaborate justification for the theft of one of the planter's chickens, but the justification presented reflected very well the concept of the world expressed in Dunbar's religious poems and in the folk tradition upon which he drew. The poet describes a world in which things are all united as a part of the Divine plan, so that nothing is intrinsically better or worse than anything else, for everything has its own justification:

> Him dat giv' de squir'ls de bush
> tails made de bobtails fu' de
> rabbits,

he says at one point. Then, at another,

> But we all fits into places dat no
> othah ones could fill,
> An' we does the things we has to,
> big er little, good er ill.
> John cain't take de place o' Henry,
> Su an' Sally ain't alike;
> Bass ain't nuthin' like a suckah,
> chub ain't nuthin' like a pike.

The notion that everything has a place and that one's situation in life is pretty much dependent upon that place echoes the ideas expressed in the "Sermon" and it had its counterpart not only in talk about freedom and in the religious songs of the people whose spirit Dunbar hoped to capture, but also in the more secular traditions on which Dunbar seems to have drawn. There were, for example, the proverbs and aphorisms which captured so much folk wisdom. Sayings such as "Rabbit know a fox track same as a houn'," [43] or "Dey's jes' ez good uh fish in de creek ez evah been caught, Dey's jes ez good uh timber in de woods ez evah been bought," [44] describe very well the kind of world which Dunbar calls up in "Accountability." Everything has its place in relation to every other thing, according to some larger plan. The rabbit's reasons for recognizing a fox track are as good as the hound's, though they may be different, just as, for the poet,

John cain't take de place o' Henry,
Su an' Sally ain't alike.

There is a sophisticated attitude of relativism captured in the proverbs—and in Dunbar's poem—which has not often been recognized in Afro-American folk tradition.

Moral questions also become a relative matter in a world where everything is a part of the Divine plan. As the poet said,

We cain't he'p ouah likes and dislikes,
if we'se bad we ain't to blame.

The maker of proverbs took the same kind of ethical posture when he noted that "folk ain't ap' to fall out wid de mockin' bird jes' 'cause he steals his songs." [45] The essence of such a relativistic posture was *not* that there was no such thing as right or wrong, but, rather, that such categories are not absolute. Instead, judgments of rightness or wrongness have to be made in the context of a given time and place, so that differences among individuals and the kinds of situations in which they find themselves are all relevant criteria for making moral judgments.

Of course, in Dunbar's poem all of the elaborate ethical discourse leads up to a punch line:

When you come to think about it,
how it's all planned out it's
splendid.
Nuthin's done er evah happens
'dout hit's somefin' dat's intended;
Don't keer whut you does, you has to,
an' hit sholy beats de dickens—
Viney, go put on de kittle, I got
one o' mastah's chickens.

We're not to blame the speaker for having expropriated the chicken. The same God who planned it all out, making both bushy-tailed squirrels and bob-tailed rabbits, also determined that given the speaker's position, taking the chicken was his best possible course of action. As the poet put it,

An' we does the things we has to,
big er little, good er ill.

"Accountability" is squarely in the tradition of the trickster stories among Afro-Americans. Although such stories are most familiar in the form of animal tales, such as the adventures of Brer Rabbit, there was also a strong tradition of "putting on old master," in which a wily slave *attempted* to overcome the obstacles posed by the plantation system through chicanery. In some cases, the trickster was after food, as in the story related by one ex-slave about "malitis"—a disease which rendered a pig inedible for the white folks, but fit for the slaves. The disease came at night and was caused by a hammer blow between the victim's eyes.[46] In other cases, the hope of the trickster was to save his own neck, as in a story collected by Zora Neale Hurston. One slave hid in a tree, while another knelt in prayer below, about to be hanged by the slave owner. When the fellow down below prayed, "O Lord, here Ah am at de foot of de persimmon tree. If you're gointer destroy Old Massa tonight, with his wife and chillun and everything he got, lemme see it lightnin'." As he prayed, the accomplice struck a match. Not only did the slave escape hanging, but he received his freedom, land, and capital.[47]

In these stories, the trickster seems to break the rule set forth in "Accountability" by manipulating the situation—albeit in limited ways—to his own advantage. Yet, if the tales are viewed in the larger context of trickster stories, they appear in a somewhat different light. The fact is, the wily slave was as likely to get caught in his act, or even be fooled by the master, as he was to succeed. There is, for example, the classic slap at otherworldly religion, one version of which was collected in Virginia around the turn of the century. In the story, an old slave went out to his prayer ground under a tree and prayed that the Lord would take him to heaven and out of slavery. The master overheard, and the next time the slave asked for a "line from heaven," the master threw him a rope which was on a pulley attached to the top of the tree. The old slave took hold, putting the "line" around his neck, whereupon the planter began to raise the old man up and to let him fall. Finally, after this had happened several times, the slave got up, took the rope off his neck, and ran home, vowing never to pray again.[48] Stories of the trickster's having been caught and punished are about as common as those in which he gets away, and though the culprit may try to get out of it, as did the man in a story cited earlier, who fell back on the Bible, one may be assured that the penalty Old Master exacted would be a harsh one.

The trickster was as much a tool of fate as everyone else. His success rate was hardly one hundred percent,[49] and he was usually assured of success only when the stakes were impressively high, as when he was fighting for his life. When the stakes were small—e.g., a stolen pig or a chicken—it was not at all unusual for the trickster-hero to get caught. The success or failure of the hero was, in other words, irrelevant to the acceptability of a story, and the fun was probably in watching him work. Since the individual was really governed by a larger plan anyway, his ability to manipulate would not be an important measure of success in life.[50]

At the same time, if the trickster's success was not relevant, neither was the rightness or wrongness of his act. In the story of the "line from heaven," it is, in fact, the master who takes on the trickster role, and the act which he performs is an act of almost barbaric cruelty, a point which is never made in the story. At the same time, the storytellers recognized that, given the context of their situation in slavery, discussions of the absolute rightness or wrongness of taking from the master had very little meaning. Such ethical relativism is, of course, consistent with a cosmology in which everything is a part of a larger plan, so that nothing is intrinsically right or wrong, good or evil. As the proverb says, one doesn't condemn the mockingbird because he steals his songs, and, in the poet's words,

> Him dat made de streets an' drive-
> ways wasn't 'shamed to make
> de alleys.

"Accountability" described the same sort of world as "An Ante-Bellum Sermon," but in different terms. The "Sermon" was a poem about the black slaves' hope for freedom and for citizenship, while "Accountability" was concerned with less substantial matters; but each derived its point from a view that the world was ordered by God according to His plan; and on a view of man as an object in that plan, acted upon and governed by forces greater than himself. Both the world view and the view of self were present not only in the two examples I have chosen to discuss, but also in Dunbar's other dialect poems, particularly those where he talked about religion. In articulating such a view of the world and man's place in it in his dialect poems, Dunbar articulated with great accuracy one basic principle in the Afro-American folk traditions of the Southern United States.

It is true that Dunbar's dialect poems were not far removed from the Plantation Tradition in which some critics have placed them. The main themes of even his best poems, including "Accountability" and "An Ante-Bellum Sermon," had echoes in the literary Plantation Tradition. Chicken stealing was a stock-and-trade theme for racist proponents of the plantation school,[51] just as it was the subject of Dunbar's poem. But the difference between the plantation-writers' treatment of that theme and Dunbar's was great. Whereas the plantation-writers' attempt *was* to ridicule the freedman so that their audience would laugh *at* black Americans, Dunbar was successful at getting the reader of "Accountability" to laugh *with* the thief. The same thing is true of "An Ante-Bellum Sermon." For the plantation writer, the preacher was exceeded as a proper figure for ridicule only by the chicken thief. White writers portrayed the preacher as ignorant, but with an unquenchable desire to use big words, and, morally, no better than his flock.[52] Dunbar's plantation preacher may have been given to flights of Biblical oratory, but he was ignorant of neither the real meaning of his words nor of the moral force behind them. The poem may have been humorous, but, once again, one laughs *with* the preacher, not at him.

Even Dunbar's most nostalgic dialect poems are more real than the parallel compositions of the Plantation Tradition. Poems such as "The News" or "Chrismus on the Plantation" are, to be sure, as offensive as anything that ever appeared in the white literary magazines of Dunbar's day, but a poem like "The Old Cabin" [53] seems to have captured very well the nostalgia that was to be found among people who were growing older. The old man in that poem expressed no love for slavery, when he was held, "In my mis'ry—ha'd an' fas'," but he could also remember when he had been young and all the "joyful" sights and sounds of his youth. The plantation writers never understood such nostalgia, and they liked to interpret it as a sign that the freedmen could not thrive in their new estate. Dunbar, on the other hand, knew the nostalgia for what it was—a looking-back at youth from the perspective of a life almost finished.

The key difference was, of course, that Dunbar knew what he was talking about and the plantation writers did not. Dunbar was capable of going beyond the level of the superficialities of black folk tradition to a deeper understanding of the world view that lay at the base of tradition. He was not the reteller of tales, but was, rather, an interpreter of a way of looking at life and at the world. And he captured, with great accuracy, but also with great feeling, a generation of Americans who had seen and endured more than any other, before or since.

NOTES

1. Addison Gayle, Jr., *Oak and Ivy: A Biography of Paul Laurence Dunbar* (Garden City: Doubleday and Company, 1971), p. 11.
2. "Unpublished Letters of Paul Laurence Dunbar to a Friend," *Crisis* 20 (1920), 73.

3. James Weldon Johnson, ed., *The Book of American Negro Poetry* (New York: Harcourt, Brace & World, Inc. 1931), pp. 35–36.
4. In Gayle, *Oak and Ivy*, p. 38.
5. Gossie Harold Hudson, *A Biography of Paul Laurence Dunbar* (Unpublished Ph.D. dissertation, Ohio State Univ., 1970), p. 127.
6. See Gayle, *Oak and Ivy*, pp. 87–88.
7. John Livingston Wright, "Three Negro Poets," *The Colored American Magazine* 2 (1901), 105–06.
8. August Meier, *Negro Thought In America, 1880–1915: Racial Ideology in the Age of Booker T. Washington* (Ann Arbor: Univ. of Michigan Press, 1963), pp. 175–76.
9. George Davis Jenifer, "The Services of Dunbar," *The Voice of the Negro* 3 (1906), 408–09. Jenifer means "vernacular" to be associated with "official," "standard" speech and "patois" to refer to Dunbar's work in dialect speech.
10. *Ibid.*
11. "Paul Laurence Dunbar," *The Voice of the Negro* 3 (1906), 173.
12. *Ibid.*, p. 174.
13. Meier, *Negro Thought*, pp. 239–40.
14. Mary Church Terrell, "Paul Laurence Dunbar," *The Voice of the Negro* 3 (1906), 272.
15. *Ibid.*, p. 277.
16. Edward H. Lawson, "Paul Laurence Dunbar," *Alexander's Magazine* 1, no. 11 (March 1906), 47. I am grateful to Mr. Eugene Metcalf for pointing this article out to me.
17. "The Passing of Dunbar," *Alexander's Magazine* 1, no. 10 (February 1906), 16.
18. In Hudson, *A Biography*, p. 10.
19. *Ibid.*, pp. 24–25.
20. *Ibid.*, p. 112.
21. Edward F. Arnold, "Some Personal Reminiscences of Paul Laurence Dunbar," *Journal of Negro History* 17 (1932), 401.
22. Hudson, *A Biography*, p. 189; Gayle, *Oak and Ivy*, p. 47. See, also, Dunbar's poem "To the South, on Its New Slavery," *Complete Poems* (New York: Dodd, Mead and Company, 1913), p. 216.
23. The story appears in the New York *Times*, August 20, 1900, p. 2.
24. Gayle, *Oak and Ivy*, p. 47; Hudson, *A Biography*, p. 180.
25. Dunbar, *Complete Poems*, pp. 13–15.
26. In Norman R. Yetman, ed., *Life Under the "Peculiar Institution": Selections from the Slave Narrative Collection* (New York: Holt, Rinehart and Winston, 1970), p. 337.
27. In *Ibid.*, p. 75.
28. W. F. Allen, C. P. Ware, and Lucy McKim Garrison, *Slave Songs of the United States* (New York, 1868. Rpt. New York: Peter Smith, 1951), p. 73.

29. Portia Smiley, "Folklore from Virginia, South Carolina, Georgia, Alabama, and Florida," *Journal of American Folklore* 32 (1919), 362.
30. Speech as printed in the New York *Times,* July 10, 1903, p. 2.
31. B. A. Botkin, ed., *Lay My Burden Down: A Folk History of Slavery* (Chicago: Univ. of Chicago Press, 1945. Phoenix ed., 1958), p. 26.
32. Benjamin E. Mays, *The Negro's God as Reflected in His Literature* (1938. Rpt. New York: Atheneum, 1968), p. 14.
33. In Clifton H. Johnson, ed., *God Struck Me Dead: Religious Conversion Experiences and Autobiographies of Ex-Slaves* (Philadelphia and Boston: Pilgrim Press, 1969), p. 16.
34. *Ibid.*, pp. 71–72.
35. Dunbar, *Complete Poems*, p. 38.
36. *Ibid.*, p. 193.
37. Allen, *et al.*, *Slave Songs*, p. 104.
38. Mays, *The Negro's God*, p. 134.
39. Allen, *et al.*, *Slave Songs*, p. 104.
40. Yetman, *Life*, pp. 263–64.
41. Dunbar, *Complete Poems*, p. 245.
42. *Ibid.*, pp. 5–6.
43. J. Mason Brewer, *American Negro Folklore* (Chicago: Quadrangle, 1968), p. 318.
44. *Ibid.*, p. 325.
45. Brewer, *American Negro Folklore*, p. 316.
46. Botkin, *Lay My Burden Down*, pp. 4–5.
47. Zora Neale Hurston, *Mules and Men* (Philadelphia: Lippincott, 1935; New York: Harper & Row Perennial Library, 1970), pp. 113–14.
48. A. M. Bacon and E. C. Parsons, "Folklore from Elizabeth City County, Virginia," *Journal of American Folklore* 35 (1922), 294–95.
49. Indeed, John's success rate was considerably less than fifty percent. In the stories I examined, all collected by black folklorists in the years from about 1890 to 1920, some twenty-nine end with John either getting caught or getting fooled himself, usually by "Old Master." Twenty-five are stories of John's success, but in half of those, John's success results in profits for "Old Master."
50. Harry Oster has noticed the same features of the "John and Old Master" stories, but has explained what it means in somewhat different terms. "Negro Humor: John and Old Marster," *Journal of the Folklore Institute* 5 (1968), 42–57.
51. Rayford W. Logan, *The Negro in American Life and Thought: The Nadir, 1877–1901* (New York: Dial Press, 1954), pp. 242–43.
52. *Ibid.*, pp. 244–46.
53. Dunbar, *Complete Poems*, p. 260.

Myron Simon

Dunbar and Dialect Poetry

Reading Dunbar, one is forcibly reminded that black poetry in America has issued from two quite different sources. One stream, beginning with Phillis Wheatley and Jupiter Hammon, and continuing with George Moses Horton, Frances Watkins Harper, James Whitfield, Albery Whitman, and Joseph Seaman Cotter, carefully observed the margins of the Anglo-American literary tradition and accordingly committed itself to formal modes of expression entirely remote from the vernacular of the black community, which was still chiefly Southern and rural during Dunbar's lifetime. The other stream, beginning with the anonymous authors of spirituals, blues, protest and work songs, was compelled by the residual experience of the black community and faithful to its vernacular until, in the last decades of the nineteenth century, transcription of the black oral tradition was initiated by white Southern writers like Irwin Russell, Joel Chandler Harris, and Thomas Nelson Page and by black writers like Daniel Davis, James Campbell, James Corrothers, and Dunbar. These writers were interested in Southern rural black speech largely as a vehicle for amiable humor and pathos, and thus employed the vernacular selectively for literary effect. Although Harper, Whitman, and Cotter occasionally wrote in the vernacular, up to the time of Dunbar the two streams had remained quite pure. Indeed, Dunbar kept them so perfectly separate in his work that he became the prototype of the black poet with two different voices: the one cultivated and non-racial or only faintly racial; the other solecistic and black.

Dunbar manifestly preferred his literary to his vernacular voice, but his mastery of both was widely praised. And he was, consequently, the first black poet to become celebrated—albeit sometimes by different audiences—for his work in both standard literary English and in the "plantation" dialect.[1] Dunbar explicitly separated the two modes only in *Majors and Minors* and *Lyrics of the Hearthside*, the second of his four "Lyrics" volumes, where "The Paradox" and "Sympathy" stand apart from "Little Brown Baby" which appears in a concluding section called "Humor and Dialect." In the other volumes, the two modes sit familiarly together on the same or facing pages, "An Ante-Bellum Sermon" close against the "Ode to Ethiopia." Thus, one of the reasons for Dunbar's great importance in the history of black poetry is that in his books the two channels through which black poetry emerged in America—the literary and the oral traditions—begin to come together: they inhabit the same mind, are bound between the same covers.

As Dunbar knew, there was abundant precedent in Anglo-American literary tradition for the introduction of the vernacular into poetic composition. In terms of theory, the classical doctrine of decorum had long sanctioned the use of ordinary or rough expression when the character represented was understood to be humble or rude or comic. In terms of practice, Dunbar could draw reassurance from the work of "standard" poets like Burns or Lowell, whose use of the Scots or New England vernaculars had been acclaimed. Burns had artfully combined the literary and vernacular styles in poems like "The Cotter's Saturday Night"; and Lowell's use of rural New England speech in *The Biglow Papers* had only enhanced his reputation as the author of "The Vision of Sir Launfal." Evidently committed to this tradition, Dunbar wrote alternately in the literary and vernacular modes from the outset of his poetic career to its very end. Two-thirds of Dunbar's poetry is in standard literary English, and the literary mode is more dominant in *Lyrics of Lowly Life* than in any of the succeeding volumes. But, overall, the balance between the two modes is rather evenly maintained throughout the four volumes which comprise the *Complete Poems*. Too much has perhaps been made of Dunbar's uneasiness over the popularity of his vernacular—i.e., dialect—poems. There is no reason to believe that, given the achievements in the vernacular by major poets of the previous century in England and America, he thought his dialect poems greatly inferior to his more dignified and elegant performances. It is more likely that he was progressively disheartened by the capacity of the poems he had written in dialect to obscure the larger part of his poetry. What he seems to have wished was a celebrity for his genteel verses equal to that which the public had bestowed upon the dialect poems.

However, what worked for Lowell did not work as well for Dunbar, since the circumstances of the two poets could scarcely have been more different. Lowell, deeply rooted in his region and the issue of its highest culture, moved easily between Harvard rationalism and Yankee village shrewdness. The "reality" underlying Hosea Biglow's dialect speech is not disjunct from the values and the sense of life which inform the self-assured wit of "A Fable for Critics." Because Hosea Biglow is as much a part of New England culture as the Brahmin editor of the *Atlantic Monthly*, there is no impediment to Lowell's employment of two quite different poetic voices. That is, Lowell occupied his region, his country, and his role as a poet unselfconsciously, without any sense that in writing "The Vision of Sir Launfal" he was shirking obligations to his contemporaries; and he could write his *Biglow Papers* playfully, without feeling that he was demeaning his literary gifts.

But Dunbar—born in a region different from the one in which his parents had been reared, the son of self-taught former slaves and largely self-taught himself—was unselfconsciously at home neither in the South nor the Midwest, neither in standard literary English nor the rural black vernacular. As Brawley tells us,[2] Dunbar was early drawn to Shelley, Keats, Tennyson, Poe, and Longfellow; and he gave most of his poetic career to writing their kinds of poetry. In consequence of his unwavering loyalty to traditional diction and prosody, most of Dunbar's genteel poems have the slightly labored, uneasy look of set pieces and imitations. Pastoral lyrics like "Retort" and "Farewell to Arcady," Longfellowesque fables like "The Seedling," a classical romance like "Ione," and dutiful exercises like "Columbian Ode," "Dirge," and "Madrigal" in their uniform facility suggest only how often Dunbar's study lamp burned late. As for the dialect poems, he wrote them—he told James Weldon Johnson self-reproachfully—to "gain a hearing," [3] i.e., to capitalize upon his facility in a form of writing which had become enormously popular during the preceding generation. Dunbar's assessment of personal motive may have been too harsh: dialect poems like "When Malindy Sings" and "The Party" almost certainly were written out of more than ambition and self-interest. His best dialect poems work not through disingenuous manipulation of the reader's emotions, but by generating their own emotion out of Dunbar's unmistakable empathy for a rural black world that seemed stable and out of his nostalgia for its close, well-defined human relationships. But, in any event, the operative conventions of "local color" writing had been effectively codified by the time Dunbar made his earliest attempts at it. The formulas by which the post-Civil War reading public was to secure more realistic representations of the full variety of American life found their principal apologist in William Dean Howells and their chief Southern practitioners in J.A. Macon, Irwin Russell, Joel Chandler Harris, and Thomas Nelson Page. Their sense of the content of plantation culture was undoubtedly assimilated by Dunbar. And both from them and James Whitcomb Riley he derived much of his sense of how rural life and speech were to be imitated in literature. Thus equipped, Dunbar found it difficult to get beyond the deceptive surface of black rural life to those ineluctable qualities for which no black poet had yet found an adequate language.

As the example of Lowell indicates, a poet may employ two widely discrepant voices concurrently without loss if, in the profoundest manner of possession, both speech styles are his own. Or, as in the case of Burns, a poet may employ two voices when one is clearly a more "natural" and powerfully wielded instrument than the other. But Dunbar's two voices, whatever their immediate popularity, evidently left him feeling dissatisfied and unfulfilled. Neither language was finally his own; neither was adequate to the task of apprehending and articulating the very reality that his black sensibility was distinctly fitted to engage. In his conversations with Johnson in 1901, Dunbar not only spoke self-reproachfully of his commitment to dialect poetry but implied that the poems he wished to write would not be in literary English. Johnson "surmised" that it was Dunbar's ambition to write poems in "straight English that would relate to the Negro." However, at the end—five years later—he could only report disconsolately to

Johnson, "I've kept on doing the same things, and doing them no better. I have never gotten to the things I really wanted to do." [4]

Little more than a decade after Dunbar's death, the emergence of the New Negro movement—with its assertions of racial pride—provoked a sharp reaction against the Plantation Tradition in black writing. Johnson led the attack on precisely those forms and attitudes in dialect poetry of which Dunbar was the acknowledged master. If the direct influence of Dunbar persisted, it was through his verses in literary English—especially the high Romantic strain, which Countee Cullen admired and successfully emulated. But less obviously and more importantly, Dunbar's central dilemma survived in a line of black poets who oscillated—early in their careers—between the two voices that he had never managed either to make his own or to reject. Although Johnson's reservations about the validity of poetry in the plantation or minstrel dialect date from the turn of the century, his first book of poems, *Fifty Years and Other Poems* (1917), is clearly in the line of Dunbar. It has a section of dialect poems that are directly indebted to Dunbar,[5] the most famous of them being "Sence You Went Away"; the poems in the other section, like "O Black and Unknown Bards" and "Fifty Years," are conspicuously accomplished, fastidious performances in literary English. In Langston Hughes's first book, *The Weary Blues* (1926), the same bivocalism is evident. Although the literary voice, under Imagist influence, has been purged of the late Romantic mannerisms so pronounced in Dunbar (see, for example, the sections "Water-Front Streets" and "Shadows in the Sun"), it is yet plainly disjunct from Hughes's vernacular voice, his slightly unsure first attempts to characterize the speech of the urban working-class black in such poems as "Blues Fantasy" and "Mother to Son." By the same token, Sterling Brown's *Southern Road* (1932) is about evenly divided between literary and dialect expression. Such carefully measured statements of near despair—in the style of Housman—as "Salutamus," "Challenge," "Rain," and "Nous n'irons plus au bois . . ." contrast oddly with Brown's dialect presentation of similar Housmanian ironies in poems like "Old Man Buzzard" and "Mister Samuel and Sam." Moreover, this radical division in the languages of black poetry was carried forward into at least the 1940s, as may be seen in Gwendolyn Brooks's *A Street in Bronzeville* (1945) and Owen Dodson's *Powerful Long Ladder* (1946). Although most of the poems in both volumes are in literary English and the occasional uses of dialect continue the endeavor of Hughes and Brown to abandon phonetic caricature for a more subtle or muted representation of black speech, there is still the effect of speech styles colliding incongruously in Brooks's "The Date" ("If she don't hurry up and let me out of here") and "Firstly Inclined to Take What It Is Told" ("Thee sacrosanct, Thee sweet, Thee crystalline,/ With the full jewel wile of mighty light") and in Dodson's "Poem for Pearl's Dancers" ("My lips taste blood, / And in they souls they's blood. / My tongue can't joy no future in this blood") and "Pearl Primus" ("Is it Cassandra as she saw the dark wolf / And caught him fast and dug her prophetic fingernails / To below the hair into the flesh / Feeling a dark blood world of hate?"). In the tension between these styles, bespeaking ultimately an alienation from both, one may perceive the crux in respect to which these very different poets are all close to Dunbar.

Although we may dissent from his reasons, Howells was surely right in pronouncing Dunbar's dialect poems more valuable than his poems in literary English. He judged some of the latter to be "very good, and even more than very good, but not distinctively his contribution to the body of American poetry":

> What I mean is that several people might have written them; but I do not know any one else at present who could quite have written the dialect pieces. These are divinations and reports of what passes in the hearts and minds of a lowly people whose poetry had hitherto been inarticulately expressed in music, but now finds, for the first time in our tongue, literary interpretation of a very artistic completeness.[6]

If we turn it around, Howells's argument suggests why Dunbar's critics, during the Harlem Renaissance and after, have usually felt more dissatisfied with his dialect poems than with those in literary English. The black experience surrounded him, still virtually untouched, awaiting "literary interpretation of a very artistic completeness"; and Dunbar's best chance to engage it lay—as Howells perceived—in the black vernacular, the "tongue" he was better fitted than any white writer to make into the authentic voice of that experience. However, Howells credited him with having achieved precisely what he failed to provide: a true and complete account of what was most distinctive in that part of the American or human experience which he really knew at first hand. Dunbar's failures in literary English, as Sterling Brown has observed, were no worse than those of "the school of American Tennysonians to which he belonged." But his failures in dialect were not so easily extenuated, even by a sympathetic critic; for he omitted much and idealized what he did not omit. Whatever the reason, "the fact of omission remains."[7] Since Dunbar's dialect poems have now come through more than a half-century of growing indifference and censure, it may be useful to examine some of the assumptions underlying those responses.

The reasons for this disaffection from poems once so popular are not always persuasive. Some of the reasons have little direct bearing upon the specific qualities of Dunbar's dialect poems. To begin with, dialect writing as a *genre* was falling into disrepute by the time of Dunbar's death. It had been so heavily associated with rural America, with all that had begun to seem most ephemeral in American life and literature, that the new artistic predilections for urban and industrial life appeared to render it obsolete. Accordingly, when Langston Hughes commenced his experiments with the language of uneducated working-class blacks who lived not in Kentucky but in Washington, Chicago, and New York, few perceived that he had selected the *dialect* of the newly emergent black urban proletariat as his model; such unprecedented literary speech sounded too natural to be termed "dialect." Rather, it was generally understood that Hughes had abandoned dialect, with its stereotypical portrayal of the Negro. Thus, Dunbar's dialect poetry shared in the general devaluation of local color writing that accompanied the introduction of subtler and tougher minded modes of realistic writing at the beginning of the new century. Moreover, the New Negro movement—with its revisionist stress upon authentic knowledge of the black community—broadened doubts about the adequacy of Dunbar's understanding of rural black life in Kentucky that had been suggested a generation earlier in Joseph Seaman Cotter's ironic "Answer to Dunbar's 'After a Visit.'"[8] Brawley is quick to point out that "Born in Dayton, in the Middle

West," Dunbar "had only limited opportunity to study the Negro."[9] Brawley's concession that Dunbar nevertheless "gave a better interpretation than any writer who had preceded him" is nicely ambiguous praise; for, despite the fact that Brawley was speaking thirty years after Dunbar's death, he restricts Dunbar's superiority to the writers who preceded him. There is, of course, a basis in common sense for such doubts; but, clearly, a poet's first-hand knowledge of his subject must be taken as a sufficient and not as a necessary condition of his art. Finally, many criticisms of the dialect poems have questioned the accuracy of Dunbar's representations of black speech in Kentucky or elsewhere in the Southern Midlands. And this has seemed a serious charge because it is generally, if erroneously, believed that the merit of a literary dialect depends upon its correspondence with actual speech. Brawley, eager to defend Dunbar's skill in the employment of dialect, if not his understanding of black life, claims that when—during his boyhood—Dunbar listened to his mother's stories of old Kentucky he was "unconsciously impressed by his mother's inimitable phrasing." "And where," he asks in reference to the artistic progress evident in *Majors and Minors*, "did the young man who had never been South get this exquisite finish for his Negro dialect? Where but in the stories heard at his mother's knee even from his earliest years?"[10] But critics before and after Brawley have more typically found Dunbar's dialect too remote from the actual speech he sought to represent, too literary in the fashion of Russell and Riley.

Dunbar's most penetrating comment on the use of dialect in literature appears in a letter to Helen Douglass:

> As to your remarks about my dialect, I have nothing to say save that I am sorry to find among intelligent people those who are unable to differentiate dialect as a philological branch from Negro minstrelsy.[11]

That is, linguistics and "minstrelsy" (here meaning poetry, not blackface comedy) provide functionally distinct reports of a dialect because, as George Philip Krapp has observed, they engage actual speech differently:

> The relations of literary dialects to "real" dialects are not easily explicable, mainly because "real" dialects themselves are elusive

> and hard to define. Literary dialects, on the other hand, depend for their success upon being positive and readily recognizable.[12]

Although the linguist undertakes to provide a full report of his elusive quarry, Krapp denies that the writer of dialect is under any obligation to conform to what the linguist takes the reality of a given variety of English to be. The linguist "at least attempts to exhaust all the details of dialect speech which can come under his observation, thus arriving at a finality of some kind"; the writer, on the other hand, "utilizes only as much of his material as he thinks he needs for his special literary purposes":

> The literary artist attempts by occasional suggestion to produce the illusion of a distinct and "real" dialect speech, but the scientist endeavors to attain a different conception of reality with an analytic method and an exhaustive examination of the material open to him for observation.[13]

Thus, in the case of Dunbar or any other dialect writer, whether literary dialect has been managed well or ill depends not upon its literal accuracy, its closeness to the actual speech which it has selectively approximated, but rather upon how well it works as a creative means of constituting the writer's experience.

Sumner Ives has noted that, despite the popularity of dialect in American literature, there has been very little investigation of the ways in which authors have represented dialects that goes beyond the pioneer chapter on "Literary Dialects" in Krapp's *The English Language in America.* Ives himself advanced the study of literary dialects by the intelligence with which he promptly applied the new evidence and insights of the Linguistic Atlas of the United States to the task of illuminating the subtle relationships between actual dialects and their literary representations in the work of such writers as Lowell, Twain, and Joel Chandler Harris.[14] But there has been no comparable study of black dialect writing, so that critics who have commented either affirmatively or negatively on Dunbar's use of dialect appear similarly unaware of the distinctions between Southern plantation speech and Southern mountain speech, on the one hand, and—yet more basically—between Southern speech and Southern Midland speech, on the other. Since these dialects are not easily differentiated and since, in any event, we have no reliable records of the black speech in these dialect areas during Dunbar's lifetime, it is impossible to say with certainty which dialect he was imitating. We know only that he derived from his mother some indication of black speech in Kentucky; that he had direct knowledge of the speech of black communities in Ohio, Kentucky, Maryland, and the District of Columbia; [15] that he was well acquainted with the conventions in dialect writing practiced by his contemporaries; and that he distinguished the poet's description of a dialect from the linguist's.

There is a sense in which Brawley could rightly imply that by the time of the publication of *Majors and Minors* early in 1896 Dunbar had nearly outgrown the influence of white dialect poets like Russell, Riley, and Will Carleton.[16] That is, he was by then no longer content to imitate them. But one must not too hastily conclude from this judgment that, as Dunbar matured, he abandoned their fundamental assumptions about how dialect was to be rendered. Krapp's principal conclusion about American dialect writers in the nineteenth century is that they were far more attentive to those characteristics of speech that were social—and, hence, cut across geographical lines—than they were to those characteristics that were purely regional. He amasses substantial evidence to show that American dialect writers conceived vernacular speech in terms of class rather than place, and notes the rudimentary ways in which a class dialect "distinguishes between popular and cultivated or standard speech":

> The impression of popular speech is easily produced by a sprinkling of such forms as *aint* for *isn't*, *done* for *did*, *them* for *those*, and similar grammatical improprieties. This impression is often assisted by what may be termed "eye dialect," in which the convention violated is one of the eye, not of the ear. Thus a dialect writer often spells a word like *front* as *frunt*, or *face* as *fase*, or *picture* as *pictsher*, not because he intends to indicate here a genuine difference of pronunciation, but the spelling is merely a friendly nudge to the reader, a knowing look which establishes a sympathetic sense of superiority between the author and reader as contrasted with the humble speaker of dialect.[17]

The first principle that guided the selections of dialect writers from actual speech was their desire to create the impression of uneducated speakers. It was largely in other ways that they sought to register regional and racial differences. Whatever the presumed locale of the speaker, his rusticity or lower-class status was made dominant by the reiteration of nonstandard forms that characterized uncultivated speech throughout the nation. And, as Sumner Ives puts it, the greater the density of nonstandard forms, "the greater the rusticity or the lower the class." [18] Whether purporting to represent the speech of New England, the Southwest, the South, the Midlands or the Negro, most dialect writing was based upon uneducated lower-class usage with a highly selective admixture of local dialect words. Consequently, the special qualities of local color in dialect literature derived far less from the language than from the subject matter itself, i.e., from setting, characterization, and incident.[19]

Krapp remarks of the transcription of black dialect provided by Joel Chandler Harris that, "If there is such a thing as classic Negro literary dialect, it is to be found in the speech of Uncle Remus." However, after careful linguistic examination of a typical passage, he concludes that the "general effect produced by the Uncle Remus stories is strongly dialectal" but that "relatively little in them is found to be dialectally peculiar":

> That the speech of Uncle Remus as Joel Chandler Harris heard it differed markedly even from Southern low colloquial is possible, but if so, his literary transcription of the dialect of Uncle Remus gives remarkably few clues which will enable one to realize this difference. The speech of Uncle Remus and the speech of rustic whites as Harris records it are so much alike that if one did not know which character was speaking, one might often be unable to tell whether the words were those of a white man or of a Negro.

He maintains, "Whether these literary transcriptions are true to the 'real' Negro dialect is one of those questions impossible to answer in the lack of any accepted definition of the essential elements of Negro English." But what seems to him more worthy of note—as a correction of received opinion—is that between the *literary* transcriptions of Negro and white rural speech there was little material difference in the writings of Harris and his contemporaries.[20] In his later study of Harris, Sumner Ives was able to refine Krapp's conclusions with respect both to the relation of literary to actual dialect and the relation of the Negro literary dialect to the white:

> Actually the field records of the Linguistic Atlas, aside from a very few Gullah records, show hardly any usages in Negro speech which cannot also be found in rustic white speech. And there are many similarities in usage as Harris wrote the dialects. However, the peculiarity of his Negro speech, in addition to the features already listed, consists in the greater density of nonstandard forms, and in the fact that the nonstandard items include, in greater number, features which are associated with Southern plantation speech rather than with Southern mountain speech. Since the same features can actually be found in the speech of both Negro and rustic white, Harris could more justly be accused of exaggerating the actual difference than of failing to indicate it.[21]

The last point is an especially telling one, for it is precisely in this regard that we can see how closely Dunbar's dialect conformed to the conventions of literary dialect which Krapp and Ives have been the first to explicate.

Like Harris, Dunbar employed both Negro and white dialect. Indeed, no less than a fifth of the dialect poems in the *Complete Poems* are in white dialect, i.e., in a dialect that Dunbar plainly distinguished from the poems in Negro dialect. Two of them, "Appreciation" and "Circumstances Alter Cases," are attempts to represent ethnic dialects, German and Irish respectively, although the former is not made entirely clear. The other white dialect poems are "The Old Apple-Tree," "The Lawyers' Ways," "The Rivals," "Deacon Jones' Grievance," "After a Visit," "The Spellin'-Bee," "Keep A'Pluggin' Away," "An Easy-Goin' Feller," "The Ol' Tunes," "A Confidence," "Speakin' o' Christmas," "Lonesome," "Growin' Gray," "My Sort o' Man," "Possum Trot," "Breaking the Charm," "What's the Use," "Bein' Back Home," "Till the Wind Gets Right," "When a Feller's Itchin' to Be Spanked," "A Summer Pastoral," and "James Whitcomb Riley."[22] These are the poems that have invited comparison with the work of Riley, and properly so; for they are unmistakably intended as representations of white rural speech. Unfortunately and unfairly, Dunbar's critics have sometimes assumed that all the poems in dialect were intended to represent Negro speech; and the poems listed above have, accordingly, seemed glaring examples of Dunbar's ignorance of or indifference to authentic black speech. But in his portrayal of rural dialect Dunbar consistently differentiated black speech from white. And he did so through reliance upon conventions that had been standardized by Harris and other white dialect writers of the period.[23]

The most obvious of Dunbar's dialect practices is his introduction of many more solecisms into Negro speech than are present in his representation of white speech. Lapses of agreement like "him dat," "we is," "we chooses," and "you does" simply do not appear in his white dialect poems. Nor do such nonstandard usages as "ax" for "ask" or "gin" for "give." And the effect of illiterate usage is greatly magnified by Dunbar's heavier reliance upon "eye dialect" in his Negro dialect poems, where "as" becomes "ez," "says" becomes "sez," "if" becomes "ef," "or" becomes "er," "take" and "make" become "tek" and "mek," "like" becomes "lak," and "sort" becomes "sawt." Some of these specimens of "eye dialect"—e.g., "tek" and "lak"—appear only in his Negro dialect. Another principle of Dunbar's Negro dialect that sets it apart from his white dialect is the replacement of medial "r" with an apostrophe, as in "ca'iage" for "carriage," "diff'ent" for "different," "f'om" for "from," "ha'd" for "hard," "hea't" for "heart," and "co'se" for "course." Moreover, the white dialectal representation of "for" as "fur" becomes "fu'" in Negro dialect. Similarly, terminal "r" or "er" or "ure" is consistently represented as "ah," as when "our" becomes "ouah," "where" becomes "whah," "master" becomes "mastah," and "censure" becomes "censuah." Following both rules, Dunbar represents "mourner" as "mou'nah." The use of "d" for voiced "th" is another clear indication that Dunbar wishes to be understood as rendering Negro rather than white rural speech. Accordingly, he represents "though" as "dough," "they" as "dey," "than" as "dan," "then" as "den," "the" as "de," "that" as "dat," "this" as "dis," "there" as "dere" or "dah," "them" as "dem," and "without" as "'dout." His use of final "f" for voiceless "th" is a similar convention, as in "souf" for "south," "mouf" for "mouth," "wif" for "with," and "bofe" for "both." The substitution of "b" for medial and final "v" is also distinctive in Dunbar's portrayal of Negro dialect, as in "heaben" for "heaven," "ebenin'" for "evening," "nebbah" for "never," and "dribe" for "drive." "Just," commonly represented as "jest" in white dialect, becomes "jes'" or "des" in Dunbar's Negro dialect poems; similarly, white "when" becomes Negro "w'en." Finally, there is more loss of initial unstressed syllables—e.g., "'case" for "because"—in the Negro dialect. Through such well-established conventions of dialect writing, Dunbar sought to impart the flavor of both Negro and white rural life in the Southern Midlands during the heyday of the "local color" movement.

But Dunbar's relation to the local color writers extends beyond the conception of literary dialect which he derived from them. He acquiesced as well in their nationalism, on the one hand, and their pastoralism, on the other. Claude Simpson finds a major stimulus to local color writing in the conciliatory spirit that emerged after the Civil War:

> The concept of the Union had been established. . . . But the difference between legal unity and cultural diversity was as great as ever, and many persons seem to have felt a pressing need for a depth of understanding that slogans and propaganda had made impossible during the era of conflict.[24]

That is, local color writers were, of course, the interpreters of regional and ethnic constituencies: interpreters, however, of one constituency to the others and, collectively, interpreters of all to the nation at large. Even while amiably asserting special modes of thought and behavior, they stressed sympathies and concerns uncontained by regional or national boundaries. Thus, Mrs. Stowe avowed that her object was "to interpret to the world the New England life and character."[25] Significantly, she was drawn not to the contemporary circumstances of her region but to "that particular time of its history which may be called the seminal period." For in the aftermath of the Civil War, the great transformation from agrarian and mercantile capitalism to industrial capitalism had radically altered the American scene and engendered a vast nostalgia for antebellum, i.e., preindustrial, times. This nostalgia for a vanishing pastoral world provided the other major stimulus to local color writing. Leo Marx has delineated the versions of pastoral to which this sense of loss gave rise, and his distinction between sentimental and complex pastoralism may be usefully applied to the local colorists.[26] Unlike such complex pastoralists as Emerson, Hawthorne, and Twain who struggled to comprehend the garden in relation to the machine, the local color writers sentimentally withdrew from history into an idealized rural past.

According to Brawley, "Dunbar's conception of his art was based on his theory of life. He felt that he was first of all a man, then an American, and incidentally a Negro." [27] There is no reason to doubt Brawley's judgment; his biography appeared so many years after Dunbar's death that any merely pious effort to brighten Dunbar's reputation might more reasonably have produced a different emphasis. Brawley's point helps us to understand the convictions that disposed Dunbar to render black vernacular as he did. I take Brawley's statement to mean that Dunbar understood poetry, in the context of Romantic expressive theory, to arise from the thought and feelings of the poet as a kind of representative man; that is, he understood poetry to be the product of impulses both deeper and more universal than questions of nationality and race. Thus, as an urban intellectual nostalgic for a lost world of innocence and peace, his impulse to pastoral expression was the controlling principle of his dialect poems. It has often been too easily concluded that Dunbar really knew very little about rural Negro speech or that he was insufficiently committed to the black community. But there is no reason to believe that Dunbar was less familiar with authentic Negro speech or less loyal to his cultural origins than James Weldon Johnson, who succeeded in revolutionizing poetic use of the rural black vernacular. It is, rather, a case of his having been committed to a theory of lyric expression which predisposed him to minimize the differences between Negro and white swains. Dunbar undoubtedly wished to interpret the Negro to the nation; but, given his conception of the poet, he placed the burden of that interpretation upon the Negro's essential humanity and not upon his blackness. If the Negro who delivers "An Ante-Bellum Sermon" is only superficially distinguished from the white populist who speaks in "My Sort o' Man," that was precisely Dunbar's vision of their identity; for they share a common humanity and the same democratic faith. As practiced by Dunbar and the other local colorists, dialect writing typically revealed many more common than individuating features. To give Dunbar his due as a dialect poet, it is necessary to view his work not normatively but within a particular historical moment and literary tradition. So positioned, Dunbar will surely survive in our literature as a major local color poet and, even more certainly, as the best of the black local color poets.

It was Dunbar's fate to achieve recognition as a dialect writer at the very time when a revolutionary change in the character of poetic language was occurring which would obliterate the distinction between the two voices he had cultivated and make his conception of dialect speech obsolete. For almost a century before Dunbar, American writers had experimented with the literary possibilities of dialect speech. And by the 1880s Twain had demonstrated that the vernacular could be fashioned into a richly expressive literary language. But the efforts of poets to achieve the sound of a resonantly human voice, what Robert Frost called the "sound of sense," [28] through a comparable use of vernacular diction and rhythms lagged behind accomplishments in the short story and the novel or were not so readily accepted. Whitman was virtually ignored by his countrymen in the 1890s, and the subtle employments of the vernacular by Robinson and Frost were not favorably acknowledged until the second decade of the new century. So it is hardly surprising that Dunbar failed to comprehend that a new, more dramatic mode of poetic speech was already supplanting both literary dialect, on the one hand, and elegant literary English, on the other.

It fell to James Weldon Johnson to come upon Whitman in 1900, and he was "engulfed and submerged" by *Leaves of Grass.* At a time when most of the poems he was writing were in dialect "after the style of Dunbar," he was "set floundering again" by his discovery of Whitman and "got a sudden realization of the artificiality of conventionalized Negro dialect poetry . . . of its limitation as an instrument of expression." He made some tentative experiments with Whitman's free verse forms, and early in 1901 confided his reservations about dialect poetry to Dunbar:

> I could not tell him what the things were that I wanted to do, because I myself didn't know. The thing that I was sure of and

> kept repeating to him was that he had carried traditional dialect poetry as far as and as high as it could go; that he had brought it to the fullest measure of charm, tenderness, and beauty it could hold.

When he showed Dunbar his new work in the style of Whitman, Dunbar expressed both dislike and puzzlement; and his response to Johnson's readings from *Leaves of Grass* was the same.[29] In order to respond differently, Dunbar would have had to reconceive his sense of the nature and function of poetry. For not content with the restriction of poetry to those experiences and ideas most amenable to direct expression in the traditional forms of narration, description, and analysis, Whitman meant to penetrate the inner reality of things and reveal their actual character without falling into the abstractness of direct expression. In his effort to suggest inner states and relationships remote from conventional literature and ordinary experience, he abandoned direct presentation and invented a persona capable of articulating the full range and complexity of human experience. Desirous of writing a poem that engaged experience in a way that was both inclusive and democratic, Whitman abandoned meter and rhyme in favor of more fluid and capacious kinds of parallelism; and he abandoned the distinction between vernacular and cultivated speech styles in favor of a new, programmatically indiscriminate language of his own which blended such vernacular expressions as "so long" (i.e., "good-bye") with literary words like "circumambient," together with assorted foreign words. It was some years later before Johnson was able to provide a clear statement of his reasons for repudiating Dunbar's dialect practice and a program outlining a new conception of the use of vernacular in black poetry.[30] But his reading of Whitman seems to have confirmed him in his belief that the "minstrel" dialect employed by local colorists like Dunbar had touched only the clichéd surface of black experience and that a new language was essential to the task of exploring its full range and complexity.

The key to Johnson's reform of the language of black poetry—which had shifted so uneasily and inadequately between literary English and literary dialect—was apparently found in his subsequent reading of John Millington Synge's folk dramas. Or, at least,

Synge's example offered a closer parallel than Whitman's to the situation of the black writer. In the first place, Synge moved between two cultures: between a sophisticated Anglo-European culture and Irish folk culture. And after committing himself heavily to the former, he turned away from it to the Irish folk culture and found there in abundance the materials for his great literary achievements. Johnson, like Synge, made a belated discovery of the richness of his folk culture and recognized an experiential range and complexity in its oral narratives, spirituals, and blues that belied the restriction of black experience to humor and pathos in the work of the plantation dialect writers. In the second, like the black writer, the Irishman had originally possessed two languages; but with the emergence of the Anglo-Irish vernacular early in the nineteenth century, the languages coalesced, Irish vocabulary, syntax, and speech rhythms blending into a rather old-fashioned standard English. By the end of the century Lady Gregory and Synge had begun to demonstrate the extraordinary literary uses to which this vernacular lent itself:

> . . . in countries where the imagination of the people, and the language they use, is rich and living, it is possible for a writer to be rich and copious in his words, and at the same time to give the reality, which is the root of all poetry, in a comprehensive and natural form.[31]

Given a rich and living popular culture of his own, the poet requires a language adequate to it and to the fictive uses he means to make of it, which he draws from the folk culture itself but imaginatively fuses with standard literary English in order to produce an expressive instrument of maximal subtlety and force. Synge based his dramatic speech upon the actual vernacular of the Irish folk; he did not, however, make a point-by-point transcription of it. Rather, he combined it with the conventions of literary English to produce a new literary language with a capacity for expressiveness that neither cultivated nor folk speech possessed when taken singly. He did not attempt to reproduce the Anglo-Irish vernacular phonetically—in the manner of Finley Peter Dunne's "Mr. Dooley" sketches—by substituting apostrophes for terminal "g" and "d" or by employing such nonstandard spellings as "dacent" for "decent" and "niver" for "never." Instead, he accurately reflected its idiom (i.e., its vocabulary) and its syntax (i.e., its word order, phrasal structure, and intonation patterns).

By 1922 Johnson had publicly rejected traditional dialect poetry because its popularity was based upon an absurdly limited conception of Negro life. He called for an expanded portrayal of that life, and named Synge as the model whom black poets should emulate.[32] But in doing so he was careful to point out that he was not repudiating dialect itself, only its conventional use. Because Johnson was not always entirely clear in his pronouncements on this subject, some critics have described Johnson as an opponent of dialect and have said that his later work—like *God's Trombones* —was written in "straight English" or "non-dialect English."[33] Synge's use of the Anglo-Irish vernacular suggested to him a way of liberating rural black vernacular from certain restrictive literary mannerisms and making it into a far more natural voice for black poets. Thus, Johnson was calling not for an end to the use of dialect but a profound alteration in the nature of its composition and the manner of its use. As an alternative to Dunbar's dialect voice, he proposed building on the actual voice of the black vernacular, which he likened to a trombone, "the instrument possessing above all others the power to express the wide and varied range of emotions encompassed by the human voice—and with greater amplitude."[34] Johnson contemplated the emergence of new black folk poets whose use of black speech was, first, valid for themselves and for their "own group" and, only second, for the larger reading public. In such poets as Don L. Lee, Nikki Giovanni, and the later Gwendolyn Brooks, his expectations appear to have been fulfilled. As for Dunbar, Johnson wrote with characteristic generosity, "I have frequently speculated upon what Dunbar might have done with Negro dialect if it had come to him fresh and plastic."[35]

NOTES

1. This familiar distinction in literary history rests, of course, upon an outmoded and largely pejorative conception of the term "dialect," which presupposed the existence of a single "correct" form of English in respect to which regional and social variants were regarded as dialectal corrup-

tions. Modern linguists employ the term neutrally, so that it is now applied to *any* socially or geographically limited set of linguistic habits which distinguishes groups within the same speech community. In this modern sense of the term, standard literary English is itself describable as a dialect. See George Philip Krapp, *The English Language in America,* I (New York: The Century Company, 1925), pp. 225–226; and Raven I. McDavid, "Sense and Nonsense about American Dialects," *PMLA* 81 (May 1966), 7–17.

2. Benjamin Brawley, *Paul Laurence Dunbar* (Chapel Hill: Univ. of North Carolina Press, 1936), p. 15. Although Sterling Brown (*Negro Poetry and Drama*) and Victor Lawson (*Dunbar Critically Examined*) speak only of Romantic influence upon Dunbar, there is evidence that he was also influenced by Robert Herrick.
3. James Weldon Johnson, *Along This Way* (New York: Viking Press, 1933), p. 160.
4. *Ibid.*, p. 161.
5. Johnson acknowledges the influence in *Along This Way*, p. 158.
6. William Dean Howells, "Introduction," *Lyrics of Lowly Life* (New York: Dodd, Mead & Company, 1896), p. xix.
7. Sterling Brown, *Negro Poetry and Drama* (New York: Atheneum, 1969), pp. 35–36, 48.
8. Cotter's poem is collected in *Early Black American Poets*, ed. William H. Robinson, Jr. (Dubuque: William C. Brown Company, 1969), pp. 199–200.
9. Brawley, *Paul Laurence Dunbar*, p. 1.
10. *Ibid.*, pp. 14, 42.
11. Letter to Helen Douglass, dated October 22, 1896, in the Paul Laurence Dunbar papers of the Ohio Historical Society.
12. Krapp, *The English Language in America*, p. 225.
13. *Ibid.*, p. 227.
14. See Sumner Ives, "A Theory of Literary Dialect," *Tulane Studies in English* 2 (1950), 137–82; and "Dialect Differentiation in the Stories of Joel Chandler Harris," *American Literature* 27 (March 1955), 88–96.
15. Sterling Brown, *Negro Poetry and Drama*, pp. 32–33.
16. Brawley, *Paul Laurence Dunbar*, pp. 27–29, 41–43.
17. Krapp, *The English Language in America*, p. 228.
18. Ives, "Dialect Differentiation in the Stories of Joel Chandler Harris," p. 89.
19. See Krapp, *The English Language in America,* pp. 236–37, 242–43.
20. *Ibid.*, pp. 248–51.
21. Ives, "Dialect Differentiation in the Stories of Joel Chandler Harris," p. 92.
22. With the exception of the two poems in ethnic dialect, I list these titles in the order they occur in *The Complete Poems of Paul Laurence Dunbar* (New York: Dodd, Mead & Company, 1913).

23. For Ives's summary of the conventions by which Harris differentiated Negro and white rural Southern speech, see "Dialect Differentiation in the Stories of Joel Chandler Harris," pp. 91–92.
24. Claude Simpson, *The Local Colorists* (New York: Harper & Row, 1960), p. 5.
25. Harriet Beecher Stowe, *Oldtown Folks* (Boston: Houghton Mifflin, 1899), p. xxiii. First published in 1869.
26. Leo Marx, *The Machine in the Garden* (New York: Oxford Univ. Press, 1964), pp. 5–11, 24–26, 362–63.
27. Brawley, *Paul Laurence Dunbar*, p. 76.
28. Lawrance Thompson, ed., *Selected Letters of Robert Frost* (New York: Holt, Rhinehart & Winston, 1964), pp. 80, 158.
29. Johnson, *Along This Way*, pp. 158–61.
30. See James Weldon Johnson, ed., *The Book of American Negro Poetry* (New York: Harcourt Brace Jovanovich, 1931), pp. 3–5, 40–42. Johnson's famous statement on dialect poetry was first published in 1922. See also the "Preface" to Johnson's *God's Trombones* (New York: Viking Press, 1927).
31. "Preface" to *The Playboy of the Western World*, in *J.M. Synge's Plays, Poems, and Prose* (London: J.M. Dent, 1941), p. 107.
32. Johnson, *The Book of American Negro Poetry*, pp. 41–42.
33. See, for example, Stephen H. Bronz, *Roots of Negro Racial Consciousness* (New York: Libra Publishers, 1964), pp. 16, 39.
34. Johnson, *God's Trombones*, p. 7.
35. Johnson, *Along This Way*, p. 159.

DUNBAR

This year; and Douglass' house in Rochester
Burned—his papers lost.
And well we all might mourn

These seven years from slavery
Suddenly turned rotten
As Freedman's Bureau beef.
The Klan-spawned violence, our Patience:
A lesson not yet learned.

The Bank failing, our
Colored Troops recalled, the grief
When Douglass dies and Booker Washington
Barters compromise for
Each week's lynched Black life.

To see hope shattered,
With a poet's eyes!
Black suffering hammered into law,
The White House shut against Black cries!

And splendid Du Bois home from Germany
To draw deep resolution from the souls
Of Black folk, fearlessly to climb
Thundering Niagara, sensing power;
To ponder that deafening roar; and more—

1906: Paul, at 34 you are
In your grave. How young you died!
This year the crime is being
Black. Events ride Black men:
Brownsville and Atlanta rage,

The earth quakes, Hope lies exhausted. You
Can forget this sad time.

But we go onward into a
Modern age of wonders
Yet see only darkness deepening
For us all. I feel a dread
Which nothing can assuage.

In Dayton it is the same:
I keep your books, your
Photograph hangs in the hall.
We do not argue now whether
You wrote best your Negro rhymes
Or your poems more traditional,

Nor how in life you could
Turn sorrow into jest. Dear poet,
Take your rest.

Raymond R. Patterson

III

THE FICTION OF PAUL LAURENCE DUNBAR

Addison Gayle, Jr.

Literature as Catharsis: The Novels of Paul Laurence Dunbar

The function of the novel as viewed by Henry Fielding—to entertain and to instruct—was one which William Wells Brown could not possibly adhere to. When he wrote *Clotel; or the President's Daughter* in 1853, he was on British shores, an exile from America; yet he remained conscious of the war for human dignity and freedom taking place in his native land. His awareness of, and his devotion to that war determined his outlook upon the new genre, the novel. Unfortunately, he left us no guidelines, no written instructions concerning the form which this new genre should take. If we look closely at *Clotel,* however, we might surmise that Brown viewed the novel as one more instrument in the abolitionist arsenal of weapons. His contemporary, Frank Webb, author of *The Garies and Their Friends* (1857), seems to come closer to accepting Fielding's stipulations. However, *The Garies and Their Friends* is as much protest against the plight of Northern blacks, who undergo varied forms of discrimination, as it is instruction to the Afro-American middle class. With the publication of Martin Delany's *Blake, or the Huts of America* (1861), the notion that the Afro-American novelist would follow the prescription of Fielding, a prescription adopted by such American writers as James Fenimore Cooper and Nathaniel Hawthorne, is soon discarded. The novel is unmitigated protest, aimed at depicting the plight of black men in America and abroad.

From the outset, then, the Afro-American novelist viewed the function of the novel differently than did his English and American counterparts. This view was shaped by the life he lived, a life which differed markedly from that of other writers. His was a life of chaos and turmoil, and, be he abolitionist or private citizen, the proscriptions which bound other black men applied equally to him: the lives of desperation lived by his fellows under bonds were similar to his own, though his was lived, usually, on a higher plane of desperation. Spurred on by an atmosphere of revolt and pregnant with incipient revolution, when he sought to construct an art form, he forged it out of the steel and iron of his own experiences, thus creating a weapon of warfare to be used in the interest of black liberation.

Looking back upon these early novelists, we know that the direction in which they moved, away from the prescriptions of the English and American novelists, was the correct one. They thought of the new genre not as a vehicle for entertainment or instruction as such, but one to spur men to action; to move nations and races towards a new morality; and to prepare the way for the New Canaan soon to be erected—or so they believed—on American shores. Yet, innovative as they were, we know now that they failed to grasp the realities of the age in which they lived; that they were ignorant of the war being waged for the minds of men. More interested in freeing men's bodies than their minds, they were oblivious of the truth articulated by Richard Wright in 1936, that they had the ability "to fuse and make articulate the experiences of men," and "to create the myths and symbols which inspire a faith in life."

In other words, they were so obsessed with the novel as a weapon in the abolitionist struggle, that they did not realize its importance as a vehicle for creating positive images and symbols of black men, images for which paradigms existed in great numbers in black communities North and South. This failure accounts for the stultifying search for identity in the literature of many black writers who followed; and it contributed, in part, to the attempt of such novelists as Paul Laurence Dunbar to seek to escape what he believed to be images of degradation, and to adopt those of positive import. With the possible exception of Frank Yerby, no Afro-American novelist has been more confused concerning his true identity or worth as a black writer than was Dunbar. And none succeeded so well in using the novel form as a vehicle for vicarious identification with symbols drawn from an alien world.

What image was he attempting to escape? There were several, and Sterling Brown, in "Negro Characters as Seen by White Authors," has enumerated them for us. The one which stands out, however, is that enunciated by the narrator of John Pendleton Kennedy's *Swallow Barn*:

> I am quite sure they [black people] could never become a happier people than here. . . . No tribe of people have ever passed from barbarism to civilization whose . . . progress has been more secure from harm, more genial to their character or better supplied with mild and beneficent guardianship, adapted to the actual state of their intellectual feebleness, than the Negroes of Swallow Barn.

It was this image—the black man as helpless, feeble-minded child—which so appalled Dunbar, and caused him to seek to escape it in his novels. His dilemma is readily apparent. In most of his short fiction and in many of his poems, he championed such images with a gusto unmatched, perhaps, even by the Plantation School of writers, who are credited with first creating the image. In his novels, however, he attempts to move outside of them in two ways: first, by adopting a persona; second, by confronting them and moving, existentially, beyond them. To suggest, with Benjamin Brawley, that he pandered to the popular taste in his short fiction and in his dialect poetry, seems too simplistic an explanation. The truth, I believe, is that he lacked literary models from his own contemporaries and forerunners. In addition, he lacked a literary tradition dedicated to validating the dignity and worth of the Afro-American. For a writer as sensitive as Dunbar, one so wracked by spiritual turmoil, such a lack produced, I believe, a schizophrenia, causing him to question whether he would see himself as black man as represented in the fiction of the Plantation School or as "the American Man" in general—he who had built the great cathedrals and railroads, created the enduring literature, and established the "official" institutions. Out of this psychological dilemma, two images emerged to dominate his writing. One is found in his short stories, dialect poetry, and in two of his novels, *The Fanatics* and *The Sport of the Gods*; the other, in his poetry written in standard English and in his two other novels,

The Uncalled and *The Love of Landry*. One image represents blacks; the other, "man," as Paul Laurence Dunbar wished himself to be: free, white, and independent.

How much this dilemma was made more acute by William Dean Howells's critical appraisal of Dunbar's poetry, first issued in 1896, and repeated one year later, is difficult to estimate, though one suspects that the limitations and proscriptions which Howells, unknowingly perhaps, dictated, did much to force the writer to assess his own value as a man and a poet. Howells wrote,

> Yet it appeared to me then, and it appears to me now, that there is a precious difference of temperament between the races which it would be a great pity ever to lose, and that this is best preserved and most charmingly suggested by Mr. Dunbar in those pieces of his where he studies the moods and traits of his race in its own accent of our English. . . . In nothing is his essentially refined and delicate art so well shown as in these pieces, which, as I ventured to say, described the range between appetite and emotion . . . which is the range of the race. He reveals in these a finely ironical perception of the Negro's limitations. . . . These are divinations and reports of what passes in the hearts and minds of a lowly people.

To understand the slight here, is to understand more about the dialect tradition than Howells probably did. We know, by the example of Douglass, Webster, and Abraham Lincoln, that one measure of intellect and manhood, for the eighteenth and nineteenth centuries, was language. At no time in American history had the old cliché, that a man is known by the words that he speaks, been better suited to actuality. Language, in many cases, therefore, was as indicative of the black man's inferiority as was the color of his skin. As a consequence, the feeble-minded, half-witted man-child of the works of John Pendleton Kennedy, Irvin Russell, and Joel Chandler Harris was clearly identifiable by his "jingles in a broken tongue." But, while white practitioners of the Plantation Tradition could escape the stigma of guilt by association, Dunbar could not. When praised by Howells for revealing "a finely ironical perception of the Negro's limitations" simply by his facility with dialect verse, Dunbar was unable, without serious, mental difficulty, to dissociate himself from the images which he had propounded.

In *The Uncalled* (1898), written after Howells's review, he made the attempt at dissociation in the longer fictional form. The central metaphor of this first novel is rebellion from the restrictions of old mores and folk ways. It is, simultaneously, however, a metaphor for freedom—freedom from the restrictions of racial stereotypes. The plot itself is slight. Freddie Brent and his mother are abandoned in the town of Dexter, Ohio, by a wastrel father. When the mother dies, the orphan is adopted by the town spinster, Hester Prime, who, against the boy's wishes, educates him for the ministry. The thematic structure of the novel is now apparent: the conflict is between the young Brent and the religious parochialism of the poeple in the town. When Brent, having achieved ordination, refuses to preach a sermon against a "fallen woman," he surrenders the pulpit and a chance at marriage and success. In so doing, he moves outside the self-imposed code voiced earlier in the novel: "When fate is fighting with all her might against a human soul, the greatest victory that the soul can win is to reconcile itself to the unpleasant which is never so unpleasant afterwards."

Here is a strange intrusion in this naturalistic novel. The protagonist, destined to a life dictated by some "fate infinitely more powerful than his own," moves, in existential fashion, outside of his prescribed destiny. When he leaves the town of Dexter, he has moved towards redefining the terms which previously governed his existence, has stepped outside the traditional patterns, in order to create new ones—of his own making. The parallels between Brent and the author are unmistakable: both had reached the threshold of success; one, the fictional creation, however, surrendered success in favor of individuality and freedom, while the other, the creator, could achieve freedom from tradition and restraint only through vicarious identification with his character. In private correspondence, in gatherings with friends, and in several of his poems in standard English, Dunbar openly revolted against what he viewed to be the limitations imposed upon him by Howells and his followers: "One critic says a thing," he related to a friend, "and the rest hasten to say the same thing, in many cases using identical words. I see now very clearly that Mr. Howells has done me irrevocable harm in the dictum he laid down regarding my dialect verse."

Instead of public revolt or confrontation with Howells, however, Dunbar sought to register his revolt by picturing himself as outside the negative images and symbols which the dialect tradition adumbrated. "He did not say," writes Saunders Redding, "that he was looking at white characters from a colored point of view. He simply assumed inherent emotional, intellectual, and spiritual identity with his characters." It is not too far wrong to suggest, therefore, that from Dunbar's perspective in *The Uncalled*, Freddie Brent was Paul Laurence Dunbar, and Paul Laurence Dunbar was Freddie Brent. In that unknown world where the author chooses his focus and point of view towards his characters, Dunbar associated himself with a character whose skin color moved him beyond the stigmata of inferiority and degradation; in so doing, he moved beyond the prescription of the Afro-American novel as handed down from Brown to Charles Chesnutt; he suggested, that is to say, that the function of the novel is to serve as the vehicle for catharsis.

This was possible, however, only in a personal sense. *The Uncalled* was published in the same year as a collection of short fiction, *Folks from Dixie* (1898). Most of the stories in this volume dealt with stereotypes; yet, *Folks from Dixie* received praise, whereas *The Uncalled* received disparagement. That Dunbar, a black man, could masquerade as a white youth, struck his audience as insincere, and they quickly showed their preference for the old image by prating about the collection of short stories far in excess of its artistic merit. Far from dissuading Dunbar from other such ventures, however, the preference of his audience for traditional images exacerbated his own personal problems and caused him to seek to negate his identity all the more. The personal problems were pressing. Marriage difficulties had occurred as early as 1899; a terrible bout with pneumonia resulted in the weakening of his lungs, which made his body susceptible to tuberculosis—later the cause of his death. The inability of his public to award him praise and recognition for his verse in standard English helped push him into alcoholism. When he journeyed to Colorado, in 1899, to revive his health, he was an invalid, and the ills which beset him were both mental and physical. *The Love of Landry* (1900) his second novel, is the result of that illness.

If *The Uncalled* was naturalistic in form, veering sharply towards an existential bent at the end, *The Love of Landry*, a romantic novel, maintains its form throughout. In this shallowly plotted work, the conflict centers about a romantic triangle. Sought after by Arthur Heathcote, an Englishman who "smells of civilization," Mildred Osborne, daughter of wealthy parents, travels west, and falls in love with Landry Thayer, a ranch hand. Defying the wishes of her parents, and rejecting the attention of Heathcote, Mildred settles upon Thayer as her mate. In true Victorian fashion, this is not accomplished until Thayer has saved the heroine's life during a cattle stampede, and is proved to be an heir and gentleman who had surrendered a fortune to fulfill his desire to live free of the restraints of civilization.

Dunbar's attempt to appropriate symbols and images for his fiction from his autobiography is even more discernible in his second novel than in the first. Mildred, like the author, suffers from tuberculosis. Despite her affliction, however, she is robust, spontaneous, and happy. Landry, whose name is too obviously a symbol of land, of earth, represents natural man in retreat from the "enslaving arms of civilization." Analogous to Freddie Brent, he surrenders one identity for another, and his daredevil rescue of the heroine evidences his freedom even from the fear of death. Though Heathcote is a poor stereotype of an Englishman, he is symbolic of an ordered, respected tradition, wherein a man's worth is evaluated in terms of his individual achievement. More personally, the attempt of the spinster aunt to separate the two lovers has its parallel in Dunbar's own life—his mother-in-law had led a long campaign to separate the poet and his wife.

The conflict, mirrored in the heroine and hero, who fight the lonely fight against tradition and restriction, is a conflict central to the author's life. A black writer, seething with silent revolt, desiring freedom from rules and restrictions, he used the medium most natural to portray revolt—the novel. And as he had done in *The Uncalled*, in order to register his protest, he dons the mask of white men, thus lending his own weight to the negative images which he despised, validating the arguments of those who championed the superiority of white images over those of blacks.

How far along this road of self-doubt and confused identity

Dunbar had traveled can be seen when he depicts a major black character in the longer fictional genre. Here the schizophrenia has reached acute form. Thus far, in *The Uncalled* and *The Love of Landry*, he had been free from confrontation with his blackness; he had refused to allow blacks entry into the genre. He wrote of Freddie Brent and Landry Thayer and affected an emotional identification with them, without being forced to disparage or denigrate the images and symbols of his Afro-American heritage. This problem was not acute in the short stories or in the dialect poetry. These were written for entertainment and held by the author in lower esteem than was the novel. Further, the poems in standard English, in their own way, satirized the material produced to satisfy the dialect vogue.

To interject a black man into the novel alongside the images which he had appropriated from the outside world, however, presented a problem—how could he depict such characters and maintain his identification with the others? Having created Freddie Brent in the image of Paul Laurence Dunbar, could he now create a black man in the same image without casting aspersion, in his own mind, upon his newly adopted identity? Such questions are answered in the negative in his third novel, *The Fanatics* (1901), where Nigger Ed, the black character, is created in the images bequeathed Afro-American literature from the Plantation School of writers.

The Fanatics, a historical romance, centers upon events during the American Civil War. Two old Ohio families, the Van Dorens and the Waters, are on opposite sides in the contest. Bradford Waters sympathizes with the Union; Stephen Van Doren with the Confederacy. The conflicts between the two scions are reflected in the citizenry of the town, who are equally divided in loyalty towards the Union and the Confederacy. The tension generated by the conflict is exemplified in the affair between Mary, daughter of Waters, and Robert, son of Van Doren. When Robert joins the Confederate forces, Waters insists that his daughter break their engagement. Mary's rebellion against parental authority is explained by the author: "She loved Bob, not his politics. What had she to do with those black men down there in the South, it was none of her business." Neither were "those men down there," the business of the town. When the escaping slaves attempt to enter the town, they are opposed by Loyalist and Union sympathizers alike: "For the time all party lines fell away, and all the people were united in one cause—resistance of the black horde." Waters, Van Doren, and the townspeople are equally fanatical concerning the black men and the war, and the keynote of the novel is sounded by the wife of Waters's son: "Every one is mad, you and I and all of us. When shall we come to our senses?"

Such a question is one which might have been asked of the age itself. Warfare between blacks and whites on the social and political front had increased tenfold by 1901. The black exodus from South to North had gained momentum; lynchings and mass murder, symbolized by the Wilmington, North Carolina, riot of 1898—the catalyst which propelled Charles Chesnutt to write *The Marrow of Tradition*—were almost daily occurrences. The compact initiated in 1895 between Booker T. Washington and the white industrialists had been all but nullified by young, courageous black men like Du Bois and Monroe Trotter. Given these historical realities, the American Civil War, the product of national strife, might have served as the metaphor for a different kind of war—that between the races, which raged as intently in its own way as that between North and South during the 1860s.

A novel of such dimensions might have been possible for a writer free from his own mental and spiritual dilemma. For Dunbar, however, beset with the old problems of marriage, identity, and the failure to achieve personal recognition commensurate with his expectations, the task was impossible. Fidelity to craft would have mandated that a novel dealing realistically with the Civil War accurately portray the black man's part in it. To do this, Dunbar would have to step objectively away from his own problem of identity, and to project positive images of black men and women. Such might have been possible before *The Uncalled*. By the time he wrote *The Fanatics*, however, he could look at black people only through the eyes of Freddie Brent, and thus his perception, for all intents and purposes, was as distorted as those of his white contemporaries.

Take Nigger Ed, for example. The plan of the novel was to show Ed's evolution from town drunkard and buffoon to town hero. The character whom we meet in the beginning of the novel, who "has a picturesque knack for lying," is analogous to Nelse of *The Leopard's Spots*, and Thomas Dixon's description of his black character is apropos Dunbar's description of Nigger Ed: "A black hero of the old regime." What Dixon praised as heroic were obsequious behavior, childlike devotion and loyalty, and quirks of speech and gesture serving to entertain white people. Both characters were drawn from the Southern mythology and folklore which created the terms by which black men were to be defined; both are the feeble-minded, darky-clowns of Southern literature. Viewed in this fashion it is impossible to take seriously the proclamation at the end of Dunbar's novel that "there were women who begged him [Ed] to come in and talk to them about their sons who had been left on some Southern field, wives who wanted to hear over and over again the last words of their loved one"; nor is it possible to believe that the town buffoon, now become hero, is accepted by the same people who refused to accept black contraband during the war: "they gave him a place for life and everything he wanted."

Dunbar himself could not have believed in the evolution of Ed; yet, in terms of his own problems of identity, he could have portrayed Ed no other way. In this first confrontation with a black character in serious fiction, he moved to validate the stereotype, to cast his voice with those who averred that Mammy Peggy, Rev. Elisha Edwards, and Gideon, from the short fiction, were representatives of a unique species of humanity. Adhering to the truncated Darwinism of his old friend, Booker Washington, he suggests now, that there are superiors and inferiors, and he has answered the question which haunted him before—to which category did he belong? Freddie Brent may have been Paul Laurence Dunbar; Nigger Ed certainly was not. Ed was the key to the resolution of the artistic question of perspective. Dunbar, having come face to face with a black man in his novels, and having portrayed him in the form of the old Plantation Tradition, could feel more secure in his own adopted identity, could pursue the route established in the short stories, step back from his material with that objective perspective which white critics deemed necessary to the creation of lasting and enduring art. *The Fanatics* freed the author to deal with black men in novel form on the same terms that they were dealt with by white writers.

To substantiate this thesis, one need only turn to Dunbar's last novel, *The Sport of the Gods* (1902). The opening lines voice the author's intention to move away from the spirit of the plantation tradition: "Fiction has said so much in regret of the old days when there were plantations and overseers and masters and slaves that it was good to come upon such a household as Berry Hamilton's, if for no other reason than that it afforded a relief from the monotony of tiresome iteration." Once Dunbar begins to deal with his black characters, however, the plan is laid aside.

Berry Hamilton, trusted, loyal, butler on the estate of Maurice Oakley, is the major protagonist. He and his wife, Fannie, their two children, Kit and Joe, are members of the black middle class, increasing in number at the turn of the century. In contrast to the old Afro-American middle class, built upon caste, this new middle class is delineated by the power and influence it exerts in the black community, and its close proximity to the real seat of power—white people. The Hamilton family are respected members of the black community. They are pillars of the black church, scions of Negro society, and they are admired and envied by blacks of lesser attainments. Like the characters of Frank Webb's *The Garies and Their Friends*, they are content to rule in hell, while paying proper obeisance to heaven.

When Francis, wastrel brother of Maurice, steals money in order to finance his playboy activities abroad, disaster strikes the Hamilton family. The loyal servant for over forty years is framed for the theft, and the employer has little trouble in accepting his guilt: "the Negroes are becoming less faithful and less contented, and more's the pity, . . . more ambitious." Circumstantial evidence points towards Hamilton's guilt; the butler is remanded to jail, and his family expelled from the Oakley estate.

The incarceration of the breadwinner, and the expulsion of his wife and children, allows Dunbar to shift his characters from South to North, and to examine black people in a new and different setting. Once again, the author travels the old Plantation Tradition road: away from the paternalistic arms of their white supporters, the family quickly disintegrates. Fannie is tricked into marriage with a brutal man; Kit enters upon a hapless career as a show girl; after succumbing to the temptation to become a dandy, Joe murders his sweetheart. Commenting on the disaster which overtakes the Hamilton family up North, Dunbar remarks, "Oh, is there no way to keep these people from rushing away from the small villages and country districts of the South up to the cities, where they cannot battle with the terrible force of a strange and unusual environment? . . . The South has its faults . . . and its disadvantages, but . . . even what they suffered from these was better than what awaited them in the great alleys of New York."

When Dunbar invokes the aid of a *deus ex machina* to reunite Fannie and Berry and to return them to their Southern environment, the point is driven home. Hamilton is released from jail after a white reporter proves his innocence and Francis's guilt; the shock of the revelation sends Maurice Oakley to an early grave. Fannie's new husband is killed in a drunken brawl, and, reuniting with Berry, the two, minus their children, travel back to the waiting arms of the Widow Oakley, who "heard of their coming, and with her own hands re-opened and refurnished the little cottage in the yard for them. There the white-haired woman begged them to spend the rest of their days and be in peace and comfort."

Paternalism is the key to Dunbar's treatment of both Nigger Ed and Berry Hamilton, and this was an attitude devoted exclusively to black characters. Both Ed and Hamilton are to be cared for by white benefactors, to be *given* everything they need for the rest of their lives. In a society of men, such charity is unthinkable, and it is not too far wrong to suggest that because Dunbar wanted to see himself as Freddie Brent, Landry Thayer, or the Waterses and Van Dorens, his psychological difficulties prevented him from regarding black men as other than wards of American society. As a result, outside of his white personae, he was incapable of viewing himself as other than the sport of the gods, incapable of imputing heroism and grandeur to those made in his own image.

Dunbar was a victim of his age. His predecessors, who had wavered between formulating a theory of literature which would redefine the old definitions and one which would serve as an instrument to assault the conscience of white men, had failed him.

The hard task of constructing new images and symbols had been left to their successors. Consequently, they failed to till the ground for such talented writers as Dunbar, who as a result, was forced to deal with the images and stereotypes of black people as laid down in the literature of Southern and Northern propagandists.

What kind of instrument might the Afro-American novel have become had its first creators set out to depict the realities of black life, to record the heroism of those who survived the holocaust of the middle passage and slavery, who lived and struggled despite terror and despondency, who dreamed always of a new world a-coming for their successors? What models for positive images and symbols might have become the material of the novel had the artist drawn upon the experiences of those many thousands gone—of Frederick Douglass, David Walker, Harriet Tubman, Nat Turner, and others too numerous to list?

Dunbar had no such models, and this lack greatly affected his art, and his life. As he came to accept the images of the Plantation School of writers, as he continued to depict such characters in his own short stories and poetry, he was forced to confront a dilemma of schizophrenic proportions: could he move outside the racial restrictions by adopting the mask of his oppressors? An examination of his life proves that he could not. For the characteristics which separated him from the Freddie Brents of the world went beyond color, to the depths of man's spiritual anguish and despair; to have surrendered this would have meant to have surrendered a body of literature still alive with meaning and promise for our times. Such a surrender would not have been salvation, but madness.

Kenny J. Williams

The Masking of the Novelist

The first recorded novel by an American Negro was published during 1853 in London and was written by William Wells Brown, an ex-slave. Entitled *Clotel: Or, the President's Daughter, a Narrative of Slave Life in the United States*, the novel created some commotion in England and in Europe. Published the year after Harriet Beecher Stowe's *Uncle Tom's Cabin*, the novel intensified the horror of human slavery by using every conceivable degrading episode to exemplify the terrorized lives of the slaves in America. Furthermore, in order to insure the "shock value" of the novel, Brown used Thomas Jefferson—the man so closely identified with the Declaration of Independence—as the father of Clotel, who is one of the first tragic quadroons in American fiction. The fate-ridden life of Clotel comes to an end as she dies, trying to escape recapture, a short distance from the White House. When it was published in this country in 1864, the novel became *Clotelle; or A Tale of the Southern States*, and an anonymous U.S. senator replaced Jefferson. As might be expected, the novel and its many revisions were strong protests against slavery and against the human degradation which resulted from it. It presented the physical, mental, and spiritual cruelty of slavery as well as the hypocrisy and duplicity generated by that peculiar institution. Through an intricate use of characters and subplots, Brown clearly explained the irony and tragedy of slavery in America. Although he was a prolific writer who produced short fiction, travel books, dramas, history, and personal reminiscences in rapid succession, Brown made perhaps his most significant contribution in his first novel. In its first and in successive editions, *Clotel* set the tone of protest which has been considered an integral part of the American Negro novel.

Shortly after the appearance of the London edition of Brown's novel Frank Webb's *The Garies and Their Friends* was also published in London. While there is an element of protest in this novel, the work is primarily concerned with the rising middle class of freedmen in the North. Published in 1857, the novel emphasizes the possibility of achieving success within the framework of the American Dream by following the laws of thrift, brotherhood, morality, and love. Although *The Garies and Their Friends* has been a "neglected work," it does provide further insight into the concerns of the early Negro novelist. Here such topics as mixed marriages, "passing," and conflicts between light-skinned and dark-skinned characters anticipate the fiction of the "color line." And the ambiguity of life in the North for all Negroes receives considerable comment as Webb makes clear that racial prejudice is not the special phenomenon of the South. Martin Delany, on the other hand, presented another point of view. His incomplete novel, *Blake, or the Huts of America*, appeared in the 1859 volume of *The Anglo-African Magazine*. He was not nearly so optimistic as Webb about the possibilities of integration into American society, nor was he willing to place great stress upon an embryonic middle class with middle-class values. Instead, he celebrated the black character on its own terms and was convinced that there would have to be a different kind of American system before the freedmen and slaves could become an integral part of the nation. And so he produced a work which is clearly a forerunner of the Marxian novels of the twentieth century. By 1880 William Wells Brown had returned to fiction and in *My Southern Home* produced a nostalgic view of the South that was most similar to the type of work produced by the Plantation Tradition in American fiction. Thus, in four early works can be seen the major themes and concerns of a fiction conditioned by the race of the authors.

Still veiled in a great deal of obscurity is James H. Howard's *Bond and Free* of 1886, which should have been subtitled *Or the American Ambiguity.* When the famous abolitionist poet, Frances E. W. Harper, turned her attention to fiction in the early 1890s, the didacticism of her poetry was simply transferred to fiction. In 1892 she published *Iola Leroy, or Shadows Uplifted.* The novel deals with the period of Reconstruction and with the inevitable "color line." While she is most convinced that hard work will produce the necessary regard for the American Negro, she is also concerned about the rising tide of immigration. At this point she compared the patriotism of her people with what she considered to be the anarchy of the foreigners; hence, of the two oppressed groups the American Negro showed far greater promise as an acceptable citizen of this nation. In dealing with the problems of employment in his novel, *The Appointed*, Walter Stowers presented a more realistic portrayal of some of the problems facing his people in America. Published in 1894, it was set in the period of Reconstruction. This was also the scene for J. McHenry Jones's *Hearts of Gold* (1896), which was, of all of these early novels, the most idealistic portrayal of Negroes in America.

Thus by 1898 and the publication of *The Uncalled*, Paul Laurence Dunbar's first novel, there had been sufficient evidence to indicate that there was a growing coterie of Negro novelists who were trying to gain the attention of the American reading public. These early novels dealt with racial matters but they did so in diverse ways. With few exceptions, notably that of Delany, a firm commitment to the American dream was combined with protest—sometimes subtle—against any system of behavior which ran counter to that dream. In short, these early novelists evinced a faith in America and a belief that by an exposure to the riddle of American life there would evolve some possibility toward solution.

Yet, the closing years of the century presented a series of problems which had to be met by the novelist. In the first place, the novel itself had not had a long and distinguished history in America. Indeed, it was a relatively new form in world literature and in spite of the traditional assertions by novelists that their works were "based on facts" it had been devoted more to entertainment rather than to purposeful social criticism and reform. The highly moralistic, sentimental novel concealed its purpose behind all of the trappings of melodrama. By the end of the century, Americans were far more interested in the sentimental novels of Fanny Fern than in either *The Scarlet Letter* or *Moby Dick*, written before the middle of the century. It was not a period of great interest in the fictional use of social issues. Romances were extremely popular; writers such as Francis Marion Crawford and Archibald Clavering wrote of Europe; other romances returned to past ages of history, as in the work of S. Weir Mitchell and Winston Churchill. In short, this period of sentimentalism produced novels of idealistic enthusiasm and equated pioneer values with American values; the characters were simple souls who usually found the "good life" close to nature. A roster of the popular novelists of the period of Dunbar's novels from 1898 to 1902 is the roster of some of the most poorly written sentimental novels in American literature. But they *were* popular, people bought them, people read them, and people apparently enjoyed them. For any writer desiring public acclaim, the formula had been established. There were, of course, strong indications that another kind of novel was being produced in America and that the work of Howells and James was not totally in vain, but generally it was a sentimental period with a popular novel which was caught between the death throes of the romantic period and the beginning of the move toward realism. Part of the difficulty faced by the Negro novelist of the latter part of the nineteenth century was a result of the literary conditions of the period. The problems with which many of them dealt were intrinsically realistic; however, they frequently used the popular romantic novel as their medium. Bridging the gap between a realistic subject and romantic conventions has always been a formidable task, and many of these early novels were doomed to failure, commercially as well as artistically.

Not only was this a transitional period in American fiction but it was also a period of great negativism toward the American Negro. This period has been well-described by Rayford Logan, who in *The Negro in American Life and Thought: The Nadir, 1877–1901* (1954) examined newspapers and magazines of the time and pointed out the extreme racism evident in them. The bitterness engendered by the Civil War had hardened into unbelievable instances of prejudice and Jim Crowism as both the North and the South heaped their scorn on the helpless black man in the United States. Yet, out of this period of shifting literary ideologies and of extreme racial hostility came a group of novelists who were determined to be heard and who—in their differing approaches to the novel—presented the dilemma which was to face the Negro novelist well into the twentieth century. In addition to the four novels by Dunbar which appeared at the turn of the century, Charles Waddell Chesnutt produced three between 1900 and 1905, and Sutton E. Griggs published five between 1899 and 1908.

Both Chesnutt and Griggs are perhaps more understandable to modern audiences. They followed the pattern of former novelists, but addressed themselves realistically to racial matters and so wrote a protest fiction which treated various facets of the race problem in America. To understand Griggs demands that the reader read his novels in chronological order, for in essence his five novels form several approaches to a single theme. Concerning himself with the solutions to the racial question in America, Griggs presented a series of alternative answers. From the apparent black nationalism of *Imperium in Imperio* of 1899 he moved to a rather pessimistic analysis of the social structure of American life in *Overshadowed* (1901) and in *Unfettered* (1902); he concludes in the latter novel, after a recitation of one tragic event after another, that the solution to the race problem in this country can result only after both whites and blacks rid themselves of their senseless prejudices. *The Hindered Hand* (1905) emphasizes the psychological effects of race upon Americans, and he sees in the concept of "passing" just one attempt to come to terms with a society which places emphasis upon color. Yet, he maintains, "passing" cannot be done without great detriment; therefore, those characters who are light enough to pass must suffer the pangs of the identification crisis. In his last novel, *Pointing the Way* (1908), he presents his solution for all of the problems which he had presented earlier. The novel attempts to convince the reader that integration is possible only when people of good will band together for the common cause.

Addressing himself to themes and problems in a perhaps unorthodox manner, Griggs, nonetheless, wrote in the tradition of Martin Delany, celebrating the black hero. Unlike many of the former novelists and unlike Chesnutt, Griggs did not find a light skin to be an advantage. Although he was virtually unknown among the white reading public, Griggs was exceedingly popular with his own people. He wanted to be published, he did not wish to yield to any pressure of editors or readers; and so in a day when publishers literally dictated what would come from their presses, he established his own publishing company and thus assured not only freedom from censorship in publication, but also, through his own control of distribution, a readership as well.

In *The House Behind the Cedars* (1900), *The Marrow of Tradition* (1901), and *The Colonel's Dream* (1905), Chesnutt concerned himself with the period of Reconstruction and the hard times imposed upon all by the emphasis upon race. Not only did he separate his Negro characters into several categories, he concluded that the professional man of color was too frequently misunderstood by white America. As he dealt with the subject of integration, he also dealt with the inevitable "color line" and presented its peculiar set of problems. As Chesnutt became more and more outspoken, he ran into difficulties not only with his publisher but also with his reading public and so laid down his pen almost twenty-seven years before his death. While he frequently spoke of writing another novel, he never did.

Dunbar, perhaps because he was determined to write through the white establishment, attempted the unexpected. In a period when the Negro novelist overtly concerned himself with race and by virtue of this wrote a protest fiction, in a period when—in fact —a Negro was expected to be a "spokesman," Dunbar veiled what he had to say. He thus managed to fulfill his own theory of literary art while at the same time giving voice to those concerns, some of which were racial, which troubled him. Even if one is to assume that the modern Negro novel is a direct outgrowth of the perspective and methodology of Griggs and Chesnutt, one must remember that at a given moment in American culture there was a novelist who looked upon race not as the controlling force of his artistic life but only as an incidental fact.

In the careers as novelists of Griggs, Chesnutt, and Dunbar is one of the best commentaries upon the American publishing scene at the turn of the century. Opting for a wide audience, Dunbar attempted to offer what that audience wanted to read. Griggs had a message, created his own audience, and provided his own publishing company to spread his word. Chesnutt refused to yield to popular pressure and insisted that his readers accept his unadorned portrait of race relations in this country. While he was perhaps better known among his own people than either Dunbar or Chesnutt at the time, Griggs has become a literary statistic. Chesnutt ceased to use the novel as a means of expression when he ran into difficulty with his publisher. Only Dunbar survived the dilemma faced by the Negro author in the America of his day.

There were other novelists writing during the period of Dunbar, Griggs, and Chesnutt. In 1900 Pauline Hopkins issued *Contending Forces: A Romance Illustrative of Negro Life North and South*, in which she dealt with the "color line" and the emerging middle class; and in 1902 John S. Durham turned his back on the American scene and used Haiti as the locale for *Diana: Priestess of Haiti*, which deals with the human degradation which results whenever racial persecutions occur. In that same year G. Langhorne Pryor's *Neither Bond nor Free* appeared, which dealt with the unique position of the American Negro in society. Although the problems are presented realistically, Pryor concludes, along with most other novelists, that through hard work the American dream could become a reality, and the success formula which he presents is substantially the same as that of Benjamin Franklin's *Autobiography*. Like Griggs, however, he too used dark characters rather than light ones.

These pioneers existed and wrote before the Harlem Renaissance and its celebration of the black experience. This was before Langston Hughes declared:

> We younger Negro artists who create now intend to express our individual dark-skinned selves without fear or shame. If white people are pleased we are glad. If they are not, it doesn't matter. We know we are beautiful. And ugly too. The tom-tom cries and the tom-tom laughs. If colored people are pleased we are glad. If they are not, their displeasure doesn't matter either. We build our temples for tomorrow, strong as we know how, and we stand on top of the mountain, free within ourselves.[1]

These early novelists were primarily concerned with artistically rendering their experiences within the context of the American experience itself. A number of factors were against them. Perhaps of primary importance was the lack of distribution and the condemnation not only of the critics but also of the white reading establishment, which somehow concluded that these novelists had no right to criticize the American scene and its dream. Furthermore, as a direct result of the prevailing racial attitudes of the period, these novelists were not only unsung but frequently unread. Dunbar, to whom success was important, dealt with some of the same issues as these other novelists, but he did so in an unorthodox manner. Nevertheless, he was read and achieved a success denied to many of the others. Dunbar's current reputation as a novelist is, for the most part, based upon a misunderstanding of his view of fiction.

When measured against the so-called "classics" of American fiction, certainly no one of these writers produced works of the highest caliber; but then, the measuring rod (for reasons which are not hard to find) has not been created to include these writers. A quick glance at the literary histories of the country reveals that these writers have invariably suffered from the "cult of silence." Perhaps one can argue convincingly that these writers did not produce universally significant works. But it cannot be denied that each writer in his own way came to grips with some very basic problems which were increasingly to become significant to the writer of fiction. In their awareness they were trailblazers—dim though their lamps may have been—for the development of the so-called Negro novel in America. And before the complete story of the growth and development of the novel in this country can be told, they must be included. These writers, as was Dunbar, were victimized by literary hostility, stereotypes which both they and white authors used, and by the racial propagandists. Hence, when one is faced with the stereotypes in Dunbar's fiction, it should be remembered that he was not alone; for the early Negro writers tended to use such type characters. Although all of them were to discover that the romantic tradition was a difficult medium for protest, it was not until the acceptance of the realistic method that a viable novel could arise.

I

By the time that he turned his attention to the writing of novels, Dunbar had already distinguished himself as a poet. But at the time there was no long and outstanding tradition in fiction upon which he could build comparable to the post-romantic traditions of poetry in which he worked. As a rather precocious youngster in the Dayton public schools, Dunbar had started writing poetry at an early age. Much of it was saved by his mother, an ex-slave. When he was twelve, his father, who had escaped to Canada from slavery and who had fought in the Civil War with a Massachusetts division, died. Young Dunbar went on to finish high school in Dayton, the city of his birth; and though he met some unpleasant racial incidents, through his friendship with such youngsters as Wilbur and Orville Wright he was able to discount them. Furthermore, he seems to have been motivated generally by a spirit of romanticism. While he was generally considered to be a good student and an active one in extracurricular activities, his graduation was delayed by one year because of a failing grade in algebra. There is evidence that he was strongly disappointed to have to delay his entrance into the "world at large"; however, with a philosophical attitude which was to become typical of Dunbar when he faced some disappointment, he repeated the year and continued to enjoy life in the virtually all-white Dayton High School. As the class poet, Dunbar further distinguished himself, and some of his poetry found its way into the Dayton *Herald*, the daily newspaper. But good student though he was, he became aware of the handicap of race when he graduated and applied to that same newspaper for a job only to be told that the paper "could not hire colored." After weeks of searching for employment, he found one of the few jobs open to him: he became an elevator operator at four dollars per week. Yet he continued to write, and in 1892 *Oak and Ivy*, his first collection of verse, was published at his own expense and with the encouragement of some of the people whom he had met through the Western Writers Conference, especially Dr. J. N. Matthews, of Mason, Illinois, who became one of his strong supporters. As one of the poets selected to memorialize the World's Columbian Exposition, Dunbar thrilled the audience with his ode. But perhaps more important, from Dunbar's point of view, was the fact that in those days in Chicago he had an opportunity to meet Frederick Douglass and his circle. He learned that his reputation as a poet had preceded him. Within three years he came to the attention of William Dean Howells, who drew national attention to the young man by reviewing his second volume of verse, *Majors and Minors.* From that moment on his success as a professional writer was assured. Later that same year his third volume of verse appeared with a Dodd, Mead & Company imprint and the now-famous introduction by Howells. From 1896 until his death in 1906 he continued to write poetry, give readings, and was generally well thought of both by those who knew him personally and by those who knew him only by reputation.

Dunbar was often cited as an example of what could be done by an American Negro. Thus, unwittingly, he became a symbol of what was expected of the Negro writer, a legend in his own time. But legends and myths oftentimes place unbearable pressures upon their subjects, and so it was with Dunbar. Too frequently he responded to the legendary with what was expected of the myth, but there were moments when both the legend and the myth were cast aside. That it was his dialect poetry rather than his poetry in standard English which attracted people to him was one of the tragedies of his career. The judgment of Howells that this poetry is a "representative interpretation of Negro life" was repeated time and time again. This, of course, came at a time when the struggling Negro middle class was trying hard to forget its slave origins. It is particularly ironic that Howells, who was a friend of the downtrodden, who was himself very intent upon the adherence to the laws of brotherhood, who later became one of the founders of the NAACP, should have been the literary critic who emphasized the very things which the supporters of the Plantation Tradition had said for years. Howells appeared to suggest that in the Negro character there was a basic happiness and joy, that the Negro character either did not or could not look upon life seriously, and reduced everything to singing in the twilight and other little earthly joys. It made little difference to those who read "When Malindy Sings" that Dunbar had never been South when his first dialect poems were written, that his dialect was in essence his tribute to his idols James Whitcomb Riley, Will Pfrimmer, and John Greenleaf Whittier, that his only contact with the days of slavery came from his parents, both of whom were ex-slaves and who had told him stories of the antebellum days, that his mother tried to keep as much unpleasantness as possible from her young son, and that he was born in Dayton, Ohio, where he grew up in a substantially all-white society.

Initially, for Dunbar, the dialect poems were done "just for fun." It was his romantic and sentimental poems which he held in high esteem; hence, he was saddened to know that what he considered his best work was largely ignored or at best tolerated. In his autobiography, *Along This Way* (1933), James Weldon Johnson recorded a conversation which he had had with Dunbar:

> We talked again and again about poetry. I told him my doubts regarding the further possibilities of stereotyped dialect. He was hardly less dubious than I. He said, "You know, of course, that I didn't start as a dialect poet. I simply came to the conclusion that I could write it as well as, if not better than, anybody else I knew of, and that by doing so I should gain a hearing. I gained the hearing, and now they don't want me to write anything but dialect." There was a tone of self-reproach in what he said; and five years later, in his fatal illness, he sounded the same tone more deeply when he said to me, "I've kept on doing the same things, and doing them no better. I have never gotten to the things I really wanted to do." [2]

But this sadness was not limited to his friends. In "The Poet" Dunbar indicated clearly that he understood his role in American letters:

> He sang of life, serenely sweet,
> With, now and then, a deeper note.
> From some high peak, nigh yet remote,
> He voiced the world's absorbing beat.
>
> He sang of love when earth was young,
> And Love, itself, was in his lays.
> But ah, the world, it turned to praise
> A jingle in a broken tongue.

But he continued to sing "of life, serenely sweet" and he probed the "deeper note" even though "the world . . . turned to praise a jingle in a broken tongue." But ill health and frustrations plagued him. By 1906, at the age of thirty-four, Paul Laurence Dunbar was dead.

The meaning of Dunbar's literary career at the end of the nineteenth century has been variously described by American social historians; it is usually summarized as being a "significant" step in the literary development of American Negroes. Certainly he was one of the first writers to gain approval from a wide reading audience, but the tragedy of Dunbar remains in the fact that he was frequently praised for his least noteworthy work. Dunbar's popularity was due to a number of different reasons, all misrepresenting, in one way or another, Dunbar's real intentions. For the white readers, his dialect poetry reinforced their beliefs in the Plantation Tradition of singing slaves who enjoyed corn pones after a day's work. For Negro Americans he became the first one of their writers to become a professional and well known. They became well aware of the fact that he was not of mixed blood, and in a period when genius was defined in terms of the amount of "white blood" a person had, Dunbar defied the current theories. Thus, in a day when slavery was not a point of pride and when being black was considered a handicap, Dunbar—the son of two ex-slaves—rose to greater popular heights than had been attained by any Negro writer prior to his time. Furthermore, in a day when proving oneself was of utmost importance, he proved that popularity could be achieved. How widespread his popularity in the white community was is attested by the fact that his poems were issued annually in gift books even after his death. At the same time, among his own people the innumerable Dunbar societies and the many schools and housing projects named for him are silent testimonies to the respect and affection which the black community held for him. Yet neither the whites nor the blacks truly understood Dunbar's literary merit. For each he was a symbol of something which each needed at the time. It is fairly obvious that Dunbar himself recognized the dilemma of being an artist in America and with regret he asserted that the world turned to praise "a jingle in a broken tongue."

He, of course, was aware that his work in standard English would not and could not get a fair hearing in spite of the support from Matthews, and that it was his dialect poetry which catapulted him into national fame. Nobody bothered then or even later to note that Dunbar knew little, if any, authentic dialect. He merely copied his favorite Western poets and added the sentimental stories from his mother. By so doing he became for the nineteenth-century white establishment the "voice of the Negro." Later in his career he sought justification for his dialect by asserting that it was his true speech, but though he recited his poems well, those who knew him were struck by the very correctness of his own speech patterns.

So pervasive in American literary history is the myth of Dunbar as a dialect verse writer that his novels are dismissed as being "poor," "nonracial," "disappointing," and damned by similar adjectives. Yet Dunbar's critics fail to realize that at a given point in American history, his novels did achieve enough success to justify their inclusion within the scope of the history of the American novel and to receive widespread circulation. Certainly they tend to illustrate Dunbar's own literary theory. Perhaps one of the most significant judgments of Dunbar came from the newspapers which were usually hostile to Negroes. As Rayford Logan has pointed out, the San Francisco *Examiner* often used Dunbar as an example of what Negroes could achieve in this country (pp. 315–16). And the noted *New York Times* considered him to be an "exception." [3]

However, it has been fashionable recently to dismiss Dunbar as a writer who refused to look forward, who refused to address himself to racial issues, and who did a disservice to his people and ultimately to himself. Writing in his *Native Sons: A Critical Study* Edward Margolies dismissed Dunbar summarily:

> Dunbar's fiction deserves brief comment. His short stories at their best are prose replicas of his dialect poems—at their worst, over-sentimentalized versions of the saccharine school of ante-bellum apologists for the South. His novels are badly written, frequently melodramatic and drearily drawn out. Their chief interest lies in the light they throw on Dunbar's social views. Of his four novels, only *The Sport of the Gods* (1902) deals mainly with Negro characters—and here he implicitly urges Negroes to submit to small town or plantation values—despite racial injustices—since cities, by their very nature, are degenerate and corrupt. However kindly a view one may take of Dunbar's problems in making his books acceptable to white readers, one cannot escape the feeling that he was himself one of his own worst oppressors.[4]

Condemnation of Dunbar has taken many different paths. Some have condemned him for his use of the Plantation Tradition, others have criticized him for not being an overt racial leader, but few have recognized either his racial concerns or his theory of literature. He believed, first of all, that an artist should not be restricted because of accidents of either birth or race. At the same time, he did recognize the effects of his environment upon him. In varying ways he ambivalently merged these rather two diametrically opposed points of view. As his biographer, Benjamin Brawley, was to say in *Paul Laurence Dunbar: Poet of His People*, in his time "black was not fashionable. The burdens still rested upon the Negro to prove that he could do what any other man could do, and in America that meant to use the white man's techniques and meet the white man's standard of excellence. . . . This was the test . . . he had to satisfy, and not many will doubt that he met it admirably."[5] What Brawley perhaps should have added was that in meeting all of these tests one had to say what the white establishment wanted to hear. This was not the day when overt and loud protests were likely to be heard. This was not the day of the support of protest because it in some way lessened the pain of latent guilt feelings. In short, this was not the day when the reading public planned to pay to read strong protests against the "American way," or when they planned to pay to be insulted. All of this was to come later. So a Negro writer had few options. He could become predominantly a protest writer and pay to have his work distributed among his own people in the manner of Sutton Griggs; he could stop writing because he did not get the kind of reception which he thought he deserved, as Chesnutt did; or he could veil his protests in such a way that they would prove to be acceptable. The latter course was—needless to say—more demanding, but this was the course chosen by Dunbar. Therefore, he donned the mask and hid his protest beneath his apparent acceptance of the philosophy and psychology of white America.

It is also important to remember that Dunbar was brought up in the romantic tradition of American literature. Much of his poetry evidences this as well as his novels. In order to achieve some verisimilitude within this movement, he sometimes used "race-less" characters as well as the melodramatic themes which were popular in romantic fiction. As American literature embraced the realistic tradition so also did Dunbar. And when he did he was able to produce a novel which spoke directly not only of his race but also of America. Yet the romantic tradition had a ready-made receptive audience, and Dunbar aimed to capture at least part of it. He did, however, face a tremendous dilemma. Dunbar believed that he could write novels which would appeal to the American reading public, but this meant including the prejudices and stereotypes which they understood. But the years of racial rejection were to take their toll, and often there does appear—in subtle ways—the use of his own experiences, which were racial in nature.

As was the case with other Negro writers, Dunbar was aware of the fact that "a liberal publisher" was a misnomer. All publishers had preconceived notions of what the Negro writer ought to say. Either he must be happy in the sense of the Plantation Tradition or he must be angry and ready to reject the entire American system, in which case he could produce fiction of social protest. In addition to dealing with the publishing establishment, a Negro writer must come to terms with his environment and with himself as well as with his views of both. But the dilemma is even more ironic. The only writer who is faced with a preconceived notion of what he must produce is the Negro author. Praise and blame—as the case may be—are offered or withheld on the basis of how well the writer lives up to what his critics think he should do. Unfortunately, this attitude is not restricted to the most active racists but is all too frequently the guiding principle of the so-called friend, the liberal. It is a result of a pervasive and persuasive racism under which the Negro writer in this country must labor. The whole matter is further complicated by the preconceived notions which his own people frequently have of him and his artistic productions.

The manifestation of this approach to criticism is still apparent today. For example, it is the vogue to expect the black writer to be angry. He must rail against the terrible system which has oppressed him and his people. He is heralded as the "new writer," the "new spokesman," or "the voice of the blacks." But pity the writer who is neither angry nor racially oriented. The general public never hears of him; for if he is published at all, it is by a small company which has no means of distribution. And so the

Negro writer today has the choice of being angry and published or of being happy and ignored. During Dunbar's day expectations were different.

Unlike Griggs, who was substantially a sociological novelist who used the novel as a supplement for his sermons and lectures; unlike the protest writers of the latter part of the nineteenth century; and unlike those writers who were attempting to portray the virtues of the rising black middle class, Dunbar had no messianic mission and viewed the novel as mainly a means of entertainment. Nurtured in the romantic tradition of literature, he saw his role as being merely that of a recorder of tales and a "worthy singer of songs." In a letter dated July 13, 1895, addressed to Dr. Henry A. Tobey, the superintendent of the State Hospital for the Insane, of Toledo, Dunbar made clear his hopes and aspirations as a writer. The letter was sent to thank Dr. Tobey for his unsolicited aid and explained in part:

> I did once want to be a lawyer, but that ambition has long since died out before the all-absorbing desire to be a worthy singer of the songs of God and nature. To be able to interpret my own people through song and story, and to prove to the many that after all we are more human than African.

In his desire to become a professional writer Dunbar was convinced that he could also interpret his own people. But to interpret his people meant to prove through deed and subject that they were no different from other human beings in America. Brawley records what is perhaps one of Dunbar's most cogent observations on the role of the Negro poet in America. According to Brawley, when he was asked to compare Negro and white poetry, Dunbar gave the following explanation:

> The predominant power of the African race is lyric. In that I should expect the writers of my race to excel . . . [however] their poetry will not be exotic or differ much from that of whites [because] for two hundred and fifty years the environment of the Negro has been American, in every respect the same as that of all other Americans. . . . We must write like white men. I do not mean imitate them; but our life is now the same.[6]

Yet the desire to interpret his people created a strange dichotomy in Dunbar's work. Both the dialect poems as well as the tales within the Plantation Tradition present one phase of the interpretation. Here, very much in the manner of the local colorists, he used the material of the antebellum South. Removed as he was from the stories and characters which he presented, it never really occurred to him that his race bound him in any but the most superficial way. Another phase of the interpretation resulted in those works which were not dependent upon race but which implicitly illustrated his ability to write as any other American. Like Poe and other earlier poets who wrote prose fiction, Dunbar thought of himself primarily as a poet. His prose was simply another means by which he might achieve a degree of financial independence. Lida Keck Wiggins has recorded in her *The Life and Works of Paul Laurence Dunbar* that Dunbar regarded prose as his effort to come to terms with his era. Said he, "The age is materialistic. Verse isn't. I must be with the age. So, I am writing prose." [7]

Those who condemn him for his lack of involvement must permit him the right to select his personal view of the role of the writer. His literary creed was certainly an expedient one for the closing years of the nineteenth century. Yet, through his sometimes "race-less" novels Dunbar was able to demonstrate implicitly—although he too was not the most skillful craftsman—that there are some human values which transcend race. For example, in his first novel, *The Uncalled*, the relationship between Freddie Brent and his guardian is a basic relationship and illustrates the conflicts which frequently arise when one person of an older generation attempts to superimpose his will upon one of the younger generation. The novel also demonstrates Dunbar's negative attitude toward the city, an attitude which he was to express time and time again and which was fully explored in his last novel, *The Sport of the Gods.* Romanticist that he was, he dealt with the small-town environment and looked at the city—as had other romantics—as a place of potential evil and degradation for the individual. But as he viewed the conflict between the agrarian values of American life and the rising interest in the city, Dunbar's novels evince a growing awareness not only of the realistic method but also of the hypocrisy of American society. Thus one can see even before *The Sport of the Gods* that Dunbar did indeed deal with social issues and with the racial struggles of this nation.

Interestingly enough, Dunbar frequently relied rather heavily upon his own experiences for his novels. In *The Uncalled* he expanded his own interest in the ministry in order to tell the story of a youngster adopted by a prudish woman of a small-town community and then literally forced by her into the ministry. While decidedly not the great American novel, it does present some realistic conflicts between characters in addition to being a sentimental story in the nineteenth-century tradition. In *The Love of Landry* his search for health in Colorado became the basis for the story of Mildred Osborne, who also goes to Colorado to seek health and who becomes greater by virtue of her association with nature. Commenting on the purpose for Mildred's trip, Dunbar muses rather pathetically in the novel:

> With all the faith one may have in one's self, with all the strong hopefulness of youth, it is yet a terrible thing to be forced away from home, from all one loves, to an unknown, uncared-for country, there to fight, hand to hand with death, an uncertain fight. There is none of the rush and clamour of battle that keeps up the soldier's courage. There is no clang of the instruments of war. The panting warrior hears no loud huzzas, and yet the deadly combat goes on; in the still night, when all the world's asleep, in the gray day, in the pale morning, it goes on, and no one knows it save himself and death. Then if he goes down, he knows no hero's honors; if he wins, he has no special praise. And yet, it is a terrible, lone, still fight.

The Fanatics turns its attention to life in Ohio, Dunbar's home state. Rather than concentrating on the idyllic nature of the small town, the novel investigated, years before Sinclair Lewis and Edgar Lee Masters exposed the small town, the hypocrisies and conflicts in a Northern community torn asunder by its own divisive attitude toward the Civil War. For those who viewed Ohio as the promised land, Dunbar certainly shattered the illusion. His treatment, however, of the racial, social, and labor problems is sometimes clumsily handled; but he wrote of the Ohio which he knew so well. Dunbar himself had made trips to Chicago and New York and knew well the lures of the night life of both cities, which he found to be inherently evil and certainly no place for the unsophisticated Southern Negro. This attitude forms the basis for *The*

Sport of the Gods as he turned his attention to the story of a Negro family forced to flee the South. Their sojourn in New York, a city for which they are not equipped, is tragic and degenerating. For the first time in his fiction he partially dropped his mask as he analyzed the effects of the environment upon the characters and concluded that the city was not only evil but also brought out the innate evil in man.

During the period of his four novels (1898–1902) the dilemma which faced Dunbar as a writer became most apparent. He was astute enough to recognize the exigencies of the American publishing scene. To get published meant giving the public what it wanted to read. And getting published was important to Dunbar, especially in view of the fact that he thought of himself as a professional writer. This does not mean to imply or to suggest that he compromised principles, although later generations have called him by that ubiquitous term, "Uncle Tom." He was aware of the growing social importance of the novel, while at the same time, he believed firmly that a writer's first commitment was to his story. Yet, in spite of his seemingly "white point of view," he did demonstrate his own recognition of not only the racial problems in this country but also of current social issues. Perhaps nowhere can the evolution of Dunbar's awareness be more clearly and consistently seen than during the period of his four novels. Certainly the novels are exercises in masking his own views, although they do—in spite of the professed goals of the writer—admirably present his comments upon some of the issues of his own day.

II

By 1898 and the publication of *The Uncalled* Dunbar was highly successful and was constantly in demand as a reader; however, his accomplishments did not always bring great financial rewards. As a result, he was ever searching for new forms of expression in order to capitalize upon his already-famous name. *The Uncalled* was a response to all of these forces. Literally stranded in London by his "manager" in 1897, Dunbar spent a great deal of time writing. As he wrote to Alice Moore, who was to become his wife the following year, "I am myself writing very hard and very steadily, the last few evenings past having seen me do sixteen thousand words in prose and about half a dozen poems." The letter, dated March 7, indicates the frenzy with which Dunbar often approached his writing. *The Uncalled,* or at least part of it, is a product of this hurried work. Purchased by *Lippincott's Monthly Magazine,* it appeared first in the May (1898) issue and subsequently in book form during that same year. This first novel is "race-less" in the sense that Dunbar does not specify what race his characters are; neither does he by speech or other mannerisms identify them more than to make clear they are all small-town Midwesterners with the speech patterns of that locale. As a first novel it does have some merit, although the extensive use of the intrusive author device seems rather self-conscious. But even this does not damage the work greatly because Dunbar apparently never intended to write a tightly constructed work. To Alice in another letter from London dated May 4, 1897, he mentioned *The Uncalled*:

> My novel grows apace, though I can hardly call that a novel which is merely the putting together of a half dozen distinct characters and letting them work out their destiny along the commonplace lines suggested by their values and environment. It has some plot but little incident and incident seems to be the thing nowadays.

The novel is set in Dexter, a small town in Ohio, and focuses on Frederick Brent's search for himself. Despite his own wishes he attends the seminary, becomes a minister, and accepts a charge really to please his guardian, Miss Hester Prime. Eventually he rejects the life of hypocrisy for what is to him a more meaningful life. The purpose of this slick magazine story—if *The Uncalled* can be said to have a purpose—is the revelation of the pettiness and deceitfulness which exist in a small town. The central theme revolves around Frederick's growing awareness of himself and of the world around him. Writing in the tradition of Edgar Watson Howe's *The Story of a Country Town,* Dunbar presented Dexter and its people with similar rural problems and moral situations. But the book does not share Howe's tragic theme. The reader is convinced at the end of the story that "they will live happily ever after" as conflicts are resolved and Frederick Brent makes a decision with which he can live.

Within the tradition of the melodramatic sentimental novel the opening chapters are most effective. It is a cold winter morning, as is typical of this type of novel. Margaret Brent has just died, leaving a fatherless five-year-old Freddie. Around her in her squalid surroundings are a number of gossiping women who discuss Margaret's less-than-exemplary life, her separation from her husband, and some minor concerns of small-town housewives. After the funeral the townswomen gather once again to decide what is to become of the child who wants to stay in his miserable hovel until "mama comes back." It is Miss Hester Prime, the most prudish of the women, who convinces the others that she should take the child in order to save him from the fate of his drunken father, who has disappeared, and of his dead mother. Hence, little Freddie becomes the ward of the most morally inflexible person of the town. The remainder of the story chronicles the growth and eventual rebellion of Freddie in this stifling atmosphere.

While *The Uncalled* seems loosely constructed, has some characters who lack dimension, is given a setting which seems barren, and has a "story line" that eventually strains credibility, it introduces themes which Dunbar consistently also pursued throughout his later novels. The most obvious is, of course, a thorough analysis of the small town as it is influenced by surrounding industrialism; however, the inevitable conflict between the small town and the city is explained in terms of personalities rather than in terms of locales. Unlike his attitude in *The Sport of the Gods*, Dunbar is not convinced that the city is of and in itself evil in this novel. When Frederick Brent prepares to go to Cincinnati, there are those in Dexter who feel that this represents perdition; however, Dunbar comments,

> It is one of the defects of the provincial mind that it can never see any good in a great city. It concludes that, as many people are wicked, where large numbers of human beings are gathered together there must be a much greater amount of evil than in a smaller place. It overlooks the equally obvious reasoning that, as some people are good, in the larger mass there must also be a larger amount of goodness. It seems a source of complacent satisfaction to many to sit in contemplation of the fact of the extreme wickedness of the world.

At the end of the novel Freddie decides to remain in the city because it represents freedom from the stifling atmosphere of Dexter. As he writes to his guardian, "I'm not so narrow as I was at home. I don't think so many things are wrong as I used to. It is good to be like other people sometimes, and not to feel yourself apart from the rest of humanity."

In *The Uncalled* there is also a concern for the psychological development of some of the characters as well as an analysis of the interpersonal relationships which occur whenever human beings with different values meet. The growth of Freddie is told not only from the point of view of his chronological growth but also in terms of the changes which occur within him. In many ways the novel represents the main character's spiritual biography. This development takes place against the backdrop of the townspeople who, with few exceptions, are petty, mean, and malicious in spite of their professed religion. As Dunbar deals with the spiritual barrenness of Dexter, he also attacks the sterility of organized religion. The reader is introduced early to Hester, whose religion had made her so stern. Next, Dunbar comments upon the sermon which is delivered at Margaret Brent's funeral:

> [It] was a noisy and rather inconsequential effort. The preacher had little to say, but he roared that little out in a harsh, unmusical voice accompanied by much slapping of his hands and pounding of the table. Towards the end he lowered his voice and began to play upon the feelings of his willing hearers, and when he had won his meed of sobs and tears, when he had sufficiently probed old wounds and made them bleed afresh, when he had conjured up dead sorrows from the grave, when he had obscured the sun of heavenly hope with the vapours of earthly grief, he sat down satisfied.

From this point on the reader is made well aware that the religious life of Dexter leaves a great deal to be desired. The intolerance of the clergy and the fear of the congregation represent a strange approach to religion. When he eventually becomes the minister, Freddie insists that religion should not be a burden, neither should church be a "place of terror." But he is practically alone. His test comes when he is expected to publicly denounce a young girl who has "gone astray." This he refuses to do, and this precipitates his own renunciation of the life which was not his choice. Certainly if being a minister meant sitting in moral judgment upon those who needed help, Freddie was convinced that he had not been "called."

Of all of the recurring motifs in Dunbar's novel, one is frequently ignored. So much has been made of Dunbar's romanticism that the sense of fatalistic determinism provides a discordant note because it goes counter to what is expected of Dunbar. In *The Uncalled* it is not nearly as pervasive as it becomes in *The Sport of the Gods* nor in the work of later naturalists, but nonetheless it does appear. The concept of fate appears in various ways in *The Uncalled*, but it is always presented as that force which exists outside of the province of man. In one instance it is explained in terms of the evil of human nature as stated by Hester Prime. "Human beings are by nature evil: evil must be crushed: *ergo*, everything natural must be crushed." Later in the novel Dunbar suggests that Fate might be tempered by man's recognition of it. "When Fate is fighting with all her might against a human soul, the greatest victory that the soul can win is to reconcile itself to the unpleasant, which is never quite so unpleasant afterwards." Toward the end of the novel, while Freddie is still a newcomer to Cincinnati he is gripped by an overpowering sense of loneliness. Once again there is a suggestion that the center of control of man is somewhere outside of his jurisdiction. Dunbar comments,

> "Whom the gods wish to destroy, they first make mad," we used to say; but all that is changed now, and whom the devil wishes to get, he first makes lonesome. Then the victim is up to anything.

While the novel generally had a favorable response, some critics were disturbed because the novelist had failed to write about his own people. *The Bookman* for December 1898 objected to the characters in *The Uncalled.* Claiming that Dunbar should "write about Negroes," the reviewer lamented that "the charming tender sympathy of *Folks from Dixie* is missing" and asserted that Dunbar was "an outsider" who viewed his action "as a stage manager."

That the conflicts portrayed in Frederick Brent were human ones which were not dependent upon race for validity was frequently ignored. Further, it is ironic that since the characters are not identified racially, critics have assumed that Dunbar intended that they should be white. It may well be that the missing ethnic labels were deliberate attempts on the part of Dunbar to relate to the dominant American social structure. The review in the Chicago *Times-Herald* for December 16, 1898, praised Dunbar for entering "bodily into the broader field of letters":

> We have no words but praise for Paul Laurence Dunbar's first effort in prose, "The Uncalled." This book has inspired certain critics to discover a color line in literature. . . . There is no color line in letters, as there is no aristocracy. Do the critics forget that Dumas was what is called in America a "negro"? But even if we admit for the sake of argument the existence of a color line, Mr. Dunbar has stepped clean over it. . . . He should be encouraged to write more.

Yet, on the whole, the critical attitude of the white establishment toward Dunbar as a novelist was perhaps best summarized by Vernon Loggins in his *The Negro Author in America.* Claiming that Dunbar should have "painstakingly avoided" writing stories without Negro characters, Loggins continued: "All of the bubbling spontaneity which he showed in his tales on blacks is replaced . . . by cheap conventional story-telling, with echoes of Dickens and the popular magazine, and with an English which is often downright faulty." The "faulty English" which Loggins found is simply an English devoid of dialect or peculiar mannerisms; it is a language of the Midwest which cannot be racially identified. While he asserted that it "came as a great disappointment to Dunbar's admirers," Loggins was forced to admit that the novel had "some commercial success." [8] And it was commercial success for which Dunbar aimed.

More recent critics who have considered Dunbar's fiction at all have responded variously to *The Uncalled.* In *Negro Voices in American Fiction*, Hugh Gloster calls it a "shallow novel," while in *The Negro Novel in America*, Robert Bone refers to it as "Dunbar's most successful novel." Both critics have asserted that the characters are white although the internal evidence does not necessarily demand this.[9]

By 1900 and the publication of *The Love of Landry* Dunbar, however, had turned to white characters. Dealing with Easterners who go West, Dunbar presents briefly the attitude of some white Americans. For example, Mildred Osborne, the protagonist, comments rather sadly upon the life of a porter while she travels on a westbound train with her father. He scoffs at her for being sympathetic:

> "Poor coloured man! Why Mildred, that man gets more out of life than I do. He has a greater capacity for enjoyment, with the paradox that less satisfies it. You think it humiliates him to take a tip? Not in the least. That's his business. He courteously fleeces us, and then laughs about it, no doubt."

Shortly after this conversation, Mildred frantically sends the porter on an errand which really was not as urgent as her voice would have indicated; however, he performed his task. Dunbar remarks,

> If that porter had been a blackbird instead of a black man, he would have flown, so great was his excitement. As it was, he came as near accomplishing that impossible feat as Nature, a narrow aisle, and a rolling car would allow him.

But then as Mildred and her father laugh at him, Dunbar adds,

> And, indeed, the coloured man was still staring at them with wide, white eyes, and when he saw them burst anew into laughter, he left the door and went back to his place, in disgust no doubt with the thought in his mind that here was another instance of white people trampling on, and making a fool of, the black man.

When her father notes that she should not have frightened the porter, Mildred asserts that she did not mean to frighten him and adds, "I'll give him an extra tip before we leave." But her father retorts, "You should make him pay you for turning him so near white, even for such a short space of time."

In a single incident the porter is used to record not only the dominant attitude of white America but also the innate feeling of the porter himself. The kind of paternalistic prejudice which is so characteristic of the North is evident in both Mr. Osborne and his daughter, Mildred. And the final remark of the father repeats an idea held by many whites that blacks would be willing to pay to change colors. While the conversation both begins and ends from a "white point of view," clearly the attitude of the porter is sandwiched between. Thus, in one episode Dunbar addressed himself not only to the majority of his readers but also managed to record the porter's own thoughts. While this is by no means a major incident of the novel, it does give some insight into Dunbar's technique, which he was to perfect in his next novel. By literally presenting two points of view he was able to speak to far more readers.

Certainly this novel is little more than a fairy tale. Dedicated "To my friend, Major William Cooke Daniels, in memory of some pleasant days spent over this little story," *The Love of Landry* utilizes the Colorado locale where the Eastern characters begin to lose the superficialities which had bound them to the East and to a more restricted society. Dunbar used an old technique of sending his characters back to nature in order that they might find themselves physically and spiritually. Within this context the novelist was able to draw the inevitable contrast between the East, which represents a traditional society, and the West, which stands for undefiled Nature. When Dr. Van Pelt, the family doctor of the Osbornes, recommends that Mildred should leave New York for a while because of her cough, Mr. Osborne questions a trip to Colorado because it is "beyond civilization." Dr. Van Pelt replies, "You know I'm a doctor of the old school, although I've kept up with the new; and it's my old-fogy opinion, sort of left over, as it were, that civilisation has always been a foe to good health."

Shortly after her arrival in the West, Mildred talks with Landry, who has abandoned a life of tradition, about her reasons for the trip West and about the fears which her aunt had displayed. One of the objections raised by her aunt was her fear that the West was not civilized. Landry answered, "Nothing is quite so conceited as what we call civilisation; and what does it mean after all, except to lie gracefully, to cheat legally, and to live as far away from God and Nature as the world limit will let." Then in order to answer her question as to why he came west, he asserts, "[Some] of us come to get breathing space, when we are stifled back there by meanness and deceit. Some of us come here to look at the great mountains and broad plains, and forget how little man is; to see Nature, and through it, Nature's God, and so get back to faith." Eventually, Mildred adopts a similar point of view. She is described as acquiring both "gaiety and health, the reward one gains by living near to Nature's heart."

In addition to the very clear distinctions which Dunbar makes between the restrictive East or "civilization" and the freedom and democracy of the West, he does make some social observations which are almost out of character with the romantic nature of the novel. For example, as Mildred and her father are on the train speeding westward, they pass through a section of the country which Dunbar calls "perfect seas of yellow corn." When Mildred asks: "What do they do with so much corn?" her father answers "grimly" that they bring down prices with it. The answer does not satisfy Mildred; for she feels that surely it must have some other use. Her father agrees and says, "They eat it, feed it to their stock, they mill it, and they corner it." Mildred then questions the meaning of "corner" to which her father replies, "My dear, there can be a corner in anything that one man has and another man wants. A corner is just the repetition of the act of the dog in the manger in the fable, with the exception that the ox is left the alternative of paying a high price to the dog or going without." Another instance of social commentary occurs when Mildred tries to convince Landry that he would have made a good soldier, he replies,

> "I don't know that I should want to be [a soldier]. . . . I know it isn't heroic, but I don't know that those fellows, brave as they may be, who are out there fighting a lot of half-naked savages are doing any more for ultimate good than we who are here, fighting the hard conditions of nature. I like a fight, but there are fights and fights, and I'd rather know that this irrigation ditch that I'm digging is going to make the land better and a lot of people happier, than to feel that I was carrying a cartridge-belt full of civilisation to folks that didn't want it."

When Mildred accuses him of being an "anti-expansionist," he defends his position by explaining:

> "No, I'm not an anti-expansionist, either. I believe in America's spreading out as big and as broad as she can, and doing all the good she can. But whenever I look around me on all this . . . I cannot help thinking that there's a good deal of expanding to be done at home."

The Love of Landry, which is reminiscent of Dunbar's own trip west on an expedition similar to that of Mildred Osborne, is not at all spectacular; but once again Dunbar had produced a sentimental story for a sentimental age. Once again he had celebrated the glory of man's relationship to nature away from the constricting influence of the city. The characters show little or no development, and the freedom of the West is articulated in simplistic fashion as the characters are immediately affected by their contact with nature. The end of the novel is contrived, to say the least, as there is once again the "and-they-lived-happily-after" conclusion.

In both *The Uncalled* and in *The Love of Landry* there are contrasts between the city and the country, between the "civilized" East and the freedom-producing West. While there are some social comments, there is far more psychological development of character in *The Uncalled* than in *The Love of Landry*. Those who look at these books and deplore the lack of Negro characters in them or the use of the porter in *The Love of Landry* are inadvertently supporting the thesis that the Negro artist should and must produce either works which are within the milieu of social protest or which are circumscribed not only by the time and place but also by the race of the author. Dunbar was not, in these novels, intent upon renouncing his race; neither was he attempting to ignore those problems which he saw daily. Rather, he was operating within the framework of his own belief that the literary artist who happened to be a Negro was not to be bound by the limitations of purely racial subjects.

At the same time, this should by no means suggest that Dunbar was uninterested in his race. During the period of these first two novels, Dunbar demonstrated an amazing awareness of the racial situation in America. On December 17, 1898, an article by Dunbar entitled "Recession Never" appeared in the Cincinnati *Rostrum*. It is one of the strongest pleas for racial understanding written during the period, and the type of conciliation often ascribed to Dunbar is totally absent. The article begins with a startling analogy between the North and South which, three years before *The Fanatics*, makes clear that Dunbar saw little difference between the two locales; for as he concluded at one point in the article, "The race spirit in the United States is not local but general." This article received widespread circulation—how wide only a perusal of every American newspaper will reveal; however, it not only appeared in many of the papers of Ohio and New York, but also in many of the Chicago papers, notably the Chicago *Record.*

While in Colorado, Dunbar spoke out frequently on the racial question in the United States with the same type of force and clarity. Many of his comments were duly reported in the Denver papers. Interestingly enough, he saw hope for the Negro in migrating westward rather than to the cities of the North. Firmly convinced that his people were totally unsuited for urban living, Dunbar saw in the West a chance to grow with the land. In an article which appeared in the Denver *Sunday Post* on September 17, 1899, Dunbar celebrated the West as being "the great and generous West, [that] has extended her hands to every nation and said: 'Come and be free.' " To those who might raise an objection to the overcrowding of the "wide open spaces" with the oppressed blacks, Dunbar notes, "if the black emigrant comes to the West it would be under circumstances far different from those under which the black slave went to the South. He went there under every condition making towards a destruction of his manhood. If he came here he would come with every element helping him towards a higher civilization." He then appeals to the West as the region which has been a refuge for the oppressed of the world, a locale which "has not refused the pauper from Europe; [which] has not turned back the criminal from the East." Dunbar raises the question: "Could she then say no to her poor black brother, who has been in the family for 250 years and whose blood and whose sweat have gone to give to the South whatever wealth it possesses today?"

Those who criticize Dunbar's use of the Plantation Tradition and his apparent interest in the antebellum South in his fiction have no idea how firm was his dislike for the city and what it represented. While he recognized the problems of the South, he viewed the section as being one where people could live close to the land. And it was the agrarian values of the nineteenth century which most impressed him. Even though he himself had lived in cities, he was never convinced that city life was the answer for the development of the highest values of life. Some of his fears of the city are apparent in *The Uncalled*, but by the time of *The Sport of the Gods* these antipathies had hardened into apparent obsessions, for he was convinced that it was the group least able to adjust to and cope with the urban demands who frequently moved into the crowded city. New York was the example which he most frequently used. Yet the problems of the South were evident in the North. An article addressed "to the editor" of the New York *Sun* sheds a great deal of light upon his attitude toward the city. As he viewed the unemployed in the city, he observed,

> They are not Anarchists; they never will be. Socialism has no meaning for them; and yet in these seemingly careless, guffawing crowds lies a terrible menace to our institutions. Everything in their environment tends to the blotting out of the moral sense, everything to the engendering of crime. Here and there sits a weak, ineffectual little mission, doing its best for the people around it, but altogether as inadequate as a gauze fan in the furnace heats of hell.

Much of his grief is predicated upon the fact that the race has "so much to overcome" that it seems unjust to add to it the problems of urban adjustment. His grief is reinforced by the general attitude of Americans toward the entire matter of race. Dunbar is aware of the fact that a white lower class also exists, but he realizes that it is not used to interpret an entire race; however, "The sight of one Negro suggests a race." Therefore, the underprivileged, unemployed city dweller stands for every Negro in the nation. As he views the unfortunates in the city, he states,

> It is natural to suppose that these poor people will produce offspring. Of what kind will they be? How can they run in the race of life when they are hampered from the start by the degradation of their parents? I pity the children because they are being cheated out of their birthright. I pity the parents because they are blind enough to damn their own progeny. Many of them are from the small towns of the South. They have been deceived by the glare and glitter of the city streets. They are great, naughty, irresponsible children. Their highest ideal is a search for pleasure, and they think they have found it when they indulge in vice. I pity them because they have come to the city to lose so much and to gain so little. They are losing the simple, joyous natures with which God endowed them, and are becoming hard and mean and brutal. They are losing the soft mellow voices which even slavery could not ruin.

> They are losing their capacity for simple enjoyment. They are growing cynical. They are losing their gentleness, their hospitality, their fidelity—all, in fact, of the good traits that distinguish them in their natural habitat. And for what? A hand-to-mouth struggle for life in a great city, and a place in the Potter's Field at last.

While Dunbar celebrates the simple virtues of the moralistic romantic, he does not deny the rights of people to seek that which gives them pleasure in life. He then compares what he considers to be the advantages of living close to the land with the handicaps of an urban existence which is at best meager:

> These people have a right to the joy of life. But they are selling their birthright for a mess of pottage—and such pottage! They have given up the fields for the gutters. They have bartered the sweet-smelling earth of their freshly turned furrows for the stenches of metropolitan alleys. They have lost the step of the brawny tiller of the soil. They do not walk like clodhoppers, but they creep like vermin. Is it an improvement? They are ashamed of all of the old simple delights, and cannot reach to the perfection of pure new ones. They have ceased, in great part, to play their simple melodies on the banjo, and strum out "rags" on the piano. The sensuousness that gave them warmth and glow has subsided into a hard sensuality that makes them gross. They have forgotten how to laugh and have learned to sneer.

As if to answer the objections which might be raised concerning the grimness of his portrait of life in the city, Dunbar asserts,

> It is not enough to say that there are intelligent, moral, and industrious Negroes in the city. Of course there are, and about them there would be no problem. But their influence for good and for respectability cannot be fully felt as long as so large a part of the race is operating in a different direction. The man who has worked along quietly buying property, raising a respectable family, educating his sons; who has held one position for twenty years and has the respect and confidence of his employers, does not attract one-tenth part of the attention that is attracted by the "burly Negro who was arrested last night for beating his wife." In the public mind the race receives the odium of the latter act, but not the benefit of the former. The voice of the brute who is lynched for an unspeakable crime sounds further than the voice of the man of

> God who stands in his pulpit Sunday after Sunday inveighing against wrong.

Dunbar readily admits that he has no solution to the problem and realizes that "it is probably wrong to introduce a problem and then suggest no specific remedy." Yet the constant migrations of people to the city who are not prepared to deal with urban life are the sources of many of the problems. Recognizing that the South is far from being a perfect place, he concludes that its "restrictions" are "better . . . than a seeming liberty which blossoms noxiously into license."

Perhaps from the vantage point of 1972 one might conclude that Dunbar's solutions were simplistic and his remedies naive. It cannot be denied that he was sincere nor can it be concluded that he lacked an interest in racial matters. The point which is highly interesting is the fact that during the time of the production of both *The Uncalled* and *The Love of Landry* he was constantly being quoted upon racial matters in this country. Although he did not view the novel as the proper vehicle for overt social criticism, he did evince a growing awareness of social concerns in his remaining two novels, *The Fanatics* and *The Sport of the Gods*.

In *The Fanatics* (1901), as in *The Love of Landry*, the major characters are white; but through his veiled approach Dunbar manages to make some profound observations upon the American racial scene. This was done, however, in such a way that none but the most astute would have been aware of it. On the surface one might conclude that the characterization of the whites is the most important formal feature of the novel. But more important is his organization, placement of dialogue, and disappointment of conventional expectations. Often what he does not say becomes a controlling force in the novel. Thus, in what may appear to be anti-Negro sections of the novel, Dunbar makes an impassioned plea for great racial tolerance and understanding while making profound judgments on the American social scene, especially of the North. Yet all of this is done in such a way as not to anger the reader who simply is searching for "a lively story."

The novel deals with the conflict between two families in Dorbury, a small town in Ohio. Bradford Waters is a strong supporter of the Union cause, and he expects all members of his family to be loyal to the Union. Stephen Van Doren sympathizes with the cause of the Confederacy. The conflict between these two families is symbolically suggestive of the general conflict in the border towns where there were apparent divisions between Northern and Southern supporters. The hostility between the two families is intensified because—in Romeo and Juliet fashion—Bob Van Doren is in love with Mary Waters. When Bob joins the Confederate Army, more to please his father than himself, Mary's father insists that she end her engagement to Bob. Because she claims that she loves Bob and "not his politics," Mary refuses. But Bradford Waters does reject his rebellious daughter, and she is forced to seek refuge with the Van Doren family. After a series of tragic events, the death of Waters's son, and the wounding of Van Doren's son, the two families become reunited in harmony after the Civil War.

As a story dealing with the effects of the Civil War upon a community, the novel demonstrates once again that Dunbar understood the psychology of the small town and the character of the self-righteous Northerner. For example, there was a growing concern in Dorbury about the many Negroes who poured into the town:

> Ohio, placed as she was, just on the border of the slave territory, was getting more than her share of this unwelcome population, and her white citizens soon began to chafe at it.

Eventually one character, Raymond Stothard, complains about the refugees and actually voices a prevailing attitude of the town which had always prided itself upon its insistence upon fair play and the "American ideals." Says he,

> "All the niggers in the South are crowding in on us, and pretty soon, we won't have a place to lay our heads. They'll undercharge the laborer and drive him out of house and home. They will live on leavings, and the men who are eating white bread and butter will have to get down to the level of the black hounds."

This attitude has been an historic part of the attitudes of America toward the invasion of what some people consider their territory by any group which appears to be different. For example, much of the urban objection to the foreign immigrant was expressed in similar terms, but that immigrant had the advantage of not being "highly visible," so that eventually he could be absorbed. Yet the very idea that somehow these people would undercut the prevailing economic system was uppermost in most minds. Stothard continues his lament by claiming and voicing another prevalent Northern attitude toward the Civil War:

> "The whole war is on their account. If it hadn't been for them, we'd have been friends with the South today, but they've estranged us from our brothers, rent the country asunder, and now they're coming up here to crowd us out of our town."

Bigot though Stothard is portrayed as being, he does echo some of the same arguments often heard and the attitudes of so many liberals who show great concern lest their own immediate lives should be drastically changed. It is a matter of not wanting these "strange people"—who are all right at a distance—too close to them. From the vantage point of the present time it would appear that Dunbar missed a tremendous opportunity to present a strong statement of social protest; indeed, even much of what he did accomplish is lost in the sentimental action between the two families. The love story between Bob and Mary, the reconciliation between the two families, and the many episodes designed to illustrate the power of honor contribute to the excessive melodrama. Furthermore, the characters are overdrawn and stereotyped. The townspeople are conveniently divided into the types which they represent with Mary epitomizing the nineteenth century maiden who strongly prefers a suffering love in the face of parental objections. But is not such stereotyping typical of the fictional milieu in which Dunbar worked? The Negroes who stream into the town as refugees from the war are used primarily in an apparent local-color tradition; only Nigger Ed, the town crier who goes to war, emerges as a warmly human character although he too might prove to be reprehensible to many readers. As might be expected, Dunbar—the author—remains detached from all of his characters as he views the fanatics on both sides—perhaps a little sadly. If one can ignore the weaknesses of the novel, he can see that Dunbar well reveals the hypocrisy of the North and demonstrates the paradoxical position into which most Negroes are forced in Northern communities. And he concludes that the attitudes of the North vary little from those of the South and in many ways are worse, for the promise of freedom there is not realized. It is at this point that Dunbar ceases to be the novelist and does indeed become the social critic. But his criticism—and there is much of it—is veiled behind the conventions of his fiction. Thus to appreciate fully *The Fanatics* one must look at the minor characters and the methods by which Dunbar introduced various incidents and episodes.

Whether or not Dunbar intended that Nigger Ed should have been similar to Twain's Nigger Jim is perhaps a moot point, but there are some points of similarity between them. For the town of Dorbury, Ed is the one Negro who is well known and with whom the entire race is identified. As Mary contemplates the meaning of the coming of the Civil War, she muses to herself,

> What had she to do with those black men down in the South, it was none of her business? For her part, she only knew one black man and he was bad enough. Of course, Nigger Ed was funny. They all liked him and laughed at him, but he was not exemplary. He filled, with equal adaptability, the position of town crier and town drunkard. Really, if all his brethren were like him, they would be none the worse for having masters.

However, when the Dorbury militia organizes, Ed volunteers and is to go to war as the servant to Horace Miller, the militia captain. The day of departure arrives for the militia, and the entire town turns out to wish the force godspeed; but when someone spies Ed in the parade, the serious moment is turned into one of derision:

> "Hi, Ed," called one, "ain't you afraid they'll get you and make you a slave?" and "Don't forget to stop at Dorbury when you get to running!"

But it is a different Nigger Ed who is presented by Dunbar. Through him the author is able to make one of his observations:

> Ed was usually good-natured, and met such sallies with a grin, but a new cap and a soldier's belt had had their effect on him, and he marched among his deriders, very stern, dignified and erect, as if the arduous duties of the camp were already telling upon him. The only reply he vouchsafed was "nemmine, you people, nemmine. You got to git somebody else to ring yo' ol' bell now." The crowd laughed. There came a time when they wept at [the] thought of that black buffoon; the town nigger, the town drunkard,

> when in the hospital and by deathbeds his touch was as the touch of a mother; when over the bloodswept field, he bore a woman's dearest and nursed him back to a broken life. But no more of that. The telling of it must be left to a time when he who says aught of a Negro's virtues will not be cried down as an advocate drunk with prejudice.

And so it is that in a few words Dunbar includes not only the prevailing prejudices of the times but also indicates something of the heroic natures of the men who often were refused permission to fight in the early days of the Civil War and who had to find their roles in other areas and yet who were as much responsible for the ultimate victory as the men who carried the guns.

When Ed first returns to Dorbury after his first tour of duty with the Dorbury militia and before that militia has gone into active service, Dunbar notes that he was "proud and happy":

> The sight of camps, the hurry of men and the press of real responsibility had evoked a subtle change in the Negro, and though his black face showed its accustomed grins, and he answered with humor the sallies made at him, he capered no more in the public square for the delectation of the crowd that despised him. He walked with a more stately step and the people greeted him in more serious tones, as if his association with their soldiers, light though it had been, had brought him nearer to the manhood which they still refused to recognize in him.

Eventually, however, Ed becomes representative to the fanatics of Dorbury of all that they hate. During one of the many meetings held in the town to deal with the issues caused by the war, there is an assembly in which two speakers are to debate the problems. One speaker is "a fiery demagogue and depended for his influence upon his power to work upon the passions of the lower element. His audience knew this. He knew it, and for an instant, paused in embarrassment." Then Dunbar adds,

> Just at that moment, "Nigger Ed" strolled up and joined the crowd. The eye of the orator took him in, and lighted with sudden inspiration. Here was all the text he needed. Raising his tall, spare form, he pointed in silence until every face was turned upon the Negro. Then he said, "Gentlemen, it is for such as that and worse that you are shedding your brothers' blood." Without another word

he sat down. It was the most convincing speech he had ever made. The unhappy advent of the Negro had put a power into the words of a man who otherwise would have been impotent. It was the occasion and the man to take advantage of it. It may have been clap-trap. But in the heated spirit of the time, it was a shot that went straight to the mark. The crowd began to murmur and then broke into hisses and jeers. Rude jests with more of anger than humor in them were bandied back and forth.

Both sides find themselves in an untenable position because as Dunbar notes,

> One side was furious that blood should be spilled for such as the Negro bell-ringer, while the other was equally incensed at being accused of championing his cause.

Eventually, of course, the meeting soon turns into a moblike group with a riot motive in their words and actions. Through it all, Ed is little more than a "thing" to most people:

> Back and forth the controversy raged, each party growing hotter and hotter. Negro Ed stood transfixed at the tempest he had raised. He looked from face to face but in none of them found a friend. Both sides hated him and his people. He was like a shuttlecock. He was a reproach to one and an insult to the other.

Soon it becomes evident that the mob is in favor of totally destroying Ed for what he is and for what he represents. It is not until Bob's father, Stephen Van Doren, reminds the crowd that Ed has done nothing to receive that kind of treatment that the mob begins to come to its senses. As they think of what Van Doren has said, Ed is able to leave the crowd unnoticed "in anger and in sorrow." At the end of the novel Dorbury has reversed its opinion of Ed. As the novelist notes,

> There were men who had seen that black man on bloody fields, which were thick with the wounded and the dying, and these could not speak of him without tears in their eyes. There were women who begged him to come in and talk to them about their sons who had been left on some Southern field, wives who wanted to hear over again the last words of their loved ones. And so they gave him a place for life and everything he wanted, and from being despised he was much petted and spoiled, for they were all fanatics.

The fact that there were other Negroes living in Dorbury totally escaped most of the residents until the anti-Negro spirit became dominant:

> Since 1829, there had been a gradual change for the better in the attitude of Ohio towards her colored citizens, but now, all over the state, and especially in the Southern counties and towns there had come a sudden revulsion of feeling, and the people rose generally against the possibility of being overwhelmed by an influx of runaway slaves. Their temper grew and ominous mutterings were heard on every side. The first great outburst of popular wrath came when Negro men began offering themselves for military service, and some extremists urged the policy of accepting them. . . .
>
> From none of the states came a more pronounced refusal than from Ohio. She had set her face against men of color. What wonder then, that their coming into the state aroused all her antagonistic blood? Here, for a time, all party lines fell away, and all the people were united in one cause—resistance to the invasion of the black horde.

Dorbury was typical of the kinds of events taking place all over the state. Dunbar makes clear the extent of the anti-Negro feeling:

> Upon one thing they were all united, and that was their hatred and disdain for the hapless race which had caused the war. Upon its shoulders fell all the resentment and each individual stood for his race. If their boys suffered hardships in the field, they felt that in some manner they avenged him by firing a Negro's home or chasing him along the dark streets as he made his way home from church. It became an act of patriotism to push a black woman from the sidewalks.
>
> It only needed the knowledge that free men of color had offered their services to the state to bring out a storm of invective and abuse against the "impudent niggers." There were some who expressed fear that the governor might yield to their plea, and threatened if he did, that they would call their sons and brothers from the army, and resent the insult by withholding all aid from the Union arms. But they need have had no fear of their governor. Strong as he was and independent, he was too wise a man not to know and to respect the trend of popular sentiment, and he heard with unyielding heart the prayer of the Negroes to be put in the blue. But the time did come when the despised race was emancipated and they were accepted in the field as something other than

scullions. The time came, yes, but this governor was not one of the men who helped to hasten it. It may have been his personal feeling, rather than his acquiescence to the will of the people, that prompted his reply to the Massachusetts recruiting agent. The New England commonwealth was recruiting her black regiments and was drawing men of color from every state. When the chief executive of Ohio was consulted, he was so far from objecting to the use of his Negroes by another state that he expressed himself to the effect that he would be glad if they would take "every damned nigger out of the state." It may have been irritation at the anxiety and annoyance that this unwelcome population had caused the good governor which brought forth this strong expression. Whether it was this or not, the fact remains that many black men of Ohio went into the Massachusetts regiments, and when they had made for themselves a record that shamed contempt, it was to that state that popular belief gave the honor of their deeds.

This forecasting of events would be entirely out of place but that it serves in some manner to show the spirit of the times in a loyal and non-slaveholding state at a crucial moment of the nation's life; it was a moment when only a spark was needed to light the whole magazine of discontent and blow doubt and vacillation into a conflagration of disloyalty.

As Dunbar recounts the many instances of fanaticism on both sides of the question of war, he demonstrates quite clearly that the differences between the North and South are more semantic than real. Perhaps in a manner too simplistic for modern audiences he makes it plain that there are good people both in North and South; but on the matter of race, there is very little difference between the two regions. This certainly is an attitude which goes counter to the romanticism of the Plantation Tradition.

Within Dorbury itself the fanaticism is best exemplified by the Union sympathizers and those of the Confederacy. Yet, there was still another group of fanatics who ultimately were forced to drop their unthinking attitudes in order to survive. The free Negroes in the town have developed their tight little colony which does not permit the admission of any outsiders. Just as in other sections of the country, this little group is secure within its own social structure, and it defies any contact with those who are not of their "class." When the problems of the influx of Southern Negroes hits

Dorbury, the whites are not the only ones to react to "the contrabands":

> The free blacks of Dorbury themselves . . . were fighting their unfortunate brothers of the South as vigorously as their white neighbors . . . but the stream kept pouring in. In spite of resistance, abuse and oppression, there was a certain calm determination about these fugitive slaves that was of the stuff that made the Puritans. As far North as Oberlin and Cleveland, they did not often make their way. If it was their intention to stop in Ohio at all, they usually ended their journey at the more Southern towns. While the spirit in the Northern towns was calmer, it was, perhaps, just as well that they were not overrun. In Cleveland, especially, numerous masters of the South, averse to making slaves of their own offspring, had colonized their discarded Negro mistresses and their illegitimate offspring, and these people, blinded by God knows what idea of their own position, in the eyes of the world, had made an aristocracy of their own shame.
>
> In Dorbury, the Negro aristocracy was not one founded upon mixed blood, but upon free birth or manumission before the war. Even the church, whose broad wings are supposed to cover all sorts and conditions of men, turned its face against the poor children of a later bondage.
>
> After much difficulty, the Negro contingent in Dorbury had succeeded in establishing a small house of worship in an isolated section known as "the commons." Here according to their own views, they met Sunday after Sunday to give praise and adoration to the God whom they, as well as the whites, claimed as theirs. and hither, impelled by the religious instincts of their race, came the contrabands on reaching town. But were they received with open arms? No, the God that fostered black and white alike, rich and poor, was not known to father these poor fugitives, so lately out of bondage. The holy portals were closed in their faces, and dark-skinned pastors . . . drew aside their robes as they passed them.

The episode comes to a conclusion when some of these new people apply for membership in the church and are rejected. When one of them protests that "we's all colo'ed togethah," the minister attempts to show them the difference "between people who had been freed three or four years before and those just made free."

But the time was soon to come when being "colored together" was important and marked the necessity for unity among the oppressed. The white people of Dorbury, or at least some of them, decide that the only way to keep these new residents in their place is to run all Negroes out of town, and so an attack is planned. Stephen Van Doren warns them of the impending disaster. As Dunbar describes Van Doren, he is

> a Southerner by birth and education [who] understood these people, who had for two centuries been the particular wards of the South. While he had no faith in the ultimate success of the Union arms, and believed that all these blacks must eventually go back into slavery whence they had come, . . . he reasoned that they were there, and such being the case, all that was possible, ought to be done for them.

Realizing that they are all endangered, there is immediate unity between the old and the new black residents of Dorbury, a unity which catches the white population of Dorbury by surprise:

> One advantage which the Negroes were to have was that in the sudden passion against their race the whites made no distinction as to bond or free, manumitted or contraband. This, of necessity, drew them all together, and they grew closer to each other in sympathy than they had yet known.
>
> The drawing together was not one of spirit only, but of fact. They began to have meetings at night after the warning, and a code of signals was arranged to call all of them together at the first sign of danger.

The long expected night of danger finally arrives. It is preceded by a confrontation between a newly arrived Negro family and Stothard, the most vocal of Dorbury's bigots. In an attempt to turn them back at the railroad station, Stothard is thwarted because this new family is protected by Van Doren, who arrives at the scene of the harassment just in time. The family consists of five people, "a father and mother, both verging on old age, a stalwart, strong-limbed son, apparently about twenty, and two younger children." When they ask the way to the section of the city in which other members of their race live, Stothard says, as much to the gathered crowd as to the family, "More niggers . . . why in hell don't you people stay where you belong?" When there is no answer to his question forthcoming, he demands an answer:

> He took a step forward, and the outcasts cowered before him, all save the son. He did not move a step and there was a light in his eye that was not good to see. It was the glare of an animal brought to bay. Stothard saw it and advanced no further.

The young man eventually tells him that they have come to Ohio because it is a free state; however, Stothard made it plain that it is a free state for "white people, not for niggers." He then attempts to scoff at Van Doren, who has come to the rescue of the new family; but Van Doren retorts, "It is to the Union's greatest discredit that it has such men as you on its side."

Stothard is not willing to accept defeat at the hands of Van Doren and so he begins to mobilize his forces. As the whites are preparing their attack, Dunbar states,

> Meanwhile on old McLean street, where stood the house of one of Dorbury's free black citizens, another gathering equally silent, equally stealthy and determined was taking place. The signal had gone forth, the warning had been received and free Negro and contraband were drawing together for mutual protection. Not a word was spoken among them. It was not the time for talk. But they huddled together in the half-lit room and only their hard, labored breathing broke the silence. To the freedmen, it meant the maintenance of all that they had won by quiet industry. To the contrabands, it meant the life or death of all their hopes of manhood. Now all artificial lines were broken down, and all of them were brothers by the tie of necessity. Contraband and the man who a few days ago had looked down upon him with supreme contempt, now pressed shoulder to shoulder, a common greyness in their faces, the same black dread in their hearts. In the back room sick with fear, waited the women and children. Upon the issue of the night depended all that they had prayed for. Was it to be peace and home or exile and slavery? Their mother hearts yearned over the children who clustered helpless about their feet. "If not for us, God, for these, our little ones," they prayed. Their minds went back to the plantation, its pleasures and its pains. They remembered all. There had been the dances and the frolics, and the meetings, but those paled into insignificance before the memory of the field, the overseer and the lash. Often, oh, too often, they had bared their backs to the cruel thongs. Day by day they had toiled and sweated under the relentless sun. But must these, the products of their poor bodies,

> do likewise? Must they, too, toil without respite, and labor without reward? They clasped their children in their arms with a hopelessness that was almost aggression.

Around midnight the mob arrives. After breaking the door down they meet a surprise:

> Instead of a cowering crowd of helpless men, they found themselves confronted by a solid black wall of desperate men who stood their ground and fought like soldiers.

Before the fight is over, Stothard comes face to face with

> the contraband boy whom he had abused the day before. A knife flashed in the dim light, and in a moment more was buried in the leader's heart. The shriek, half of fear, half of surprise which was on his lips, died there, and he fell forward with a groan, while the black man sped from the room.

Almost as if to apologize to his readers for presenting such a graphic portrait of the confrontation between the whites and the blacks of the town of Dorbury, Dunbar added,

> The wild-eyed boy who went out into the night to be lost forever, killed Stothard, not because he was fighting for a principle, but because the white man had made his mother cry the day before. His ideas were still primitive.

And so, one might say today, were Dunbar's views of the novel. Yet, before realism was convincingly used in racial fiction, before Americans were really ready to accept the fact that distinctions between the racial attitudes of the North and South were actually minimal, before mob scenes were portrayed with power, and before the sad plight of Negroes in so-called free territory had been exposed, Paul Laurence Dunbar—the man accused of always operating within the Plantation Tradition—had shown that even though he wrote for the popular mind and for popular acceptance he was aware of racial injustice in America and could use it artistically in fiction.

In his first letter to Alice he asked her opinion on whether Negroes should write only of their race. In a letter dated May 7, 1895, she had replied,

> I haven't much liking for those writers that wedge the Negro problem and social equality and long dissertations on the Negro in general into their stories. It is too much like a quinine pill in jelly. . . . Somehow when I start a story I always think of my folk characters as simple human beings, not of types of a race or an idea, and I seem to be on more friendly terms with them.

It is apparent that Dunbar was also opposed to putting quinine pills in the jelly, but the time was to come when the very nature of the social conditions in America forced him to look at racial concerns. But when he did, he began by subtly examining Northern attitudes toward his people. He discovered in *The Love of Landry* that the broad-minded Northerner thought little of the Negro when he thought of him at all; and he exposed in *The Fanatics* the mania which provoked such free states as Ohio into the kind of behavior which traditionally has been relegated to the South. At the same time he analyzed the attitudes of Northern Negroes toward their less fortunate brothers. Unlike Chesnutt and many of the writers of the latter part of the nineteenth century, Dunbar was not ready to excuse separatist behavior based upon either color or profession. Until the lowliest man was elevated, he agreed with his unnamed character, "we're all colored together."

In *The Sport of the Gods* (1902), his last novel, there is an apparent shift toward a more open protest and toward the use of the naturalistic method. While racial elements are important in this work, it is fundamentally a protest against the evil influence of the city, a theme which had been subtly introduced in *The Uncalled* and in *The Love of Landry*. Now Dunbar investigates what happens to the Southern Negro when he is placed in an urban environment which is not only hostile but also one for which he is ill-prepared. While the situations are not always believable, *The Sport of the Gods* marks the extent to which a spirit of pessimism had pervaded Dunbar's own artistic spirit.

The novel first appeared in the May 1901 issue of *Lippincott's Monthly Magazine* and in book form in the following year. It was published in England as *The Jest of Fate*. Although only a few years separated Dunbar's last three novels, the unnamed porter of *The Love of Landry* as well as Nigger Ed and the host of unnamed Negroes, both free and contraband of *The Fanatics*, were worlds away from the Berry Hamilton family of *The Sport of the Gods.* While one might conclude that this is reflective of Dunbar's growing racial awareness, one must also take into account the fact that this is also a result of the drastic shifts in attitude which had occurred in America. The optimism which had prevailed during the latter part of the nineteenth century, when there was a consideration of racial matters, gave way to the fact during the opening years of the twentieth that "the problem" was far from being solved.

As *The Sport of the Gods* opens, the reader is introduced to the Berry Hamilton family. Here is a family that has followed all of the rules for success. They work hard, save their money, go to church, and generally have faith in the future. Yet, when Berry Hamilton is accused of stealing money from his employer's brother, his virtues are quickly forgotten in the small Southern community. Once again the meanness of the small town is described. Before his trial, which is a farce, he is rejected not only by Maurice Oakley, his employer who knows that he has always been a good and honest worker, but also by the Negro community which fears reprisals if anyone should show mercy or sympathy for the Hamiltons. Dunbar does not find white rejection unusual, but expected. But he does attack those Negroes who are afraid to support Hamilton or to acknowledge his integrity. Once again, at the turn of the century, Dunbar makes it quite clear that the race must unite and stand together when any one member is attacked unjustly. Particularly, he finds the rejection of the church to be out of keeping with the mission of the purpose of religion:

> It seems a strange irony upon the force of right living, that this man, who had never been arrested before, who had never even been suspected of wrongdoing, should find so few who even at the first telling doubted the story of his guilt.
>
> The A.M.E. church, of which he has been an honest and active member, hastened to disavow sympathy with him, and purge itself of contamination by turning him out. His friends were afraid to visit him and were silent when his enemies gloated. . . . In the black people of the town the strong influence of slavery was still operative, and with one accord they turned away from one of their own kind upon whom had been set the ban of the white man's dis-

> pleasure . . . not then, not now, nor has it ever been true, although it has been claimed, that Negroes either harbour or sympathize with the criminal of their own kind. They did not dare do it before the sixties. They do not dare do it now. They have brought down as a heritage from the days of their bondage both fear and disloyalty.

Thus victimized by both Negro and white society, Hamilton goes to prison while his wife and two children escape to New York City in search of anonymity. In the city they are caught in a web of conditions over which they have no control, and the closely knit family is doomed to defeat. Pathetically, each character tries to hold to the ideals which he had maintained in his Southern home, but the urban environment is too much and takes its toll as these unsuspecting people surrender one by one. As Dunbar observes in the novel,

> Whom the gods wish to destroy they first make mad. The first sign of the demoralization of the provincial who comes to New York is his pride at his insensibility to certain impressions which used to influence him at home. First, he begins to scoff, and there is no truth in his views nor depth in his laugh. But by and by, from mere pretending, it becomes real. He grows callous. After that he goes to the devil very cheerfully.

Joe, the son, is fascinated by the social life of the city with its clubs and nightly entertainment. He becomes involved in the life of the Banner Club and eventually kills a jaded chorus girl, whom he had been dating. Kitty, the daughter, becomes aware of her own beauty and what it can bring in the city. She becomes a chorus girl and loses not only her beauty but her ideals as well. Even Mrs. Hamilton is not secure. She becomes involved with a gambler whom she eventually marries. Through the good offices of Skaggs, an inquisitive crusading Northern newspaper reporter, Berry Hamilton is freed from prison. In a contrived situation Mrs. Hamilton's second husband is killed, thereby paving the way for the reunion of the broken couple. Through a series of intricate subplots, the mystery of the stolen money is revealed. Maurice Oakley, in an attempt to protect his brother, who had lost the money in gambling and who had then lied about it at first, loses his mind. To protect not only his brother but also the family name exacted a heavy toll from Oakley. As the novel ends, Berry and his wife are once again in their old house near that of the Oakleys. As they sit "together with clasped hands listening to the shrieks of the madman across the yard," they think, "of what he had brought to them and to himself." Dunbar concludes the novel: "It was not a happy life, but it was all that was left to them, and they took it up without complaint, for they knew they were powerless against some Will infinitely stronger than their own."

Of the many elements of the novel which seem significant, the most obvious is the attitude toward the city which is displayed. At first, the city promises happiness:

> They had heard of New York as a place vague and far away, a city that, like Heaven, to them had existed by faith alone. All the days of their lives they had heard of it, and it seemed to them the center of all the glory, all the wealth, and all the freedom in the world. New York. It had an alluring sound.

But the promises are short-lived. After a series of melodramatic episodes and coincidences where the deterministic nature of the city predominates, Dunbar notes that the everlasting migrations of Negroes from the South "would continue to flow up . . . dashing itself against the hard necessities of the city and breaking like waves against the rock—that, until the gods grew tried of their cruel sport, there must still be sacrifices to false ideals and unreal ambitions."

Eugene Arden emphasized the significance of *The Sport of the Gods* by referring to it as "a nearly forgotten but nearly great novel which was the forerunner of the whole school" of Harlem novels. He viewed it as "the first novel to treat Negro life in New York seriously and at length." [10] Of course, much has been made of the use of Harlem by both white and black writers during the years following the First World War. One of the characteristics of the postwar search for a new form of expression was the use of exoticism and primitivism. And where else, but in Harlem—many thought—were these two elements merged? Carl Van Vechten, a member of that postwar generation, presented Harlem in his *Nigger Heaven* (1926) but he claimed no distinction for his setting; rather it was to Dunbar and *The Sport of the Gods* that Van

Vechten gave credit. He saw Dunbar's novel as the description of "the plight of a young outsider who comes to the larger New York Negro world to make his fortune, but who falls victim to the sordid snares of that world, a theme I elaborated in 1926 to fit a newer and much more intricate social system." [11] Yet the New York described by Dunbar could have been Chicago or any other large urban area where Negroes have migrated looking for a promised land. Thus it was not New York *per se* but the demands and indifference of the city which attracted Dunbar.

Throughout the novel Dunbar makes it quite clear that the "cheerful" journey to the Devil is not really the doing of the characters themselves but rather a result of the hypocrisy and deceitfulness of a society which can imprison a man because he is black, thus forcing the man's family to flee to a world for which the members of that family are not prepared. The paternalistic white man of the Plantation Tradition no longer survives in Maurice Oakley, who does nothing to protect his trusted servant; the love and affection which members of the race ought to display toward one another falls victim to behavior directed by self-interest; and the land of freedom or promise—the North—does little to help the newly arrived immigrant adjust to a world which he certainly never made. Underlying the action of *The Sport of the Gods* is a powerful message to white and black America. Although Dunbar's approach to fiction did not allow him to spend much time or creative energy in the realm of social-protest fiction, two of the most outstanding documents dealing with the hostility of the urban northern environment are *The Fanatics* and *The Sport of the Gods.* Thoroughly convinced that the city was a place of evil, Dunbar chose to present, usually, the idyllic small community; for when man lived close to Nature there was at least hope for growth and development. He did not believe that the South was perfect, but in many ways he accepted the point of view that "the Devil one knows" is infinitely better than the unknown Devil.

III

Before one dismisses Dunbar's four novels for what he did not do, one must consider what he accomplished. For the first time, an

American Negro writer gained widespread acceptance with the reading public. He aimed for success and achieved it. Upon his return from England in 1897, he was interviewed by a New York paper. Referring to his first novel, *The Uncalled*, the journalist noted,

> He is at work upon a novel. He does not know, he says, whether it is a good novel or not, but if he sells it for a good price he will be inclined to think that it has literary value. This shrewd reservation of judgment is quite consistent with all the young man's views of a world that he regards as a very satisfactory one to live in without regard to sex, color, or previous condition of servitude.

Thus it was that he equated success, literary value, and financial gain. He wrote at a time when the romantic tradition was still currently the vogue, and initially cast his novels within this tradition. When realism and naturalism began to make their impact upon American fiction, so too did Dunbar demonstrate a growing awareness of these forces within his fiction. Like the other naturalists who were to follow him, Dunbar was firmly convinced that there were forces outside of man which controlled his destiny. When these forces were applied to the racial situation they produced a record of the hostility in America and proved that racial antagonism was not merely sectional. The South could not bear the guilt alone.

Thus, romantic though much of his work is, in the four novels there is a growing awareness not only of the social problems of America but also of the problems created by an urban environment and an urban society. The city, for example, as an evil force reached its culmination in *The Sport of the Gods* but certainly is present in *The Uncalled.* By the time of his last novel the element of sorrow which had always been a part of Dunbar the man was exhibited. Fate seemed to play a large part in his own attitude toward life. And while he achieved publication in the leading magazines of his day and a national reputation which resulted in his knowing the outstanding men and women of his time, a part of him remained unfulfilled. He knew that he had traveled a long way from being a four-dollar-a-week elevator operator, but he also knew the handicaps of racism in America, subtle though these sometimes were. Howells became his patron, but he became aware of the harm which had resulted from Howells's well-intentioned support. He enjoyed his many white friends, but the black pride of "Ode to Ethiopia" was often voiced as he realized that until the lowliest man was elevated, people would continue to think of him as the exception rather than the rule. So when he sang of the "caged bird" and claimed affinity with it, it was as if he himself had come to terms—at least in part—with his own life.

One can only surmise what direction Dunbar would have taken had he lived beyond 1906. It is likely that he would have turned more to the naturalistic form, since that best mirrored his own growing pessimism. But by veiling his views of life and masking his ideas of society behind characters who would be acceptable to the reading public, he was able to produce in rapid succession four novels which enjoyed a measure of success. He must have been fully aware of the demands which the times made upon the novelist who desired popularity and who sought the approval of the American reading public at the turn of the century. His own sense of disillusionment is expressed better in his poetry than in his novels; yet poetically, he expressed not only the ambivalence of the black writer in America but also that of the black man in America when he wrote,

> We smile, but, O great Christ, our cries
> To thee from tortured souls arise.
> We sing, but oh the clay is vile
> Beneath our feet, and long the mile;
> But let the world dream otherwise,
>   We wear the mask!

In his novels Dunbar frequently wore that mask. Nevertheless, from the conflicts between two generations as well as between the city and the country of *The Uncalled*; through what he called the "conventional love story" of *The Love of Landry*, which is certainly a slick Western story; into *The Fanatics* with its evident concern for the hypocrisy of Northerners who mouth one thing about race relations but who in reality thought as little of the Negro as did their Southern brothers; and finally into *The Sport of the Gods*, which viewed life in terms of some powerful force outside of man, Dunbar slowly dropped his mask and showed a growing awareness of the use of racial subjects in the novel. At no point did he substitute his own pride and dignity for the mess of pottage which was to be his reward for critical acclaim. Neither, however, did he have the power to protest against injustice in the manner of a social-protest novelist. In fact, he did not view the novel as a medium for social change. Yet by his life and works he proved that achievement was possible in spite of race, that the black novelist could join the mainstream of American fiction—whatever that mainstream might be—and, in so doing, address himself to the American reading public. Through it all he demonstrated that the creative spirit of man was not to be fettered by such superficialities of life as race. And though he wore the mask, he permitted glimpses behind it. By writing often on two levels of meaning, he demonstrated even greater talent and understanding than those who never felt compelled to wear the mask.

One of the fallacies of American criticism is the expectation that the Negro artist must concern himself with racial materials. But if he is not conditioned by racial matters, can he be expected to be a voice upon these matters? While this question frequently goes unanswered, there is the repeated assumption that the Negro novelist must write about his own people. In addressing himself to his subject, he is often expected to have the "answers"; thus he is expected to be not only a storyteller but a psychologist, a clergyman, a sociologist, and a political scientist rolled into a single person. Even today one is frequently amazed to see the number of writers listed among those who are expected to have the solutions for racial problems. Needless to say, to a large extent the art of the novelist in America has been conditioned by the exigencies of publication. Up to the time of Dunbar the Negro novelist had been primarily concerned with racial themes. Dunbar—recognizing the unwritten code of being accepted by a large reading audience—attempted initially to deal with universal themes in the most entertaining way, for nurtured as he was in the belief in the American dream, he believed that he could sing of life "serenely sweet." Without a doubt, his creative spirit was a product of the environment into which he was born. As he matured, he became more aware of the ambiguity of American life; the American dream and the American reality were far apart.

It is, of course, clear that the writer can neither expect to live in a societal vacuum nor exist in an aesthetic one. By its very nature the novel is a product of the society which produces it; thus it does observe society and possibly make judgments upon it. But the novel is ultimately aware of its limitations as a social force because it must consider the aesthetics of its form. Thus creative spirit and narrative skill become important. Because of the mandates of the realistic method as well as those of the naturalistic school of writing, many readers have come to expect that the novel —a manifestation of a given society at a given time—must use the world as it is known and must observe, analyze, and judge that world. Within this framework readers have insisted along with many critics that the novelist assume many roles, and—if he has any energy left—he is expected to be the artist. To this we have added that the Negro writer must be a racial leader and demonstrate in all his work his own racial awareness. Thus, one is hard pressed, for example, to evaluate the work of a Phillis Wheatley, whose adherence to the principles of neoclassicism left little room for a soaring indictment of slavery, or of a Frank Yerby, who makes no apology for being a popular historical novelist. In his definition of literature in *Ideas in America*, Howard Mumford Jones addressed himself to some of these issues:

> Literature . . . is not just a mirror reflecting social trends and economic predilections. It is not a faithful but amateurish replica of philosophical ideas only. These may influence it and furnish some part of its substance, but literary history is also a study of the relation of the forms of art to the development of sensibility in that portion of society which responds in a given epoch to literary appeals. The writer is neither wholly the embodiment of a primitive, irrational, creative urge, nor wholly the half-conscious product of sociological and economic determinants. His appeal is of course to thought and feeling, but his emotive direction like his emotional apperception is a part of the sensibility of his time, and his intellectual energy is not confined to the ideational content of what he writes but is also expended upon the conscious manipulation of form for the sake of aesthetic freshness.[12]

The novel of social protest is a product of an optimistic belief in the American experience. It is predicated upon the supposition that to know a set of conditions is to change them. Unlike pure naturalism, whose methods it often uses, social-protest fiction does not assume that this is a mechanistic world or that man is programmed in a deterministic way but that there are elements of free will still operative, and from these elements stem the power to change the world. But social-protest fiction also places a great emphasis upon the power of the written word, an emphasis which is not totally consistent with the history of the success of the form itself.

The American novelist who is concerned with realistically recording the American experience is faced with a strange ambiguity. On the one hand, the American experience itself emphasizes individualism, free will, and a belief in the possibility of all things. Yet, on the other hand, there are the inevitable problems which result when man comes face to face with situations not of his own making and often finds himself in a vise of circumstances over which he has no control. Thus the environment becomes more powerful than the articulation of the American dream. Hence, since the latter part of the nineteenth century, the American novelist has been peculiarly aware of the dichotomy between the American dream and the American reality. Periodically, of course, the American novelist has attempted to forget the entire matter and has, as a result, produced romantic works which often have little relationship to the life which he knows.

The Negro novelist has not only been aware of this strange dichotomy and these unusual ambiguities but has also generally addressed himself to them. Thus, the element of protest has figured rather prominently in the Negro novel itself. But the elements of protest are based not on the premise that the injustices of American society are unchangeable but rather upon the faith and hope in the possibility of change. On one level and taken collectively, the Negro novel has represented the conscience of the American experience.

While the Negro novelist has traditionally examined the role of his people within the framework of the ambivalent American Dream/American Reality concept, he has often been aware of the fact that sheer propaganda cannot substitute for art. He has been concerned with the universality of his themes and characters because he recognized that in the final analysis his creative urge must be evaluated not as a single voice but as the universal voice of man. Thus, the experiences which he recounts must be ultimately the experiences of man at a given juncture of human history. His voice becomes the voice of the oppressed throughout the world. Frequently, the critic has been so intent upon relegating the Negro novelist into a particular nationalistic framework—that is if he even includes his work at all—that whatever might have been his prevailing literary theory has been totally lost. Nor have white critics alone been guilty of this. Many Negro critics have judged their own novelists upon how well that writer fit into some predetermined racial mold, forgetting that while racial concerns are important they may not be the *sine qua non* of every writer.

At the turn of the century Dunbar faced the challenge of being a writer in America. Perhaps he chose methods and techniques dismissed by a later generation. Perhaps, had he lived, he himself would have made a dramatic reversal. But a reevaluation of Dunbar at present provides an opportunity to reevaluate those biases which have hitherto prohibited an objective view not only of Dunbar but of the Negro artist in America. There was a time, of course, when Dunbar with the hope of youth saw himself as a part of American culture and of the American literary scene. At a time when a man was expected to prove his worth according to some predetermined standard, he dared to become a professional writer in spite of the odds against him. Throughout his life he exhibited a dominant strain of optimism, which is reflected in his extensive use of the romantic tradition both in poetry and in prose. But the strange ambiguity of race was not totally forgotten, for it too was part of America. And if the Paul Laurence Dunbar of the Plantation Tradition still seems paramount, if the Paul Laurence Dunbar who seemed to deny racial issues seems to speak most loudly in his novels, if the career of Paul Laurence Dunbar seems totally surrounded by the aura of a decadent romanticism, it must be remembered that behind all of the veils there was the Paul Laurence Dunbar who more than anything else wanted to be a successful writer. It might be well that the present will judge him merely in terms of accommodation or conciliation, but before the final chapter on Dunbar is written, one must consider the productivity of his brief career. Before he died at the age of thirty-four, he had published, in addition to the four novels, five collections of short stories (*Folks from Dixie*, 1898; *The Strength of Gideon and Other Stories*, 1900; *Ohio Pastorals* for *Lippincott's Monthly Magazine*, 1901; *In Old Plantation Days*, 1903; and *The Heart of Happy Hollow*, 1904). He had written and published over five hundred poems as well as numerous essays and articles. In spite of his biographers, who portray the happy and opportunistic Dunbar, it is fairly certain that he was aware of the ambiguities of his life. And there were times—perhaps not many—when he did reveal the man behind the mask. Nowhere did the spirit of resignation or the desire to be judged in terms of his own capabilities seem more apparent than in "Equipment":

> With what thou gavest me, O Master,
> I have wrought.
> Such chances, such abilities,
> To see the end was not for my poor eyes,
> Thine was the impulse, thine the forming thought.
>
> Ah, I have wrought,
> And these sad hands have right to tell their story,
> It was no hard up striving after glory,
> Catching and losing, gaining and failing,
> Raging me back at the world's raucous railing.
> Simply and humbly from stone and from wood,
> Wrought I the things that to thee might seem good.
>
> If they are little, ah God! but the cost,
> Who but thou knowest the all that is lost!
> If they are few, is the workmanship true?
> Try them and weigh me, whate'er be my due!

NOTES

1. "The Negro Artist and the Racial Mountain," *Nation* 122 (June 23, 1926), 694.
2. James Weldon Johnson, *Along This Way* (New York: Viking Press, 1933), pp. 160–61.

3. Rayford Logan, *The Negro in American Life and Thought: The Nadir, 1877–1901* (New York: Dial Press, 1954), pp. 310–16.
4. Edward Margolies, *Native Sons: A Critical Study* (Philadelphia: Lippincott, 1968), pp. 29–30.
5. Benjamin Brawley, *Paul Laurence Dunbar: Poet of His People* (Chapel Hill: Univ. of North Carolina Press, 1936), p. 77.
6. *Ibid.*, pp. 76–77.
7. Lida Keck Wiggins, *The Life and Works of Paul Laurence Dunbar* (Naperville, Ill.: J.L. Nichols & Company, 1907), p. 75.
8. Vernon Loggins, *The Negro Author, His Development in America* (New York: Columbia Univ. Press, 1931), p. 316.
9. Hugh Gloster, *Negro Voices in American Fiction* (Chapel Hill: Univ. of North Carolina Press, 1948), p. 47; Robert Bone, *The Negro Novel in America* (New Haven: Yale Univ. Press, 1958), p. 30.
10. Eugene Arden, "The Early Harlem Novel," *Phylon* 20 (1959), 25–31.
11. Carl Van Vechten, "Introduction," to James Weldon Johnson, *Autobiography of an Ex-Coloured Man* (New York and London: Alfred A. Knopf, 1944), p. vii.
12. Howard Mumford Jones, *Ideas in America* (Cambridge, Mass.: Harvard Univ. Press, 1945), p. 42.

Bert Bender

The Lyrical Short Fiction of Dunbar and Chesnutt

Paul Laurence Dunbar and Charles W. Chesnutt were among the first to find "all but irreconcilable" the American Negro writer's "war between his social and artistic responsibilities," as James Baldwin has put it.[1] Struggling to maintain a balance between these responsibilities, Dunbar and Chesnutt responded differently in their fiction because their experiences and their temperaments were different. Chesnutt's "war" was far more socially aware and militant than Dunbar's. But to say of Dunbar that he sought "to amuse rather than to arouse his audience" badly misrepresents his artistic achievement.[2] He had—as do all writers—far more options open to him than simply to amuse or to arouse. In some of their short stories, at least, Dunbar and Chesnutt opted similarly by choosing to approach their material lyrically. They were engaged in another felt but undeclared "war" that was primarily artistic: Dunbar and, to a lesser extent, Chesnutt, were clearly in tune with other serious writers of the day who resisted the restrictive demands of the popular "Short-story" form in order to express themselves lyrically.

The model for the "Short-story" form of the late nineteenth century was taken directly from Poe's theory about the short prose tale. In "The Philosophy of Composition" (1846), Poe held that the writer of tales must keep "the *dénouement* constantly in view" in order to "give a plot its indispensable air of consequence, or causation"; and in 1884 Brander Matthews held similar views in his essay of a similar title, "The Philosophy of the Short-story" ("'Short-story' with a 'Capital S' and a hyphen [in order] to emphasize the distinction between the Short-story and the story which is merely short").[3] Poe's ideal tale would be composed, he had said, "with the precision and rigid consequence of a mathematical problem," and it is this idea that seems most to have fascinated editors and critics in the late nineteenth century. The form, with its machinelike precision, was taken to be peculiarly American. It was both manufacturable and teachable; indeed, as F. L. Pattee has noted in his history of the American short story, "by the later 'nineties the short story had become so established an article of merchandise that the production of it became a recognized industry with numberless workers." [4] The "Short-story" was required first, of course, to be of a certain marketable length (as James learned from his editors' "dull view [that] a 'short story' was a 'short story,' and that was the end of it. Shades and differences, varieties and styles, the value above all of the idea happily *developed*, languished, to extinction, under the hard-and-fast rule of 'from six to eight thousands words' " [5]). But mainly it was required to have "originality, ingenuity, compression," and, above all, plot.[6] With an eye always to plot and denouement, writers produced stories like Frank Stockton's famous riddle, "The Lady or the Tiger?" (1882, later a model of the "Short-story"); but O. Henry finally outdid them all by perfecting his famous ending with a twist.

Once you got the trick of it, there was no problem. By the end of the century, production was up and the formal dogma was itself a highly marketable product in the form of handbooks on how to write and sell short stories. But before the form had culminated in successful mass production at the hands of O. Henry, it was first blessed and used by some of the chief defenders of genteel literary values in America—Matthews himself, and his models, Thomas B. Aldrich, Frank Stockton, and H. C. Bunner. These men used the form sometimes playfully, sometimes piously, but the prevailing tone in their stories was of light comedy: as Matthews emphasized, the "Short-story," with its "brevity and brilliancy," was more like "*vers de société*" than anything else.[7]

The genteel, comic realism of the "Short-story" distinguishes it from the lyrical short fiction of such writers as James, Crane, Jewett, and frequently, Dunbar. Though the lyrical stories of these writers were then considered to be minor achievements, we value them today because their seriousness, their tragic sense, places them well within what we now see as the mainstream. As H. S. Canby wrote in 1901, "the Short Story was adapted to the needs of the time and the tastes of the people"; [8] but the needs and the tastes then, as determined primarily in the market place, were for crisp and efficient affirmation of prevailing values, rather than for lyrical expressions of such culturally isolated characters as James's lonely artists or, especially, of Dunbar's and Chesnutt's blacks. The "Short-story" was particularly suited to, and was the embodiment of, the complacent reiteration of American values which held that business enterprises and machines—and by extension, marketable, machinelike art—could bring a kind of progress. As Canby concluded in 1901, "Men of genius found through [the short story] a new voice, and the attempt to perfect, to give laws and a form to the instrument, progressed because of the men who tried." [9]

Foremost among the writers of lyrical short stories between the late eighties and 1910 were Henry James, Stephen Crane, and Sarah Orne Jewett. While these writers are in most ways worlds apart, they are alike in that, in their best stories, they approach their material with a lyrical attitude. In the lyrical stories by these writers, the author, a narrator, or a central character attempts to contend with something larger than himself—perhaps a god, a mystic, transcendent sense, or simply a sense of his own helplessness. And, feeling the futility or inappropriateness of a reasoned response or of a conventional fictional attempt to understand his situation, he responds lyrically, in a way like that of Emily Dickinson who, in coping with her "terror," found that her response was to "sing, as the Boy does by the Burying Ground, because I am afraid." [10] The "singer" in such a situation is alone; the lyric mode is basically tragic. As Northrop Frye has suggested, the lyricist turns "his back on his audience"; [11] he tends to abandon what Frye calls "discursive" or "continuous prose" rhythm—a characteristic of conventional, realistic prose fiction—in favor of the essentially alogical and lyrical "rhythm of association." [12]

The lyrical short stories in America between the late eighties and 1910, then, are not simply stories marked by "poetic" language; they are fictions which, deriving from a tragic sense of isolation, emphasize the "singer's" emotional awareness rather than the development of plot. The lyrical writer's effort during this period is typically to seek consolation either by expressing his emotional comprehension of his situation or by projecting a fictional or hoped for solution to his troubles. Some notable examples of this kind of fiction in Dunbar's time are James's stories of life-renouncing artists or of such tragic egotists as John Marcher in "The Beast in the Jungle"; Stephen Crane's "The Open Boat," in which the intense lyrical center of the story is reached when, "to chime the notes of his emotion, a verse mysteriously entered the correspondent's head"—the verse about "a soldier of the Legion who lay dying in Algiers"; or Sarah Orne Jewett's elegiac idylls about the lonely people around Dunnett Landing in *The Country of the Pointed Firs.*

Dunbar is usually remembered as "the first Negro poet to win national recognition and full acceptance in America." [13] William Dean Howells's review of Dunbar's *Majors and Minors* (1895) served as the pronouncement from the established white literary community that "here was the first instance of an American Negro who had evinced innate distinction in literature." [14] In his introduction to Dunbar's next collection of poems, *Lyrics of Lowly Life* (1896), Howells emphasized (in, from the perspective of the 1970s, an oddly condescending way) his preference for Dunbar's dialect poems, remarking that they "best preserved and most charmingly suggested" the "precious difference of temperament between the races which it would be a great pity to lose." [15] Howells goes on to express his appreciation of Dunbar's "finely comical perception of the Negro's limitations, with a tenderness for them which I think so rare as to be almost quite new" and to predict (with unfortunate accuracy) that "this humorous quality which Mr. Dunbar had added to our literature . . . would most distinguish him, now and hereafter" (p. xvii). To have been recognized in this way by the American literati was a financial help but an artistic restriction; for Dunbar wanted most to be remembered for his poetry in standard English, while he had to yield to the public demand for songs and for readings of his dialect poems. He went on, however, after *Lyrics of Lowly Life,* to publish four volumes of short stories and four novels. He depicted in his work, and he undeniably *had*, more faces than that of the smiling, humble, benevolently enslaved black. Perhaps the best comment on critical assessments which treat him as Howells did or as later critics have (who have disapproved of Dunbar's lack of militance) is his own poem "We Wear the Mask." Ironically, it is included in the volume which Howells introduced.

It is true that even in his fiction Dunbar often romanticizes plantation life in the South, as is suggested by the titles to three of his volumes of stories, *Folks from Dixie, In Old Plantation Days,* and *The Heart of Happy Hollow*. But this tendency in Dunbar is what Robert Hemenway has called his "interest in the pastoral idyll (and its antithesis, an evil, threatening city)"; his romanticizing "suggests that he was as much a victim of popular American mythology as his white countrymen. As a result, his fiction becomes a curious blend of white myths and black stereotypes, muted black protest and indirect white injustice."[16]

But alongside his broadly humorous and—from the point of view of his white audience—harmless stories in dialect, Dunbar published stories which were more directly expressive of the emotional discontent in black America. These stories are informed by a lyric impulse—Dunbar's dream of freedom and equality for his people—and the impulse arises in reaction to various kinds of real oppression. There are stories about white oppression in the South (as in "The Ingrate" and "The Lynching of Jube Benson"), stories—in keeping with literary interests of the day—about economic oppression (as in "Jimsella" and "At Shaft 11"), and stories about oppressive superstitions and political struggles within the black community (as in "The Scapegoat" and "The Faith Cure Man"). These stories frequently attain a lyrical intensity by portraying the emotional light and dark of the black world, or by evoking the underlying, prayerful mood which is characteristic of much of our early black literature. Such a mood in Dunbar gives rise—as in his poem "Sympathy," in which he speaks of a singing caged bird—not to

> . . . a carol of joy or glee,
> But a prayer that he sends from his heart's deep core,

> But a plea, that upward to Heaven he flings—
> I know why the caged bird sings!

"Anner 'Lizer's Stumblin' Block" is one of Dunbar's stories that is set on a plantation but which focuses on a problem within the black community itself—the severely moralistic restrictions of evangelical religion. Only in the opening paragraphs is the black-white relationship mentioned, and then its function is to emphasize the darkness of the blacks' religion rather than to suggest either an oppressive or benevolent master-slave relationship:

> It was winter. The gray old mansion of Mr. Robert Selfridge, of Fayette County, Ky., was wrapped in its usual mantle of winter somberness, and the ample plantation stretching in every direction thereabout was one level plain of unflecked whiteness. At a distance from the house the cabins of the Negroes stretched away in a long, broken black line that stood out in bold relief against the extreme whiteness of their surroundings.

In this setting, Anner 'Lizer, the acknowledged belle of the estate, is contrasted to her lover, Sam Merritt. He is natural and physical, and he is an "unconscious but pronounced skeptic"; she, however, is religious, and, as the story proceeds, she becomes "more and more possessed by religious fervor." At the Baptist revival, "the weirdness of the scene and the touch of mysticism in the services" move her nearly to religious ecstasy. Though she prays both to keep Sam and to "get religion," she and Sam become separated. The mystical black religion is a barrier between Anner and Sam; she is required to deny her sexual being until she can publicly display her religious enthusiasm. Finally, after having been able neither to attract Sam nor to experience religious ecstasy, she is allowed to achieve both. She is reunited with Sam one night when she finds him alone in the woods, away from the strangely oppressive influence of the revival. Then, as a result of the consummation of her love with Sam, she finally "set the whole place afire by getting religion at home early the next morning." The ending is ironic; for, though the church had told her that Sam was her stumbling block to getting religion, "the minister announced that 'de Lawd had foun' out de sistah's stumblin' block an' removed it f'om de path.'" The story, then, is based on a struggle between oppressive religious fervor and natural, physical drives. It is impressive in its handling of Anner's psychology, but it is also impressive in the way it vividly dramatizes the fervor of the revival meeting and captures in the rhythmical dialect the strange mixture of fear, ecstasy, and incantation:

> Earnestly he besought the divine mercy in behalf of "de po' sinnahs, a-rollin' an' a-tossin' in de tempes' of dere sins. Lawd," he prayed, "come down dis evenin' in Sperit's powah to seek an' to save-ah; let us heah de rumblin' of yo' cha'iot wheels-ah lak de thundah f'om Mount Sinai-ah; oh, Lawd'ah, convert mou'nahs an' convict sinnahs-ah; show 'em dat dey mus' di an' cain't lib an' atter death to judg-a-ment; tu'n 'em aroun' befo' it is evahlastin' an' eternally too late." Then, warming more and more, and swaying his form back and forth, as he pounded the seat in emphasis, he began to wail out in a sort of indescribable monotone: "O Lawd, save de mou'nah!"
>
> "Save de mou'nah!" came the response from all over the church.
>
> "He'p 'em out of de miah an' quicksan's of dere sins!"
>
> "He'p, Lawd!"
>
> "And place deir feet upon de evahlastin' an' eternal rock-ah!"
>
> "Do, Lawd!"
>
> "O Lawd-ah shake a dyin' sinnah ovah hell an' fo'bid his mighty fall-ah!"
>
> "O Lawd, shake 'em!" came from the congregation.
>
> By this time every one was worked up to a high state of excitement, and the prayer came to an end amid great commotion. Then a rich, mellow voice led out with:
>
> "Sabe de mou'nah jes' now,
> Sabe de mou'nah jes' now,
> Sabe de mou'nah jes' now,
> Only trust Him jes' now,
> Only trust Him jes' now,
> He'p de sinnah jes' now;"
>
> and so to indefinite length the mournful minor melody ran along like a sad brook flowing through autumn woods, trying to laugh and ripple through tears.

Though Anner began "to sway backward and forward like a sapling in the wind, and she began to mourn and weep aloud," she couldn't get religion. But the natural attraction that finally brings Anner and Sam together has its mystery, too. In what is a kind of symbolic dialectic, Dunbar depicts the reunion of Anner and Sam by completing the story's pattern of contrasted light and dark. Praying alone in the woods, Anner cried "aloud from the very fullness of her heart, 'O Lawd, sen' de light—sen' de light,'" and "as if in answer to her prayer, a light appeared before her." Remembering the church song "Let us walk in de light," she struggled through the darkness toward the light: "How it flickered and flared, disappeared and reappeared, rose and fell, even as her spirits, as she stumbled and groped her way over fallen logs and through briers." Anner finally breaks through to a clearing to find Sam, who is carrying a lighted taper which he is using to catch a treed coon. The story ends on an odd note of mixed allegory, comedy, and irony. Though Dunbar treats the restrictive Baptist religion ironically, he sees its undeniable hold on the people, for Anner returns to the church: life on the plantation remains pretty much the same. The tone of the story is like the "mournful minor melody" that Dunbar described in the revival meeting; like "a sad brook flowing through autumn woods," it tries "to laugh and ripple through tears."

In the better of his two stories of lynchings, "The Lynching of Jube Benson," Dunbar treats the problem of racial injustice in an effective, indirect way—from the perspective of a white man who has taken part in a lynching. As the white man tells his story, it becomes clear that he is one who Dunbar optimistically imagines to have awakened from the world's dream that he speaks of in "We Wear the Mask." By focusing on obsessive images in the mind of the white man, Dr. Melville, Dunbar brings out the psychological reality of Dr. Melville's horror over having lynched an innocent man. As the doctor prepares to tell his story, he gazes "abstractedly into the fire," and then begins, "I can see it all very vividly now." The story unfolds, then, in a series of intense recollections that crescendo in the doctor's mind until he repeats at the end, "something kept crying in my ears, 'Blood guilty! Blood guilty!'"

Dr. Melville had fallen in love with his landlord's daughter, Annie, and he had been assisted in his courtship of Annie by the black handyman, Jube Benson, who became a loyal friend of the doctor. As the doctor tells his story, it becomes apparent that even now he is not completely free of the "false education" by which he tries to account for his guilt: It was "a false education, I reckon, one false from the beginning." For, ironically, Dunbar has him recall how Jube had been "a perfect Cerberus" in keeping other suitors from Annie. Then, recalling how he had fallen ill and how Jube had cared for him in his sickness, he describes the dream-like "chimerical vision" he had of Jube. In his "fight with death" he had seen "only a black but gentle demon that came and went, alternating with a white fairy, who would insist on coming in on her head, growing larger and larger and then dissolving." Prepared, then, by his false education, he had seen, as he recalls—after Annie had been murdered and after the suspected Jube had been trailed down—Jube's "black face glooming there in the half light, and I could only think of him as a monster." Despite Jube's pleas in "the saddest voice" the doctor had ever heard, he was lynched by the mob. The doctor's vivid recollection haunts him:

> Hungry hands were ready. We hurried him out into the yard. A rope was ready. A tree was at hand. Well, that part was the least of it, save that Hiram Daly stepped aside to let me be the first to pull upon the rope. It was lax at first. Then it tightened, and I felt the quivering soft weight resist my muscles. Other hands joined, and Jube swung off his feet.
>
> No one was masked. We knew each other. Not even the culprit's face was covered, and the last I remember of him as he went into the air was a look of sad reproach that will remain with me until I meet him face to face again.

The lynchers learn too late that they have lynched the wrong man and that Annie had been murdered by a white man whose face was "blackened to imitate a Negro's." Realizing what he has done, Dr. Melville gasps, "God Forgive me," but it is, of course, too late. Examining the skin under the dead girl's fingernails to find proof, he reads his "own doom" when he sees that the skin is white. With the cry ringing in his ears, "Blood guilty! Blood guilty!", he helplessly respects Jube's brother's fierce refusal to be helped home with the body. The story ends with the doctor sitting silently with his head in his hands and then rising to say, "Gentlemen, that was my last lynching." But Dunbar does not give us a naïvely optimistic ending. Rather, the tone is of qualified hope or prayer that the situation might improve. Though Dr. Melville appears to have unlearned much of his "false education," we see that his thinking is still slightly infected. The hope is that the men to whom Dr. Melville tells his story will be moved emotionally to see the injustice of their system. Dr. Melville tells his story in Gordon Fairfax's library, where a group of men have been discussing a recent lynching, and after one man has callously said, "I should like to see a real lynching." The scene implies that education and reasoning, alone, will not solve the problem. Something else is needed, like Dr. Melville's confessional display of his emotions. Dunbar's story, then, is operative in several ways; it is a *cri de coeur,* yet it is an effort to show the way; it is a longing dream of improvement, yet the dream is highly qualified; and, like Dunbar's "caged bird's song," it is a lyric plea to a higher power.

A lyric poet before he was a writer of fiction, Dunbar attained a full-blown lyricism in his short fiction. But the situation was different with Charles Waddell Chesnutt. Chesnutt's temperament led him into active concern with the racial problem, as a teacher, newspaperman, and lawyer. In his fiction he had constantly to contend with his anger. So while his short fiction does not resemble many popular "Short-stories" in tone, subject matter, or form, neither does it resemble the open lyricism of Dunbar's. Chesnutt's short stories sometimes have lyrical tendencies, but in them the lyric impulse is always muted.

Writing of Chesnutt's second novel, *The Marrow of Tradition* (1901), William Dean Howells said that, "like everything else he has written, [it] has to do with the relations of the blacks and whites, and in that republic of letters where all men are free and equal he stands up for his own people with courage which has more justice than mercy in it. The book is, in fact, bitter, bitter. There is no reason in history why it should not be so, if wrong is to be repaid with hate, and yet it would be better if it were not so bitter." [17] Chesnutt objected to Howells's attitude, and he wrote his publishers, Houghton Mifflin & Company, "My friend, Mr. Howells, who has said many nice things about my writings—although his review of *The Marrow of Tradition* in the *North Amer-*

ican Review for December was not a favorable one as I look at it—has remarked several times that there is no color line in literature. On that point I take issue with him. I am pretty fairly convinced that the color line runs everywhere so far as the United States is concerned."[18] It is easy to see why Chesnutt would object to Howells's remarks, for Howells scarcely suggests that he comprehends the immense aesthetic problems faced by the pioneer black writer. Chesnutt had to cope with his overwhelming sense of racial injustice; yet he had chosen to write for the general American audience. In order to keep his fiction from exploding into caustic propaganda, he learned to control his potentially explosive material with either a humorous or a kind of hard-boiled treatment. He first took the humorous approach in *The Conjure Woman* (1895), in which he ingeniously reworked the humorous and nostalgic Plantation Tradition. His black storyteller in this collection of stories, Uncle Julius, is, with his amusing dialect, like Uncle Remus. But Uncle Julius is very shrewd; he invariably gets the best of the whites in these stories, demonstrating their gullibility and lack of common sense. He is good-natured, but from behind his mask he has a firm control over his world. As with Dunbar and his dialect poems, Chesnutt was encouraged to write more of these "conjure" stories, for they were light, harmless, amusing.

The bitterness of which Howells complained is present below the surface in the "conjure" stories, and it becomes darker in Chesnutt's three novels. After 1905—discouraged by such developments as the disenfranchisement of blacks in the South, race riots in the North, and, later, mistreatment of black soldiers during World War I—his direct work with the race problem helped displace his efforts in fiction. However, his bitterness had begun to surface in 1895, in *The Wife of His Youth.* The stories in this volume treat the problem of prejudice within the black community—of light for darker people, for instance—even as they treat the ever-present problem of Southern prejudice and brutality. The tone of the stories set within the black community is either ironic (as in "A Matter of Principle") or sentimental and tragic (as in "The Wife of His Youth"); and the tone of the other stories is tragic (as in "The Bouquet" or "The Web of Circumstance").

In any case, the stories in this volume are different from the "conjure" stories (and similar to the novels which followed) in that they present powerfully emotional situations with a firmly set jaw. Chestnutt tells his stories in a way that resembles the response of Ben Davis, the falsely accused black in "The Web of Circumstance": "In the stolidity with which he received this sentence for a crime which he had not committed, spoke who knows what trait of inherited savagery? For stoicism is a savage virtue." [19] The quietness of such a response is—as F. O. Matthiessen has said of similarly stoic replies by characters in the stories of Mary Wilkins Freeman—"deafening." [20]

Working from this stance, Chesnutt seldom breaks into open lyrical expression. His social realism is deadly serious and purposeful. He said of *The Wife of His Youth* that "it was written with the distinct hope that it might have its influence in directing attention to certain aspects of the race question which are quite familiar to those on the unfortunate side of it." [21] Yet the stories have an underlying urgency which, controlled though they may be, occasionally reaches lyrical intensity. There are such moments, for instance, in "The Bouquet," in which Sophy, a young black girl, is prevented, because she is black, from placing her bouquet on the grave of the white teacher whom she idolizes. And, typically, characters in such stories have dreams of improved conditions and happier lives only to have their dreams turn to nightmares of reality, in which they remain black and abused. In "Cicely's Dream," [22] for example, Cicely has a vague but vivid dream of a happier life: "She had dreamed a beautiful dream. The fact that it was a beautiful dream, a delightful dream, her memory retained very vividly," but she couldn't recall it exactly. She could only enjoy the "memory of it in a vague, indefinite, and tantalizing way." The dream is an effort to transcend her blackness, and, tantalizingly, it is nearly realized in her relationships with her mulatto lover and her white teacher. But in the end, she is alone; for her teacher and her lover discover that they are lovers who had been separated by the war. Her dream turns to darkness, for it "had been one of the kind that go by contraries."

Even though Chesnutt's mulatto characters dream tragically of being whiter, and even though his blacks' dreams often turn to nightmares, there is an underlying sense of hope in some of his short fiction that gives rise to a pervasively prayerful mood, like that in Dunbar. The impulse from which these stories issues is contained in the paragraph with which he concludes "The Web of Circumstance":

> Some time, we are told, when the cycle of years has rolled around, there is to be another golden age, when all men will dwell together in love and harmony, and when peace and righteousness shall prevail for a thousand years. God speed the day, and let not the shining thread of hope become so enmeshed in the web of circumstance that we lose sight of it; but give us here and there, now and then, some little foretaste of this golden age, that we may more patiently await its coming!

These are Chesnutt's last words in *The Wife of His Youth* (1899), his last collected short fiction. From 1900 until 1905 he wrote three novels in which, as Robert Bone complains, "he became an overt propagandist, to the detriment of his art." [23] Then, as an artist, he became altogether silent. In his short fiction he had struggled with his anger, managing to control it first with irony and then—like his character, Ben Davis—with quiet stolidity. Chesnutt's active efforts in behalf of his race were effective; and even his eventual silence as a writer has, today, a kind of resonant eloquence—as profound as the final unabashed silent gaze of Babo in Melville's "Benito Cereno."

Both Dunbar and Chesnutt struggled against the mechanical formula fiction which prevailed during the time they were writing—Dunbar by lyricism and Chesnutt by irony. They thus not only helped to alter the social attitudes of their audience, they began to undermine the assumptions of the "Short-story." Like Henry James, even as they began to see the nature of society more clearly, they undertook to create a new aesthetics by which to represent that world, and they helped to usher in a new kind of short story.

NOTES

1. Baldwin in a review of poems by Langston Hughes. Quoted here by Nat Henthoff in a radio discussion entitled "The Negro in American

Culture," in *The Black American Writer, vol. I: Fiction*, ed. C. W. E. Bigsby (Deland, Florida: Everett/Edwards, 1969), pp. 79–108.

2. Robert Bone, *The Negro Novel in America* (New Haven: Yale Univ. Press, 1958), p. 39.
3. Brander Matthews, "The Philosophy of the Short Story," *Lippincott's Monthly Magazine* (October 1885). Quoted here from Matthews's *The Philosophy of the Short Story* (New York: Longmans, Green & Co., 1901), p. 25. Reprinted in part in *What Is the Short Story?*, eds. E. Current-Garcia and W. R. Patrick (Chicago: Scott, Foresman & Co., 1961), pp. 36–41.
4. F. L. Pattee, *The Development of the American Short Story* (New York: Harper & Row, 1923), p. 337.
5. "Preface" to *The Lesson of the Master*, vol. 15: *The Novels and Tales of Henry James* (*New York Edition:* Charles Scribner's Sons, 1909), p. viii.
6. Matthews, *The Philosophy of the Short Story*, p. 30.
7. *Ibid.*, pp. 29–30.
8. Henry Seidel Canby, "On The Short Story," *Dial* 31 (October 16, 1901), 273. Reprinted in Current-Garcia and Patrick, *What is the Short Story?*
9. *Ibid.*, p. 273. In fairness to Canby, it should be noted that he came gradually to modify this view. In 1915 he called for free short fiction, and he hoped that "the form, the *formula*, will relax its grip upon the short story." See Canby's "Free Fiction," originally in *Atlantic Monthly* 116 (July 1915), reprinted in Current-Garcia and Patrick, *What Is the Short Story?*, pp. 59–69.
10. Emily Dickinson in her second letter to T. W. Higginson, in *The Letters of Emily Dickinson*, ed. Thomas Johnson and Theodora Ward (Cambridge: Belknap Press of Harvard Univ. Press, 1958), vol. II, p. 404.
11. Northrop Frye, *Anatomy of Criticism: Four Essays* (Princeton: Princeton Univ. Press, 1957), p. 271.
12. Frye's terms in his entry "Verse and Prose," in *Encyclopedia of Poetry and Poetics*, ed. Alex Preminger (Princeton: Princeton Univ. Press, 1965), pp. 885–90.
13. From editor Abraham Chapman's biographical note on Dunbar in *Black Voices* (New York: New American Library, 1968), p. 354.
14. Howells had said this in his first review of Dunbar, as he recalls here in his introduction to Dunbar's *Lyrics of Lowly Life* (New York: Dodd, Mead & Company, 1896), p. xvi.
15. *Ibid.*, pp. xvii–xviii.
16. *The Black Novelist*, ed. Robert Hemenway (Columbus, Ohio: Ohio State Univ. Press, 1970), p. 34.
17. Quoted in Helen M. Chesnutt, *Charles Waddell Chesnutt, Pioneer of the Color Line* (Chapel Hill: Univ. of North Carolina Press, 1952), p. 177.

18. *Ibid.*, p. 147.
19. *The Wife of His Youth and Other Stories of the Color Line* (Ann Arbor: Univ. of Michigan Press, 1968), p. 313.
20. "New England Stories," in *American Writers on American Literature*, ed. John Macy (New York: Horace Liveright, 1934), p. 408.
21. Chesnutt, *Charles Waddell Chesnutt*, p. 129.
22. In *The Wife of His Youth.*
23. Bone, *The Negro Novel in America*, p. 38.

PAUL LAURENCE DUNBAR: 1872–1906

One hundred years of headrags, bandages,
a plantation tradition gone sour;
in the smokehouse of Newport, RI
is the knotted metaphor collapsed in foyer,
Miss Ann finally understanding the elevator
where you sang your standard
imperfect lyrics.

Minstrel and mask:
a landscape of speech and body
burned in verbal space,
the match cinder unstandard:
double-conscious brother in the veil–
double-conscious brother in the veil–
double-conscious brother in the veil–

Michael S. Harper

–(written on the 100th anniversary
of his birth, in continuum, in modality)–

IV

HISTORICAL

Gossie H. Hudson

The Crowded Years: Paul Laurence Dunbar in History[1]

"Down these roads they came . . . as drained as the sand on their feet. But white. God-white and immaculate . . . white as Jesus . . . once more to put the nigger in his place. And sometimes there was laughter, or drawled words of voices not unkind in sound and now without humor; but eyes were hard and hating as they hunted a black victim to sacrifice to an unknown god of whom they were sore afraid." [2] Lillian Smith's lament of the 1940s might just as well be written about the turn of the twentieth century.

Accounts printed in the daily press show that 1,665 blacks were lynched in the decade ending 1900. James Weldon Johnson wrote that "numbers of them were lynched with a savagery that was . . . nothing short of torture, mutilation and burning alive at the stake." [3] Indiana and Mississippi mobs had alike been lynching innocent blacks. Such horrible occurrences gave Paul Laurence Dunbar a theme for a strong poem of hostility, "The Haunted Oak."

The ballad is the wail of an oak tree on which an innocent victim has been hanged by a mob. Mayor Brand Whitlock, a white "Progressive" and patron from Toledo, Ohio, criticized the poet's usage of the word "innocence" in the verse:

> From those who ride fast on our heels
> With mind to do him wrong:
> They have no care for his innocence,
> And the rope they bear is long.

Dunbar defended his choice of nouns, indicating that had "innocence been left out, . . . it would have destroyed our element of dramatic powers . . . our feeling at a crime committed against a criminal is never so deep as that of one injustice done to any innocent man."[4]

Even uglier than lynching is the fact that in a number of instances the black victim was hanged merely because of the color of his skin. In a collection of short stories by Dunbar, a story entitled "The Lynching of Jube Benson" indicated the murder of an innocent black. In the story, after the lynching of Jube the mob left. This gave the protagonist not only the opportunity of trying to resuscitate Jube, but also time to inspect the body of the rape victim: "Carefully, carefully, I searched underneath her broken finger nails. There was skin there. I took it out, the little curled pieces. . . . It was the skin of a white man, and in it were embedded strands of short, brown hair or beard." A "white ruffian" had committed the crime and had smeared his face with dirt "to imitate a Negro's."

At the beginning of the twentieth century not many voices were raised in defense of the rights of black people as citizens of the United States. Both Northerners and Southerners had abandoned Reconstruction, and reactionary attitudes joined with the triumph of imperialism in the Spanish-American War. For example, Thomas Wentworth Higginson, former devout abolitionist, commander of a black regiment and founder of a school for blacks in Alabama, contended that giving the suffrage to all blacks as a class was a mistake; and that no white community would ever consent to the political supremacy of black people.[5]

Rayford Logan called this new century the "nadir," a lowest point shaped by racism and violence, and the solidification of disenfranchisement and segregation.[6] The period saw the new imperialism and the jingoism of James G. Blaine, and it also observed immigrant restrictions, condoned race riots, and increased lynchings. On January 20, 1900, George W. White, black Representative from North Carolina, introduced the first bill to make lynching a federal crime. The bill died in committee, and 105 blacks were lynched that year.[7] Samuel Eliot Morison labeled the age "the most lawless . . . that America had ever known."[8] The 1890s was mired in discriminatory laws and practices, none of the reforms had much meaning for the minority groups, and segregation was declared constitutional.

That blacks could have accomplished anything noteworthy during this decade, the worst period for "other Americans," is difficult to conceive; but a few did endure and accomplish much. The black professional class included 21,267 teachers; 1,734 doctors; 212 dentists; and 52 architects, designers, draftsmen, and inventors. Approximately twenty-four percent of American blacks owned their own homes. There were four black banks; and Charles P. Graves, president of Gold Leaf Consolidated Company of Montana and Illinois, a mining company, reported his property at a value of one million. He was the first black millionaire.[9]

By 1900 there had been over twelve hundred black writers of pamphlets and books. The early writers began in areas like Philadelphia, Boston, New York, Baltimore, and Washington. Of particular interest is the pamphlet literature, since it shows to what extent black people became thinkers and scholars in days when it was a crime to teach blacks to read and write. These souls without a country and without favor not only became educated, but what they wrote contributed greatly to the political, religious, and social questions of the day. How to destroy slavery and bring freedom and equality to the enslaved was the burden of most of the first black authors. After the passage of the Thirteenth Amendment, a number of blacks gained fame as contributors to American history. Among these were George Washington Williams, Bishop Daniel A. Payne, J. Cooper, Booker T. Washington, W. E. B. Du Bois; the literary productions of Dunbar and Charles W. Chesnutt represented contributions to literature at the end of the 1890s.

Living under the new consequences of the Reconstruction era, Dunbar sometimes forgot his real existence. His other existence was within an imagination where he, like other romantic poets, satisfied his hunger for the sentimental. There his thoughts were unshackled, and his imagination could play with time and space, shaping the superficiality of the plantation epoch. Even in his own day militant blacks criticized Dunbar's caricatures, but the whites enjoyed literature in the "shadow of the plantation." Some of the blacks did too!

His age was strange, puzzling, corrupt, and passing through the twin revolutions of industrialism and science. For all the corruption of the period and the ugliness of a new industrial complex, it was nonetheless a robust, fearless, generous era, full of gusto, joy, and living.[10] In the poet's home, Dayton, Ohio, lived a generation luxuriating in unblushing pretense, in a time of false fronts of artificial protuberances, and of light speech and mannerisms. Charlotte Conover, Dayton historian, called the era "a decade of beginnings"—gay, sentimental, romantic.[11] This burst of romanticism, mixed with the realism of the times, coalesced into the birth of the new century, and in it, Dunbar achieved fame and distinction. Yet despite the success of a black poet, it was not a satisfactory time for his people in America.

One hundred years ago, Paul Laurence Dunbar was born black and poor, and he was born in America. Therefore, he was born to troubles and hardships and cruel conditions and restrictions which no white child, however handicapped by poverty and ignorance and crime, can ever experience. Yet he sang his song with a passion and pathos, with racial concern, and with a humor and melody altogether his own.[12]

On several occasions in the late 1890s, he was asked to write an autobiography. In almost every instance, he began by relating that his life was uneventful and "that there is little in it to interest anyone." [13] In response to a letter written to him by a Mrs. A. S. Lanahan in 1898, Dunbar mentioned that he was born at Dayton, Ohio, twenty-five years earlier. He attended the common schools there and was graduated from Dayton High School. "This," he said, "constituted my education." About his parents, he intimated that they had been slaves in Kentucky, and that his grandparents had been slaves on the eastern shore of Maryland. He told Mrs. Lanahan that he began writing early, when about twelve, but published nothing until he was fourteen. "Then the fever took me," he exclaimed, "and I wrote ream upon ream of positive trash when I should have been studying English." These included plays, verses, and stories—but, he added, he seldom tried to publish. The poet remembered that his school life was pleasant. He was the only black fellow in his class and was apparently popular with his teachers and school chums. He was made president of the literary Philomathean Society, and afterwards elected editor-in-chief of the school paper. Continuing with his life story, Dunbar stated that after graduation there was nothing for him to do but find menial employment, just as other Negroes did.[14]

His first published poetry collection, *Oak and Ivy,* appeared in 1893. About that time Dunbar began reading from his own work throughout the Midwest. During the 1893 Chicago World's Fair, he was employed in the Haytian Building by Frederick Douglass. About this time, also, he also turned his energies to journalism, working on the Chicago *Record* as well as on several Ohio papers. Later, he assumed editorial charge of the Indianapolis *World.*

His second book of poems, *Majors and Minors,* was published in 1895. The edition was nearly exhausted when a favorable review by William Dean Howells in *Harper's Weekly* helped him to attract a larger audience and led to the republication of the first two books as one, *Lyrics of Lowly Life.*[15]

In February 1897, his advisers sent him to England to read, where he remained for six months, and returning, took a place in the Library of Congress, Washington, D. C. *Folks from Dixie* was published and *The Uncalled* followed in the May issue of *Lippincott's* magazine. To his mentor and patron, Colonel R. G. Ingersoll, the author wrote: "From the depth of this the meanest, most unliterary time in America I send you a copy of my first long story, *The Uncalled.* Whether there be much or little to it, I mean all I say in it and mean it very much." [16]

He was married in Brooklyn, New York, on March 6, 1898, to Alice Ruth Moore, a teacher in one of the public schools of the city and a native of New Orleans, Louisiana.[17] In 1899, the author and his wife left Washington and journeyed to Colorado, where he settled at Harmon, a small town near Denver. There he was befriended by Major William Cooke Daniels, a young Denver merchant and millionaire. To him Dunbar dedicated his novel *The Love of Landry.* This novel was followed by a book of short stories, *The Strength of Gideon.*

The turn of the century saw the poet on the floodtide of success and prosperity. May of 1899 was like "a dream come true," according to Dunbar. The board of trustees of Atlanta University voted to confer upon him the honorary degree of Master of Arts.[18] At Tuskegee he gave a number of lectures on English composition before the two advanced classes of the school. On his return trip to Washington he read at other schools in the South, including schools in Atlanta and Nashville.[19]

In recognition of his distinction in literature, on January 15, 1900, Dunbar was invited to become a member of the Executive Council of the American Social Science Association.[20] By now, he was lionized wherever he went. There was a steady and welcome market demand on his pen and he was considered a successful magazine poet. American magazines reached the zenith of their popularity in this era. Mark Twain, Henry James, William Dean Howells, and most of the other leading writers submitted short stories to magazines for first publication, and even serialized their novels.[21] Several prominent magazines accepted Dunbar's stories, poems, and articles: the *Atlantic Monthly, Harper's Monthly,* and the *Century*, to name a few. As a platform reader, poet, novelist, and essayist, he was "a master sentimentalist who in the space of seven years secured a recognized standing among men of letters both home and abroad." [22] And he sustained this reputation.

I

Dunbar did not achieve his popularity through the sacrifice of his racial integrity, though he was not so outspokenly militant as those blacks who would walk barefooted to Niagara Falls, Canada, with W. E. B. Du Bois in June of 1905. He believed that the race problem would be solved "all the sooner if those interested in it will talk and write less and work more." He believed that "race prejudice will die in time," but he was not altogether satisfied with Washington's program: "I should have been very unhappy if condemned to follow a handicraft. Give the Negro thorough industrial training, and if any among them are able to get above this, let them do it." [23] Then too, the writings of Dunbar differed essentially from those by the Southern apologists. The black man in the hands of most white dialect writers was a subject for ridicule and served to document social notions about superior and inferior races. Thomas Nelson Page, Irvin Russell, and Joel Chandler Harris, for example, wrote black dialect verse or fiction that was an apology for slavery. Their works pictured the black man as docile and happy in servitude. However, Dunbar's productions achieved a measure of reality and genuine pathos and humor which other dialect writers did not delineate. His dialect pieces possessed a certain subtle flavor, a peculiar richness of tone which white authors had striven after, more or less unsuccessfully. Ironically, he grew to detest the dialect style that made him so famous. "I'm tired of dialect," he wrote to a friend, "but the magazines aren't. Everytime I send them something else they write back asking for dialect. A Dunbar just has to be dialect, that's all." Unfortunately, this kind of black minstrelsy hardened into the stereotypical speech and behavior of the black man. Moreover, the glee and jamboree songs of Dunbar became "coon songs" and "darkey" poetry in the hands of others. Consequently, many regarded the black man's medium of expression as limited. Dunbar sometimes fretted that people gave more attention to his jingle and less to his verses in standard poetry. He confessed to it in "The Poet":

> He sang of love when earth was young,
> And Love, itself, was in his lays.
> But ah, the world, it turned to praise
> A jingle in a broken tongue.

And he admonished a critic:

> Dear critic, who my lightness so deplores,
> Would I might study to be prince of bores,
> Right wisely would I rule that dull estate—
> But, sir, I may not, till you abdicate.

The period during which Dunbar wrote has been described as the age of triumphant enterprise, the age of robber barons, the Social Darwinist era, or the age of Washington. To some the century appeared as an uplifting time when industry boomed, capitalists grew rich, and the world was their oyster. But for others, American progress "was inevitably bound up in injustice and racism." [24] The poet was keenly aware of racism and freedom. The second-class citizenship accorded the Negro brought vehement denunciation from Dunbar. "Like a dark cloud pregnant with terror and destruction, disfranchisement has spread its wings over our brethren of the South," he wrote in 1903.[25] In an article on higher education he said that in the Northern cities, blacks had been crowded out of the many occupations held by immigrants; "it happened because prejudice preferred the alien to the citizen."

Dunbar called this "the prejudice of a narrow people which allowed it." [26] "We may not work save when the foreigner refuses to," he lamented.[27] No less concerned about Africa, the writer, in an undated essay, called for more missionary zeal among his people in the United States:

> It is especially toward Africa that the eyes and attention of the colored missionary should be turned and it is right and proper that this should be his chief field of labor abroad.[28]

And in another place, he sings of Ethiopia's glory. Defining the black leader in 1903, he judged, "To have achieved something for the betterment of his race rather than for the aggrandizement of himself, seems to be a man's best title to be called representative." [29] In a speech Dunbar praised the work that Washington had done for Tuskegee "down there in the Black Belt of the South where our own people are brothers and sisters and their children have so little opportunity for development along the best lines." [30]

Dunbar often called attention to the failings of of American democracy in many of his prose stories. Old Judge Davis in the story "The Scapegoat" exhibits the racism of the times: " 'Asbury,' " he said, " 'you are—you are—well, you ought to be white, that's all. When we find a black man like you we send him to State's prison. If you were white, you'd go to the Senate.' " Dunbar castigated the Republican Party for exploiting blacks in the story "Mr. Cornelius Johnson, Office Seeker." Having confronted consistent bureaucratic racism in his bid for a political office, Johnson finally lashed out: " 'Damn you. Damn you,' " he cried; " 'damn your deceit, your low cruelties, damn you, you hard white liar.' "

"Unless we live lives of protest, and few of us are willing to do that," he wrote Mayor Brand Whitlock, "we are as guilty as the lynchers of the South," "we are all tarred with the same stick." [31] Earlier, he indicated in his own newspaper, "You know well, that the Afro-American is not one to remain silent under oppression or even fancied oppression. When kicking is needed they know how to kick." [32] "But," he later added, "you know that some will persist in kicking a dog until he bites." [33]

In 1903, he protested against the race riots in Evansville, Belleville, and Wilmington. He stated the irony of the United States' sending a note of protest to Russia over the brutal treatment of prisoners at Kishineff while yet, even on Independence Day there existed in America injustice and prejudice, "and yet we celebrate." "And we have done it all because we have not stopped to think just how little it means to us." [34] The same year he spoke out against the industrial ideas of Booker T. Washington, seeing the danger of "educating the hand to the exclusion of the head." [35]

When Dunbar wrote *The Sport of the Gods* he presented a sensitive awareness of the relationship of the past to the present. In a letter to a Mrs. Lucy B. Robinson he wrote: "I hope you will see it and understand the sermon I have tried to preach." [36] This, the author's fourth novel, treats the problem of blacks in the Northern ghettos. The thesis of the book is that ill treatment of blacks in the South was no worse than what awaited them in the alleys of New York. In a way, the book is a protest novel speaking to the black man's condition in America. Charles Nilon says that the book is "a social history, a portrayal of the Black and White relationships in the late 19th century"; it is a clear prelude to sociological studies such as Gilbert Osofsky's *Harlem: The Making of a Ghetto* and Kenneth Clark's *Black Ghetto*.[37]

II

These crowded years in the early 1900s brought an unquenchable ambition which aided Dunbar in accomplishing an unbelievable amount of work. His life would be all too short, but he crowded into it all that was possible. Under great stress he persisted in producing stories, novels, poetry, and essays. Early in 1902, the poet and his gifted wife separated. Rifts and separations had followed one after the other and people talked publicly about Dunbar's treatment of Alice in public. The separation hurt him deeply. He sent telegrams and letters from New York and Boston and received no answer. He also wired a friend to ask Alice if she would see him at the Wilmington station. Her reply was no. "She is the cruelest person that God ever made and I hope never to make another advance to her. I have wasted my time and efforts," Dunbar wrote his mother.[38] In one poem after another he poured forth his tale of longing, gentle grief and sadness. Such poems as "The Monk's Walk" and "To a Violet Found on All Saints' Day" were all veiled with references to his personal problems with

Alice. Treating the situation lightly, on the other hand, he wrote "Jilted":

Lucy done gone back on me,
  Dat's de way wif life.
Evaht'ing was movin' free,
  T'ought I had my wife.
Den some dahky comes along,
Sings my gal a little song,
Since den, evaht'ing's gone wrong,
  Evah day dey's strife.

Dunbar's health declined considerably by 1904: "I have been very ill and glad to be here at home where good nursing and good air ought to do me good, but I am afraid I am not going to be allowed a chance to stay, as the doctors are crying California, California, even as before they cried Colorado." [39] Nevertheless, he was well enough to write a campaign poem of four stanzas for Theodore Roosevelt. (The President acknowledged the poem by sending Paul two volumes of his speeches inscribed, "To Paul Laurence Dunbar, with the regard of Teddy Roosevelt, November 2, 1904.") Unfortunately, though, he was a victim of pulmonary troubles. An attack of pneumonia turned into tuberculosis. Usually he disobeyed the doctors' advice and for a nightly bedtime snack he ate a raw onion with salt and drank a bottle of beer.[40] Sometimes his condition was relieved, but he was never cured.

Dunbar's excessive and daily consumption of whiskey and ale was one of the big problems in his short life. When faced with speaking engagements or a publisher's deadline, he bolstered his weakness by strong spirits. He came to depend upon liquor and beer. Some biographers claim that the quarrels and recriminations that developed between Dunbar and his wife were a result of his problems with alcohol.[41]

Dr. A. M. Curtis, the author's doctor, and other Washingtonians who knew Dunbar intimately, recalled that he had an ungovernable habit of drinking.[42] And in an interview, Bob Turner, a sportsman, told of the times that Dunbar and he spent together in an old drinking tavern in New York. Turner remembered that the poet, during drinking sprees, would "sit for hours listening to 'roustabouts' and absorbing odd expressions which he would later [utilize] in his poems." [43]

During Dunbar's last years, some of the most prominent men in the country recognized and respected his contributions to the world of letters. Perhaps the most signal honor bestowed upon the author was an invitation to participate in President William McKinley's inauguration in 1901. President McKinley conferred on him the honor of a commission to act as aide with rank of colonel in his inaugural parade. Dunbar accepted the invitation and rode in the procession on March 1, 1901. He was also invited to participate in the inauguration-day ceremony. Theodore Roosevelt, like McKinley, commissioned him to serve as aide of the Third Civic Division with the rank of a colonel on March 4, 1905.[44]

As an elocutionist and lecturer, Dunbar gained a popular reputation; he often appeared on the stage with Booker T. Washington and W. E. B. Du Bois.[45] His lecture tours carried him to all sections of the country. Even before 1900 he had recited for Mrs. Jefferson Davis: "I recited yesterday for Mrs. Jefferson Davis and she was delighted. The Southern people have taken me up wonderfully. One of them took three books, another two and another wants five. I have order[ed] 200 books to be here Thursday." [46] On the platform Dunbar was an excellent reader, unfailingly pleasing. He read with expression and taste. People who listened to the man were slow to forget the tender notes of his rich musical voice and the artistic rendering of his choice selections. What made him most effective were his facial expressions and his knowledge of the actor's art. He had a natural style of delivery, and his rich musical voice served to bring out all the better the pathetic and humorous selections he gave. He knew how to make a nice blend of the quaint and deeply serious. The Knoxville *Sentinel* claimed that his selections were rendered with genuine pathos, and the *Mail Express* commented that he rendered selections with "a fervor and intensity which compelled the closest attention of his audience." [47] Usually, he invited audience participation during public recitations. The audience was generally moved to great enthusiasm when he recited his poems. Dunbar's voice "was a perfect instrument and he knew how to use it," James Weldon Johnson once said of him.[48] Thus, his picturesque personality and great ability as a reciter of humorous poems in which he so cleverly delineated the character of the plantation black made him a much-sought-after reader on programs.

Paul Laurence Dunbar put laughter in his songs and many there were who laughed with him, little dreaming, as they laughed, of the bitter tears and the blood which flowed just beneath his sunny humor and rhyme. The poem "We Wear the Mask" may reveal why he so often chose to write of the black man as a happy-go-lucky creature of the plantation:

> Why should the world be overwise,
> In counting all our tears and sighs?
> Nay let them only see us, while
> We wear the mask.

Four days before his death Dunbar received a satirical letter of encouragement from an old friend and patron, H. A. Tobey:

> Poor boy you are resting easy. Wish you had to fight like I do. You would forget you ever had what someone called tuberculosis . . . you poor black discouraged dying wretch, I envy you.[49]

Dunbar died at 3:30 P.M., on Friday, February 9, 1906, at his residence, 219 North Summit Street, Dayton, Ohio.[50] His last words were a fragment of the Twenty-third Psalm. He repeated, "Yea though I walk through the valley of the shadow–" There was a gasp and Paul Laurence Dunbar was no more.[51] But he left a legacy of twenty-five books, fifteen essays, more than one hundred poems, thirty-five song lyrics, twenty-four short stories, over fifteen magazine articles, nine musical shows, and four plays.

The final chapter in the career of Dunbar was closed on Monday afternoon, February 12, 1906, with the consignment of his earthly remains to the receiving vault at Woodland Cemetery, Dayton, Ohio. His life's work was eulogized by four of the black leaders in the Dayton Community: J. C. Farrow, John M. Butler, D. E. Bush, and H. O. Williams. They resolved that because of "the invaluable service rendered by Dunbar to his race, the nation, and to the world of letters, he is held by us as a precious legacy and a constant inspiration to go forward in the work of uplifting, and unifying the race." [52]

Paul Laurence Dunbar was perhaps one of the most eminent

writers of his time, and despite the radical and rebellious tone of some of his works the greater part has nothing whatsoever to do with racial problems. If cries of protest or reform and even rebellion are sometimes heard in his works, the form is usually literary. In a larger sense, therefore, one must consider Dunbar's poetry not as productions from a representative of a racial group but as a manifestation of the American creative genius. Yet, by his pronouncements in his poems of social protest and criticism, by his recognition of the race problem which is still with us, and by his concern over the tragic consequences which may arise if these social ills are not remedied in time, Dunbar was the poet of the future.

One hundred years later, his niche in American letters is unquestioned. His verse was both serious and sweet. He wrote because he was moved to write, and his poetry expressed his own spirit giving value and permanence to some of the folklore of black people in America. Indeed, he created in the hearts of his generation an interest in the lowly people, people who made a virtue out of endurance. During the 1900s, Dunbar offered an example of black leadership which young blacks admired and respected; his triumphs were their triumphs. Benjamin Brawley claimed that "young blacks recited his poems and saw in turn what was possible for them." [53] The name of Paul Laurence Dunbar invoked a feeling of black pride and dignity. Writing from Jacksonville, Florida, Dunbar himself exclaimed, "Down here one finds my poems recited everywhere. Young men help themselves through school by speaking them, and the schools help their own funds by sending readers out with them to the winter hotels." [54]

In our own time the poet merits recognition and public applause, not simply because his work was creditable to a black man but because it would have been creditable to anyone. He was a voluminous writer. He literally worked himself to death. And although marital, health, and alcohol problems plagued him, he was destined never to lay down his pen and rest. Indeed these were crowded years. For during the last five years of his life he published six volumes of poetry, two volumes of short stories, and two novels. Certainly, his vein was an inexhaustible one.

Genius or not, the poet left for humanity a gift of example: a paradigm of a creative spirit overcoming the odds of racism and injustice.[55] Today, he earns an indelible place in American history. A former girlfriend, Rebekah Baldwin, might not have been wrong when she predicted that Dunbar's "fame [would] sound his melodious name adown all the line of ages."[56]

His biography is simply the record of human effort, of the success of an individual who, in his own way, made a pathway for other writers. Though born in obscurity, he died in honor as a literary giant of distinction and prominence. One of his more recent biographers, Virginia Cunningham, concluded that, "As long as people could read, Paul's poems would say—Here is a poet, a poet and his song."[57] Indeed, "Paul was a poet not of his race alone, but the poet . . . of men everywhere," Brand Whitlock observed. "For Paul was a poet," he continued, "and I find that when I have said that I have said the greatest and most splendid thing that can be said about a man."[58]

NOTES

1. This paper is based upon the writer's doctoral dissertation, "A Biography of Paul Laurence Dunbar" (Columbus: Ohio State University, 1970).
2. Lillian Smith, *Strange Fruit* (New York: Reynal & Hitchcock, 1944), p. 328.
3. James Weldon Johnson, *Along This Way* (New York: Viking Press, 1933), p. 158; William Loren Katz, *Eyewitness* (New York: Pitman, 1967), pp. 344–45; Ralph Ginzburg, *100 Years of Lynchings* (New York: Lancer Books, 1969), pp. 253–70.
4. Dunbar to Brand Whitlock, December 26, 1900, Dunbar Papers (Ohio Historical Society, hereafter O.H.S).
5. Charles Flint Kellogg, *NAACP*, vol. I (Baltimore: Johns Hopkins Press, 1967), pp. 3–4.
6. Rayford W. Logan, *The Negro in the United States* (New York: D. Van Nostrand Company, 1957), pp. 57–61, 90.
7. Peter M. Bergman and Mort N. Bergman, *The Chronological History of the Negro in America* (New York: New American Library, 1969), p. 330.
8. Samuel Eliot Morison, *The Oxford History of the American People* (New York: Oxford Univ. Press, 1950), p. 788.
9. Bergman and Bergman, *The Chronological History of the Negro in America*, pp. 329, 332.
10. Gossie Harold Hudson, "Paul Laurence Dunbar: Black Poet in History." *Negro History Bulletin* (February 1972), 30–31.
11. Charlotte Conover, *Dayton and Montgomery County* (New York: Lewis Historical Publishing House, 1932).

12. This paragraph is based upon an unpublished essay found in the Archibald Grimke Papers (Moreland Collection, Founders Library, Howard Univ.).
13. These brief sketches or letters written in Dunbar's hand and sometimes typewritten are found in his papers located in the O.H.S., Library of Congress, and the Dayton City Library.
14. Dunbar to Mrs. A. S. Lanahan, February 17, 1898, Paul Laurence Dunbar Papers (Manuscripts Division, Library of Congress).
15. Dunbar to D. J. Weese, December 6, 1898, Dunbar Papers (O.H.S.).
16. Dunbar to Col. R. G. Ingersoll, October 2, 1898 (Manuscript Collection, Columbia Univ. Library).
17. Invitation found in the Dunbar Papers (O.H.S.). Certificate also on file in the Bureau of Records of the Department of Health in the City of New York.
18. Frederick Means to Dunbar, February 21, 1899, Dunbar Papers (O.H.S.).
19. Dunbar to Matilda Dunbar, February 21, 1899, Dunbar Papers (O.H.S.); Booker T. Washington, *An Autobiography* (Atlanta: J. L. Nichols & Company, 1901), p. 271.
20. Newspaper clipping, Box 1, Dunbar Papers (O.H.S.).
21. Martin S. Day, *History of American Literature* (New York: Doubleday & Company, 1970), p. 305.
22. Notice of Dunbar's achievement and promise appeared in several German, Swedish, and English newspapers during 1900. Dunbar Papers (O.H.S.).
23. *The Denver Republican*, September 13, 1899; *World Herald*, October 7, 1904. See also Dunbar's correspondence with Washington on December 19, 1901, January 19, 1902, and Febrary 22, 1902 (Manuscripts Division, Library of Congress).
24. Daniel Walden, *W. E. B. DuBois, A Biography* (unpublished manuscript, 1971).
25. *The New York Times*, July 10, 1903.
26. Newspaper clipping, July 28, 1900, Dunbar Papers (O.H.S.).
27. *The New York Times*, July 10, 1903.
28. Box 1, Dunbar Papers (O.H.S.).
29. *The Negro Problem: A Series of Articles by Representative American Negroes of Today* (New York: James Pott & Company, 1903), p. 189; Dunbar wrote one of the essays. Before writing his article that would include Booker T. Washington, Dunbar wrote to Washington, requesting facts about himself "which would be of interest in an article which I am writing upon Representative Negroes." Dunbar to Booker T. Washington, February 20, 1903 (Manuscripts Division, Library of Congress).
30. Undated speech in the Dunbar Papers, Box 1 (O.H.S.).
31. Dunbar to Brand Whitlock, December 26, 1900, Dunbar Papers (O.H.S.).

32. *The Tattler*, vol. 1, December 7, 1890; this paper was published by Dunbar and Orville Wright.
33. *The Denver Republican*, September 13, 1899.
34. Frederick Douglass raised the same question in his Rochester, New York, speech of July 4, 1852, "What to the Slave is the Fourth of July?", Alice Dunbar, ed., *Masterpieces of Negro Eloquence* (New York: Bookery Publishing Company, 1914), pp. 42–47.
35. Paul Laurence Dunbar, "Sweet Land of Liberty I Sing;" *The Chicago Socialist* (July 18, 1903), pp. 25–26; Virginia Cunningham, *Paul Laurence Dunbar and His Song* (New York: Dodd, Mead & Company, 1947), p. 282.
36. Dunbar to Lucy B. Robinson, January 7, 1901, Dunbar Papers (O.H.S).
37. Charles Nilon, ed., *The Sport of the Gods* by Paul Laurence Dunbar (New York: Macmillan Co., 1970), pp. 6, 8.
38. Dunbar to Matilda Dunbar, July 1, 1902, Dunbar Papers (O.H.S.).
39. W. E. B. Du Bois, "Unpublished Letters from Paul Laurence Dunbar to a friend," p. 76.
40. Johnson, *Along This Way*, p. 160.
41. Grace Goulder, *Ohio Scenes and Citizens* (Cleveland and New York: World Publishing Company, 1964), p. 28.
42. *The Afro-American*, September 28, 1935, p. 13.
43. *Ibid.*, October 5, 1935, p. 8.
44. Certificates in the Dunbar home, 219 Summit Street, Dayton, Ohio.
45. Louis A. Harlan, *The Booker T. Washington Papers* (Urbana: Univ. of Illinois Press, 1972).
46. Dunbar to Matilda, August 25, 1896, Dunbar Papers (O.H.S.).
47. Newspaper clipping, Box 17, Dunbar Papers (O.H.S.).
48. Johnson, *Along This Way*, p. 160.
49. H. A. Tobey to Dunbar, February 5, 1906, Dunbar Papers (O.H.S.).
50. Box 16, Folder 4, Dunbar Papers (O.H.S.).
51. *Ibid.*
52. Cleveland *Gazette*, February 16, 1906.
53. Benjamin Brawley, *Paul Laurence Dunbar* (Chapel Hill: Univ. of North Carolina Press, 1936), p. 9
54. Lida Keck Wiggins, *The Life and Works of Paul Laurence Dunbar* (Naperville, Ill.: J. L. Nichols & Company, 1907), p. 95.
55. Houston A. Baker, Jr., "Paul Laurence Dunbar: An Evaluation," *Black World* (November 1971), p. 37.
56. Rebekah Baldwin to Dunbar, September 24, 1893, Dunbar Papers (O.H.S.).
57. Cunningham, *Paul Laurence Dunbar and His Song*, p. 265.
58. Brand Whitlock, *The Letters and Journal of Brand Whitlock* (New York: D. Appleton Company, 1936), pp. 21, 50.

Nikki Giovanni

AFTERWORD

I remember once I saw a photograph, probably in a *National Geographic*, of the giant redwood trees. They don't really do anything—they just are, and being, they must be protected. I think it must have been very difficult to keep the Grand Canyon from being sold to someone like Howard Hughes for a little hideaway. I'm even surprised Hugh Hefner hasn't purchased the Carlsbad Caverns for some grand night club scheme turning the land itself into a giant Bunny. It does not surprise me that Richard Nixon is so fond of Florida—it being the biggest phallic symbol in the United States—nor that he would, at the risk of great scandal, have to own a piece of the tip. There is little history to show that those who have the means also have the will to protect the nation's natural resources. It has been the unknown warrior, the Sunday-school matron, the high school principal, the workman who sacrificed a day's pay, or the housewife who perhaps took in laundry who have fought for our beautiful giants.

Paul Laurence Dunbar is a natural resource of our people. He, like all our old prophets and preachers, has been preserved by our little people. Those who could command words and images, those whose pens thundered across the pages, those whose voices boomed from lecterns, those who set policy for our great publications then, as now, were quite silent. Not ever quite knowing what to do about one of America's most famous poets, when they spoke his name it was generally to condemn his dialect poetry—as if black people aren't supposed to laugh, or more as if Dunbar's poems were not the best examples of our plantation speech. One gets recitation after explanation of Dunbar's poetry, his love of his "white poems," his hatred of his need to please the white critics, but something rings quite hollow to me. I refuse to believe Paul Dunbar was ashamed of "Little Brown Baby, come sit on my knee." The poem has brought too much happiness to me. I categorically reject a standard that says "A Negro Love Song" should not make me feel warm inside. If Dunbar is only a poet with a gift in jingle tongue then there is no need for a critique. He is clearly much more.

I remember I had a conversation with a poet who told me Richard Wright wished he was not black. I waited. "Isn't that something?" she exclaimed. "But why is that unusual?" I asked. "Who would wish to be black during Wright's coming of age? For that matter, who would wish to be white now?" "But," she went on, "his greatest disappointment was that white people didn't judge him as a writer but as a black writer." Again I missed the point, saying, "But Wright was a black writer." "But don't you see he would be very hurt if he heard you call him that." "But don't you see," I said, "I don't care. Wright doesn't have to like me for me to draw strength from his writing. I'm not looking for a lover—I want a writer." And that's the way I feel about Dunbar and his plantation poetry. Dunbar preserved a part of our history. And accurately. It would be as foolish to say all blacks struggled against slavery as it would to say all acquiesced to it. The truth lies somewhere in the blending. Perhaps Dunbar's greatest triumph is that he has survived all those who would use his gift for their own dead-end purposes.

Every artist, should he create long enough, will come full cycle again and again. The artist is a political animal as well as a sensitive being. Like any person the artist is a contradiction. Dunbar will speak of the good ole days, then say "We Wear the Mask." The message is clear and available to us if we invest in Dunbar the integrity we hope others will give us.

It seems somehow strange to me that critics are so colorless—despite claims to deeper insights should they share an ethnic or religious background with the subject. One need only view how similar the critics are concerning black movies. Both black and nonblack critics think the movies are for the most part awful. Their agreement strikes me as being somehow unnatural. Our poets have suffered from this same unnatural colorlessness. The black critics condemn for not being black enough, the white for not being white enough or, as in Dunbar's case, he was black enough for the white but not white enough for the blacks. Pandora has a little gray box with a pop-up question for black artists: Are you an artist who happens to be black or a black artist? Derek Walcott said, "What's the difference?" I agree. If your skin is colored, and most certainly if your mama's is, you are on our side of the ledger. Our question is, how can we as a people gain strength from your travail?

One looks to the critics, if one looks, to point the way to reasons for pride—to the essence of strength. Generally, one finds insipid gossip guaranteed to turn you off either the critic or the artist. And that's sad. Black criticism is a premature baby, though with proper attention one would like to feel some weight will be gained. It is important, I feel, that the critics like their subject. We cannot kill by condemnation, only by silence. As we invest life, therefore, we should also communicate joy. We must look at what the subject actually did, not what we wish he had done. We must understand the times in which our subject lived and created. And we must not be afraid to say our subject is good because we found him to be good. The printed word is not awesome; it was created to further communication, not to obscure it. We must draw comparisons that are meaningful from the field in which the artist worked. Dunbar, for example, is peerless. There is no poet, black or nonblack, who measures his achievement. Even today. He wanted to be a writer and he wrote. He survived, not always well, by his pen. He probably did not want to be hassled by his peers, who through Dunbar's efforts were enjoying greater attention. He probably was plagued by as many doubts as any other person. Yet he dared to persist in hope.

It is only fitting at Dunbar's centennial that we take stock of the poet. It is equally correct that we apply what we know about then to our situation now. Dunbar, the poet, was quite different from other poets of his era. Our intellectuals of today must be quite different from other thinkers also. We must bring the sweet juice, not just the dried bones, alive to our young people. There is a reason Shakespeare is still read today; there is a reason Dostoevski is still venerated; there is also a reason Phillis Wheatley is sneered at when her name is mentioned; there is also a reason Pushkin is mostly just a name to our young; and a great part of those reasons turn on criticism. The reasons turn on one group's determination to keep its writers alive and another group with less determination. We spend far too much energy trying uselessly to control the creating artist instead of defining those whose creations are complete. Academia is a lonely endeavor. But it is within the mind, with the pen, within the will to keep alive those works of art upon which our history turns.

One hears a great deal about the energy crisis. In a decade coal and gas as we now know them will be depleted. The scientists are looking for some synthetic forms of energy. We do not have to seek synthetic energy when we have a million suns—a billion suns, should we ever cease our fear of offending the gods that be. Inside the dusty old books, with the clap of the preacher's hands or the shrill scream of a child running "Home free!" in hide-and-seek we must determine to define for ourselves. We must cease the fear that our callused hands do not grip the pen as well as those which have not suffered. We must trust our judgment as Paul Dunbar trusted his. We must be ready to chance a great failure for a great success. Paul Laurence Dunbar did. And he lives on. So can we all.

Notes on Contributors

JAY MARTIN organized the Centenary Conference on Paul Laurence Dunbar at the University of California, Irvine, at which most of the essays included in this volume were first delivered. He is the author or editor of works on Conrad Aiken, American literature between 1865 and 1914, Nathanael West, and T. S. Eliot.

BERT BENDER teaches English at Arizona State University. His work on Dunbar is part of a longer book-in-progress on the lyrical novel in America.

ARNA BONTEMPS was born in 1902 and died in 1973. Winning literary prizes as early as 1927, he became a leading figure in the Harlem Renaissance and an important critic. His works include many anthologies, such as *The Poetry of the Negro 1746–1949;* poetry, books for children; three novels, and several biographical and historical books. He conferred distinction upon every literary field in which he worked and achieved a permanent place in American literature.

DICKSON D. BRUCE, JR. taught Comparative Culture at the University of California, Irvine. His book *And They All Sang Hallelujah* has won the James Mooney Award for Studies of New World Societies and Cultures. He has published numerous essays on Southern folk culture and other subjects.

JAMES A. EMANUEL is the author of *Langston Hughes* and of several volumes of poetry, including *The Tree House and Other Poems.* He co-edited *Dark Symphony: The Development of Negro Literature in America.* He has taught in France and now is a professor of English at the City College of New York.

ADDISON GAYLE, JR., has edited several books. These are *Black Expression: Essays by and About Black Americans in the Creative Arts, The Black Situation*, and *The Black Aesthetic*. He is working on a history of the black novel and teaches English at the Bernard M. Baruch College of the City University of New York. *Oak and Ivy* is his biography of Paul Laurence Dunbar.

NIKKI GIOVANNI has taught and lectured at several universities. Her books of poetry include *Black Feeling, Black Talk, Black Judgement*; *Re:Creation*; and *My House*, and she is also a distinguished essayist.

MICHAEL S. HARPER currently teaches in the writing program at Brown University. His poems have appeared in such magazines as *Poetry* and *Burning Bush*, and have been gathered into *Dear John, Dear Coltrane*, *History Is Your Own Heartbeat*, and *Song: I Want a Witness and Debridement*.

GOSSIE H. HUDSON is Chairman of History and the Division of Social Sciences at Lincoln University. His studies of Paul Laurence Dunbar have appeared in several journals. He is at work on a biography of the poet.

RAYMOND R. PATTERSON teaches in the City College of New York. His poetry has been published in *Twentysix Ways of Looking at a Black Man and Other Poems*. He has also written a syndicated column, "From Our Past," on Negro history. He is director of Black Poets Reading, Inc.

SAUNDERS REDDING, professor at Cornell University, has written or edited many books on the history and literature of black Americans. Among these the best known are *To Make a Poet Black*, *They Came in Chains*, *On Being Negro in America*, *An American in India*, *The Lonesome Road*, *The Negro*, and *Cavalcade: Negro American Writing from 1760 to the Present*.

MYRON SIMON is a professor of English and Comparative Literature at the University of California, Irvine. In addition to his work on Robert Graves, Georgian poetics, and the Transcendentalists, he is the editor of *Ethnic Writers in America*.

LORENZO THOMAS is the author of *Fit Music* and of other poems in such anthologies as *Black Fire* and *New Black Voices*. His work has appeared in the *Massachusetts Review*, *Art and Literature*, and other journals.

DARWIN T. TURNER is the Director of Afro-American Studies at the University of Iowa. He has edited books on the fiction, poetry, and essays written by black Americans, as well as writing his own short stories, drama, and poetry, the last collected in *Katharsis*. His critical works include *Nathaniel Hawthorne's The Scarlet Letter* and *In a Minor Chord*.

MARGARET WALKER has published poetry and fiction of the highest quality and significance. Her volumes of poetry are *For My People* and *Prophets for a New Day*. Her novel, *Jubilee*, has been highly praised.

KENNY J. WILLIAMS is a professor of English at Northern Illinois State University. Her critical history of black writing in America, *They Also Spoke*, is a standard work in the field. Her most recent book is a study of the literature and architecture of Chicago.

Index